Chasing Mosby,
Killing Booth

Chasing Mosby, Killing Booth

The 16th New York Volunteer Cavalry

JAMES CARSON

McFarland & Company, Inc., Publishers
Jefferson, North Carolina

LIBRARY OF CONGRESS CATALOGUING-IN-PUBLICATION DATA

Names: Carson, James, 1944– author.
Title: Chasing Mosby, killing Booth : the 16th New York Volunteer Cavalry / James Carson.
Description: Jefferson, North Carolina : McFarland & Company, Inc., Publishers, 2017.
Identifiers: LCCN 2017019138 | ISBN 9781476663296 (softcover : acid free paper) ∞
Subjects: LCSH: United States. Army. New York Cavalry Regiment, 16th (1863–1865) | New York (State)—History—Civil War, 1861–1865—Regimental histories. | United States—History—Civil War, 1861–1865—Regimental histories. | United States—History—Civil War, 1861–1865—Cavalry operations. | Confederate States of America. Army. Virginia Cavalry Battalion, 43rd. | Mosby, John Singleton, 1833–1916. | Booth, John Wilkes, 1838–1865—Death and burial.
Classification: LCC E523.6 16th .C37 2017 | DDC 973.7/447—dc23
LC record available at https://lccn.loc.gov/2017019138

BRITISH LIBRARY CATALOGUING DATA ARE AVAILABLE

**ISBN (print) 978-1-4766-6329-6
ISBN (ebook) 978-1-4766-2813-4**

© 2017 James Carson. All rights reserved

No part of this book may be reproduced or transmitted in any form or by any means, electronic or mechanical, including photocopying or recording, or by any information storage and retrieval system, without permission in writing from the publisher.

Front cover: *Federal Cavalrymen Fording Bull Run* (1862) © 2017 Picturesnow; *insets* John S. Mosby, C.S.A. (left), and John Wilkes Booth (Library of Congress)

Printed in the United States of America

*McFarland & Company, Inc., Publishers
Box 611, Jefferson, North Carolina 28640
www.mcfarlandpub.com*

Acknowledgments

This book is dedicated to my wife, Margaret Kress Carson, my best friend, companion, advisor, and a superb reviewer. She has spent countless hours visiting libraries, museums, and historic sites and has helped me mine volumes of research files. Without her encouragement, editorial advice, and support over the years this project would not have been possible.

I also am especially indebted to Lincoln historian Steven G. Miller of Lake Villa, Illinois, who shared valuable advice as well as material on the 16th New York Cavalry from his personal holdings on "Lincoln's Avengers," and to Mr. John Fincham of Winchester, Virginia, who spent many hours searching the Internet for photos and information on the 16th New York. Between them, Steve and John saved me months of work searching for that proverbial needle in the haystack.

Several other individuals were kind enough to share their personal files on members of the 16th New York. Rod MacDonald of Stratford, Ontario, Canada, and Robert Keays of northern California provided extensive material related to Capt. William J. Keays. Louise Brown of Witney, Oxfordshire, England, graciously shared her collection of letters written home by Capt. James H. Fleming before his death at Fairfax Station in August 1864. Kathy Manese of New Jersey and Robert Snapper of Kew Gardens, New York, provided valuable biographic and family information on Captain Joseph Schneider, the fearless defender of Annandale's "Fort Schneider." Wayne Diercks of Rochester, Minnesota, shared his research and written materials on regimental drummer Private Louis Abend.

I am also grateful to the following individuals and institutions for their guidance and research assistance: Ellen Adams, Curator, Alice T. Miner Museum, Chazy, New York; Jennifer Bulriss, Town Historian, Mooers, New York; Jan Couture, Town Historian, Saranac, New York; Julie

Dowd, Clinton County Historical Association, Plattsburgh, New York; Anastasia L. Pratt, Clinton County Historian, Plattsburgh, New York; the Andersonville Guild and Drummer Boy Museum, Andersonville, Georgia; the Colgate University Libraries Special Collections and University Archives, Hamilton, New York; the New-York Historical Society, New York, New York; the New York State Military Museum and Veterans Research Center, Saratoga Springs, New York; the New York State Archives and New York State Library, Albany, New York; the State University of New York at Plattsburgh, Special Collections, Plattsburgh, New York; the Thomas Balch Library, Leesburg, Virginia; the University of Michigan, William L. Clements Library, Ann Arbor, Michigan; the U.S. Army Heritage and Education Center, Carlisle, Pennsylvania; the U.S. Library of Congress; and the U.S. National Archives and Records Administration, Washington, D.C., and Bethesda, Maryland.

I also am indebted to my close friend and fellow Civil War buff, Tom Boltz, of Reston, Virginia, for his advice and guidance through several drafts of this manuscript and to Ken Jones of Midlothian, Virginia, for his outstanding efforts in preparing the maps. Finally, I must give special credit to the late Mayo Stuntz and his wife Connie of Vienna, Virginia, for introducing me to Vienna's rich history and the role that the 16th New York Cavalry played in it.

Table of Contents

Acknowledgments	v
Preface	1
Introduction	3
One: A Regiment Is Formed	13
Two: Colonel Lazelle Joins His Regiment	50
Three: The Spring 1864 Campaign	63
Four: July–August 1864: More Challenges, More Losses	75
Five: September–October 1864: More and More Losses	94
Six: A New Colonel and Brigade Reorganization	112
Seven: Victory and Tragedy	129
Eight: At War's End	143
Nine: Postwar Fortunes and Failures	152
Appendix A: Roster of Officers and Sergeants	183
Appendix B: Regimental Deaths in Andersonville and Other Prisons	225
Chapter Notes	228
Bibliography	242
Index	251

Preface

In October 1864, Army Chief of Staff Henry W. Halleck described the men of the 16th New York Volunteer Cavalry as "cowed and useless" because they had been "so often cut up by Mosby's band." Six months later, the regiment would celebrate when 26 of its men, led by Capt. Edward P. Doherty, captured and killed President Lincoln's assassin, John Wilkes Booth, at Richard Henry Garrett's Farm near Port Royal Crossroads in Caroline County, Virginia.

Initially known as the Sprague Light Cavalry, after New York State Adjutant General John T. Sprague, the 16th New York was a troubled unit almost from the start. An amalgamation of three partially formed regiments, it was plagued by early desertions, poor leadership, and a near mutiny as its first battalion prepared to march to Washington. Arriving at Vienna, Virginia, in October 1863 to bolster the outer defenses of Washington, the 16th spent most of its time reacting to guerrilla attacks by Col. John Singleton Mosby and his band of rangers.

Despite a mixed operational record, the men of the 16th New York were selected on April 16, 1865, to serve in the military escort for President Lincoln's funeral procession down Pennsylvania Avenue from the White House to the Capitol building. Ten days later, Capt. Doherty and his men caught up with and killed the President's assassin in Richard Garrett's tobacco barn.

This is the story of the 16th New York Cavalry, and its officers and men, from its initial recruitment and mustering in Plattsburgh and Staten Island, through its numerous and sometimes successful efforts against Mosby's Rangers and other Confederate forces in northern Virginia, to its final mustering out of Federal service in September 1865.

The *Official Records of the War of the Rebellion* provide a factual "framework" and timeline of the actions and operations of the regiment. However, the real story of the 16th can only be told by the officers and men who served. To the degree that diaries, letters, and memoirs are available, I have endeavored to let the men speak. Several collections were of particular value. These include Commissary Lt. Albert B. Wilbur's diary with nearly daily entries covering all of 1864 and 1865 through the end of the regiment's service; letters written home to Ireland in 1863 and 1864 by Capt. James H. Fleming, the only 16th New York officer killed in action; letters to his mother from Charles F. Moore (2nd Lt., Co. A and 1st Lt. Co. C) from June 1863 through April 1865; a series of articles written by QM-Sgt. Cyrus G. Shepard in 1897 for the *New York Evening Post* about his experiences in the war; "Reminiscences of Civil War Experience," a manuscript written by Pvt. Francis T. Hagadorn (Co. F); and letters written to his parents by Cpl. Albert G. Martin (Co. B), who would perish from disease February 1864 while a prisoner at Belle Isle in Richmond, Virginia. Letters written home by Cpl. Valorus Dearborn of the 2nd Massachusetts Cavalry, and an autobiographical manuscript written by 1st Lt. Augustus Green of the 13th New York Cavalry, about their joint operations with the 16th New York also provided some rich perspective.

I also have tried, where appropriate and possible, to tell both sides of the story, focusing on Mosby's perspectives. In this regard, Mosby's own memoirs provided his personal take on many of his operations against the New York cavalrymen. Mosby Ranger James J. Williamson's well-documented 1896 memoir also provided rich material, sometimes in greater detail than, and other times at odds with, that in the *Official Records*.

I have made every effort to ensure the historical accuracy of this account, and I accept full responsibility for any factual errors that may be found. In drawing upon the writings of members of the regiment, I have sought to corroborate their statements of "fact" with reports from the *Official Records* and/or additional primary sources. I also have endeavored to confirm all newspaper accounts.

Introduction

It was October of 1863 and the "autumn leaves were bright along the Eastern Branch, as the jolly procession of carriages rolled across the Navy Yard Bridge." Seeking a moment's diversion from the daily reminders of war, Washington society was going to the "trotting races" at the newly built "National Race-Course" near the city's insane asylum.[1]

Although significant fighting "had shifted to a safe distance from the earthworks that ringed the capital," the potential threat posed by General Lee's Confederate forces to the south was always on the mind of Washington's residents. Indeed, earlier in October they had "heard of sharp skirmishes on its immediate front, as General Lee began a flanking movement, and [General] Meade's army retreated all the way to Centreville."[2]

Two years earlier, following the defeat of Federal forces at the first battle of Manassas in July 1861, Maj. Gen. George B. McClellan, who had replaced Brig. Gen. Irvin McDowell in command of the Army of the Potomac, had turned his attention to building up the garrison defenses of Washington so he could "free his growing army for field work." By early 1863, Washington had become "a fortress city," surrounded by a "chain of fortifications, connected by lines of earthworks mounting the most powerful guns of the period ... some fifty-three enclosed works and twenty-two batteries."[3] In addition, Washington's early warning system of picket posts, lookouts, railroad guards, and "sentinels at road junctions"[4] was being pushed outward from the city, partly in response to Confederate General J.E.B. Stuart's cavalry raids.

Although General Lee's Confederate Army had never seriously threatened Washington—he had set his sights, instead, on Maryland and Pennsylvania—Secretary of War Stanton still worried that the city's defenses would prove inadequate to a Confederate assault. In September 1862, he had ordered Maj. Gen. Samuel P. Heintzelman, commanding troops in

Washington, to establish "lines of battle in addition to the defenses of the works" and to see that "lines of communication are kept open in their rear, so that any point of attack may be readily reinforced. Great care should be taken to establish the outposts, and to have the picket service efficiently performed."[5] In October, Stanton also had appointed a commission of senior officers to study Washington's defenses and recommend necessary improvements.

Three days after Christmas in 1862, General J.E.B. Stuart led 1,800 cavalrymen, among them his Aide, Lt. John Mosby, out of Fredericksburg through Culpeper and Prince William County, across the Occoquan River, and into Fairfax County. Raiding Burke Station on the Orange and Alexandria Railroad near Fairfax Court House, they captured the telegraph operator and some mules. Before cutting the telegraph lines, Stuart sent a short message to Washington, complaining about "the quality of the Yankee mules."[6]

Just days after Stuart's raid on Burke Station, Secretary Stanton's commissioners reported their general satisfaction with "the lines established and of the works," around Washington, suggesting only minor additions and modifications. However, they did recommend that manning be increased to a permanent garrison force of 25,000 infantrymen and 9,000 artillerymen, augmented by 3,000 cavalrymen "for outpost duty, to give notice of the approach of any enemy."[7] This was a good deal more than the 19,000 infantry, artillery and cavalry troops that Brig. Gen. James S. Wadsworth, then commanding the Military District of Washington, had reported present for duty in April 1862.[8]

Responding to the commission on February 2, 1863, the War Department issued General Order No. 26, establishing the 22nd Army Corps, commanded by Maj. Gen. Heintzelman, composed of troops from the Department of Washington, and charged with the protection of Washington. The Corps was organized into two districts, Washington and Alexandria, and two commands that formed the outer defenses of the city: the Defenses North of the Potomac (from Piscataway Creek to Annapolis Junction to the mouth of the Monocacy River) and the Defenses South of the Potomac (from Goose Creek and the Bull Run Mountains to the mouth of the Occoquan River).

Typically, a Union army corps was composed of infantry, artillery and cavalry organized into two or more divisions. Each division was made up of two or more brigades with anywhere from four to six regiments. Infantry and cavalry regiments typically held ten companies, each with 100 men at full strength. The 22nd Corps, however, was somewhat unique in that its

Introduction 5

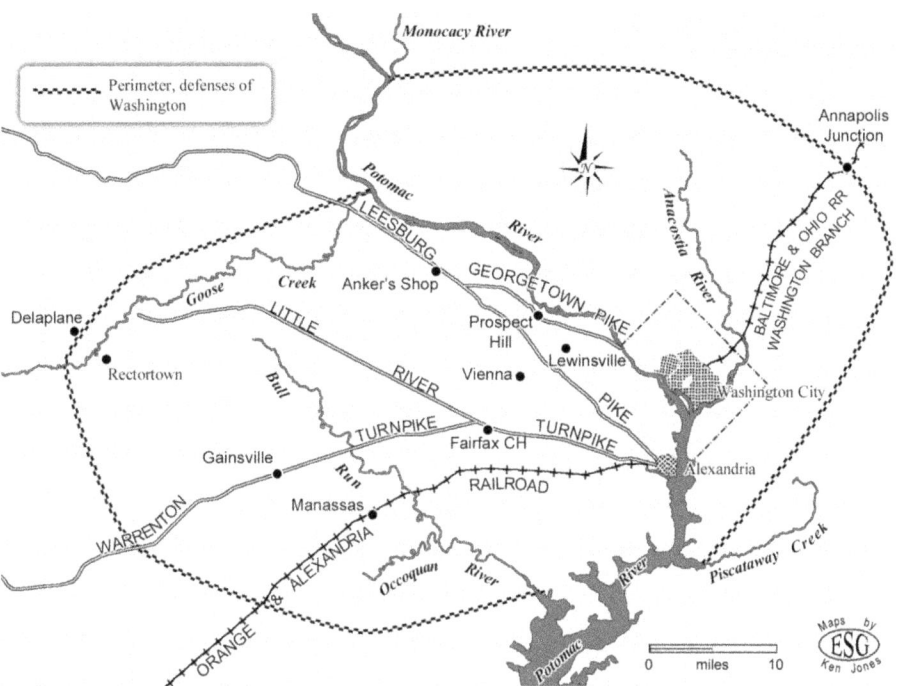

Organization of the 22nd Army Corps, 1863.

composition was highly fluid as a number of its regiments moved in and out of Washington.

Cavalry units assigned to 22nd Corps initially were organized into an Independent Cavalry Brigade, commanded by Col. R. Butler Price of the 2nd Pennsylvania, with six regiments (the 2nd and 18th Pennsylvania, 1st Vermont, 5th New York, 1st West Virginia, and 1st Michigan) and two companies of the 1st Ohio. By late March 1863, cavalry forces in Washington had grown substantially and were consolidated into a Cavalry Division, with three brigades (12 regiments), commanded by Maj. Gen. Julius H. Stahel.[9]

Throughout the spring of 1863, Secretary Stanton was torn between two requirements. On the one hand, he needed to maintain adequate defenses around Washington in the face of continuing "pesky raids" by Confederate cavalry units[10] and the incipient threat posed by Lee's movements northward. On the other hand, he needed to respond to increasing calls for reinforcements from Maj. Gen. Joseph Hooker, commanding the Army of the Potomac. On May 23, Stanton queried General-in-Chief Henry W. Halleck about the ability of Hooker's forces and those stationed around Washington to deal with Confederate raiding and, specifically, how the cavalry should be employed. Halleck responded that, in his view, the cavalry forces of the Department of Washington (22nd Corps) were properly deployed "on and in front of the outer line of pickets south of the Potomac" and sent out as scouts "on the roads to feel the enemy and give notice of his movements."[11]

Moreover, Halleck believed, Hooker had sufficient troops to deal with Confederate raids, particularly if they were "either stationed nearer to the Orange and Alexandria Railroad" or "employed in again attacking and breaking up the enemy's cavalry." Secretary Stanton concurred with Halleck's assessment and recommended to President Lincoln the following day that "the large cavalry forces of the Army of the Potomac should be so disposed as to afford protection against the enemy's cavalry raids upon our military depots and exposed points."[12]

Three days later, Hooker—responding to reports of enemy cavalry movement toward the Orange and Alexandria Railroad, which he considered his "duty to look after"—recommended that Stahel's cavalry be instructed "to look into the Shenandoah Valley and see what is going on over there." Stanton was emphatic in his response: "There is no other cavalry force about Washington than that of General Stahel, which is now engaged on scouting duty toward Bull Run Mountains, and in picketing Bull Run and Occoquan Rivers. If it be removed, there will be no force in front to give notice of enemy's raids on Alexandria or Washington."[13]

In June 1863, as General Lee's Army of Northern Virginia moved into Maryland on its way to Gettysburg, pressure mounted on Heintzelman to free up reinforcements for Hooker's Army. On June 20, Stahel, his division now essentially seconded to the Army of the Potomac, reported from Hooker's Headquarters at Fairfax Court House that he had concentrated his forces there, "broken up my camps, sent all the surplus property and quartermaster's stores to Fairfax Station," and that his command was "ready to march, provided with eight days' rations." The following day Hooker ordered him to undertake a "reconnaissance in force" toward Warrenton and the Upper Rappahannock and "attack, destroy, capture or disperse" a Confederate brigade reported at Warrenton.[14]

On June 24, Hooker once again ordered Stahel to move his command, this time to Harper's Ferry, where he was to report to Maj. Gen. William French, commanding Harpers Ferry District.[15] From there, his cavalry

Opposite: Map of the Potomac River Region (Library of Congress, Robert K. Sneden Diary).

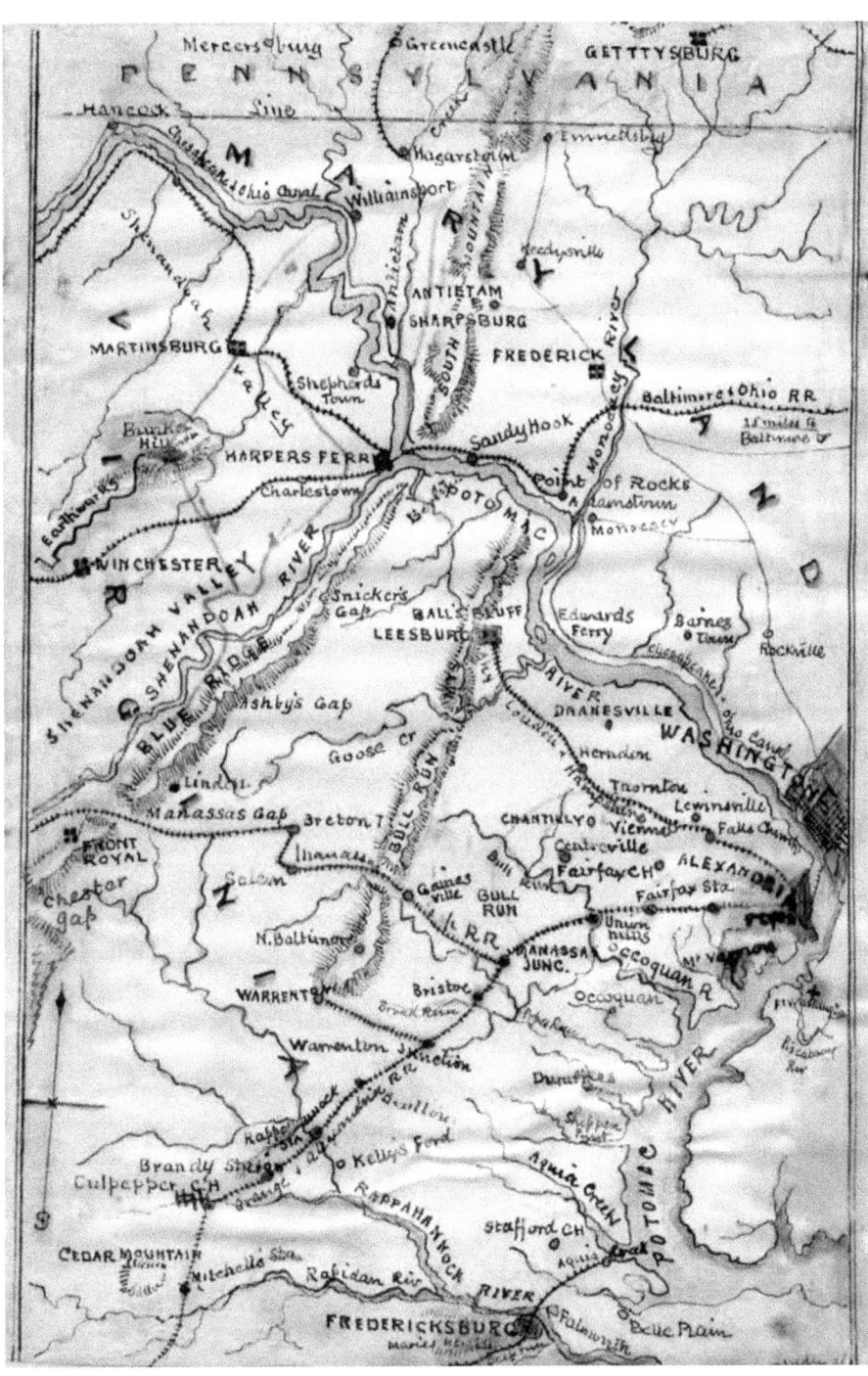

troops were sent across the Potomac into Maryland. On June 26, Stahel reported from Frederick City, Maryland, that he had positioned a brigade and artillery, along with troops from 11th Corps, at Crampton's Pass; a regiment in South Mountain Pass; another brigade and artillery in Middletown; and two regiments near Frederick. According to Stahel, "the whole rebel army" was marching toward Harrisburg, and "Ewell's whole corps" had recently passed through Hagerstown and Smithsburg.[16] The Union and Confederate armies would soon clash at Gettysburg.

On June 26, 1863, Stahel's Cavalry Division was transferred officially to the Army of the Potomac. Assigned to the Army's Cavalry Corps, all of the regiments would see action at Gettysburg. Two days later, as command of the Army of the Potomac passed from Hooker to Maj. Gen. George Meade, Stahel was relieved of duty and ordered to Harrisburg to "organize and command the cavalry in the Department of the Susquehanna."[17]

Meanwhile, Washington's defenses had been stripped to bare bones, so much so that Maj. Gen. Heintzelman's Chief Engineer was discussing the need to hurriedly arm, train, and organize into companies and battalions some 12,000 to 15,000 "citizens and transient persons," to help garrison the city. Heintzelman, particularly concerned that his cavalry screen had been stripped away, reported to General Halleck on June 25, that "as all of my cavalry has been taken from the other side [of the Potomac], should the Army of the Potomac move from my front, the first indication of the approach of the enemy would be their appearance at our works." Three days later, Army Quartermaster-General Montgomery C. Meigs also complained that "all the cavalry of the Defenses of Washington was swept off by the army, and we are now insulted by burning wagons 3 miles outside of Tennallytown."[18]

Even those few cavalry forces that Heintzelman could still count as his own were pulled away to support the Gettysburg Campaign. These included recently mustered companies of the 2nd Massachusetts Volunteer Cavalry, which had been organized early in 1863. Five companies had initially moved from Camp Meigs in Readville, Massachusetts, to Fortress Monroe, Virginia, in February, and then on to Gloucester Point, Virginia. Attached to the Cavalry Command of the Fourth Army Corps in the Department of Virginia, they performed picket and outpost duty. Another seven companies left Readville for Washington, D.C., in May 1863, and were attached to Casey's Provisional Troops, 22nd Corps.

In late June 1863, five companies of the Second, commanded by Col. Charles R. Lowell, were stationed on the Potomac at Poolesville, Maryland, covering the river fords in the rear of the Army of the Potomac. On June 27, Lowell reported back to Washington that Gen. Hooker had ordered

Introduction

him to report with his command to XII Corps Commander Maj. Gen. Henry W. Slocum at Knoxville, Maryland, east of Harpers Ferry. Lowell was told immediately that he was not to obey any order from Hooker "until you have instructions from these headquarters."[19] Lowell and his men stayed in Poolesville, and in July following Gettysburg, the 2nd Massachusetts was assigned to King's Division ("Not Brigaded") of the 22nd Corps.

All of the regiments in Stahel's original Cavalry Division remained with the Army of the Potomac following Gettysburg. However, on August 1, 1863, Heintzelman finally got his cavalry screen back. An Independent Cavalry Brigade was reestablished and placed under command of Col. Lowell. Initially manned by the 2nd Massachusetts Cavalry, it would include the 13th and 16th New York Cavalry Regiments by the end of 1863.

The 13th New York Cavalry ("Seymour Light") was organized on June 20, 1863, at Staten Island by consolidating several incomplete cavalry organizations. Its first six companies left for Washington on June 23, another two on August 14, and the final four the winter of 1863–1864. Several companies of the Thirteenth performed "patrol duty" in the rear of the Army of the Potomac during the Gettysburg Campaign. Another two companies served in New York City during the July 1863 draft riots before deploying to Washington. The regiment completed mustering and arrived in Vienna, Virginia, in December 1863.[20]

Mosby's Confederacy

Early in March 1863, a "strange man" had appeared at Fairfax Court House, "dressed as a Union captain," asking the servants of Union Brig. Gen. Edwin Stoughton, commander of the 2nd Brigade of Vermont Infantry, about the number of troops in the area, where they were billeted, and whether the general "kept his horse saddled at night."[21] A week later, the stranger, Capt. John S. Mosby, former aide to General J.E.B. Stuart, returned to

John S. Mosby (Library of Congress).

Fairfax Court House with 29 men in the middle of the night, taking Stoughton prisoner along with "two captains, 30 other prisoners, together with their arms, equipments and 58 horses." Stuart later characterized Mosby's raid as "almost unparalleled in the war" as it was "performed in the midst of the enemy's troops at Fairfax Court House, without loss or injury."[22]

The brazen capture of Brig. Gen. Stoughton by a small band of cavalrymen, a classic guerrilla operation, was the first of many exploits that would only reinforce in the minds of Generals Halleck and Heintzelman the dangers of leaving Washington undefended. This early incident:

> ... put Washington in a frenzy. A number of prominent citizens of Fairfax were arrested and placed in prison. So was Antonia Ford, a pretty daughter of a local merchant who was accused of being in league with Mosby. The incident stirred humor in only one person in the Union capital. When told of what had happened so close to the banks of the Potomac, Abraham Lincoln is said to have remarked: "Well, I'm sorry for that—I can make brigadier generals, but I can't make horses."[23]

John Singleton Mosby, the so-called "Gray Ghost," would come to dominate the attention of Union forces across a broad swath of northern Virginia that became known as "Mosby's Confederacy." Roughly bounded by the Bull Run Mountains, the road from Aldie to Snicker's Gap, the Blue Ridge Mountains, and a line in the south running from Manassas Gap to Thoroughfare Gap, it encompassed some 2,000 square miles of Loudoun, Fairfax, Fauquier, and Prince William counties.[24] Mosby's operational forays frequently carried him into Union-held territory close to Washington in Fairfax and Loudoun counties and south of Alexandria.

Born west of Richmond in 1833, Mosby had attended local schools and majored in Greek and mathematics at the University of Virginia. Allegedly, one of his favorite books in his youth recounted the guerrilla warfare exploits of Francis Marion, the legendary "Swamp Fox" of the American Revolution.[25] Expelled from the university after an incident that also garnered him a short jail sentence, Mosby went on to study law, establish a practice in rural Washington County in 1855, and marry a young woman from a prominent Kentucky family.

In 1860, Mosby and two friends enrolled in the local militia company, the Washington Rifles. When Virginia seceded from the Union in April 1861, Mosby and the men of the Washington Rifles headed to Richmond. From there, they joined Brig. Gen. Joe Johnston's army in the Shenandoah Valley and were eventually incorporated into the 1st Virginia Cavalry under then–Col. J.E.B. Stuart.[26]

Under Stuart's tutelage, Mosby earned his spurs and advanced in rank

Introduction 11

Mosby's Confederacy. From John Scott, *Partisan Life with Col. John S. Mosby* (New York: Harper & Bros. Publishers, 1867).

to captain. He established the 43rd Battalion, Virginia Cavalry on June 10, 1863, near Rectortown in Fauquier County when, with Stuart's blessing, he raised its first company. General Robert E. Lee had granted permission for the unit under the 1862 Partisan Ranger Act of the Confederate Congress, which authorized the establishment of partisan, or ranger, units. By the fall of 1863, when the regiments of the 22nd Corps' Independent Cavalry Brigade set up camp in Vienna, Virginia, Mosby and his rangers had already achieved considerable notoriety.

1st Lt. Augustus P. Green of the 13th New York Cavalry characterized Mosby's men as "bushwackers" who were "too lazy to enter the confederate service where they would be disciplined," but he also acknowledged the effectiveness of their guerrilla tactics:

Introduction

> They never would attack a body of our troops face to face but would always lie in ambush and when they had a small body of men in an advantageous spot would then attack front and rear. And if they found they were being worsted would scatter like wild geese and disappear by the by-paths I have mentioned and then meet by nights at some haunt agreed upon, talk it over, and lay their plans for some fresh outrage. Belonging to that band there was [sic] some of the most notorious cut-throats and outlaws in all Virginia, who would think nothing when they needed money of throwing a train off the track, setting fire to it, and then robbing the defenseless women and children of everything they possessed, even going so far as to pull the earrings out of their ears. They employed every means to hide their horses.
>
> The men themselves, in almost every one of their houses, they had places fixed, ready for concealment at any time day or night, secret entrances, small closets out in the walls with sliding doors into which one or two could enter and close the door and then watch our men searching for them like rats watching a cat from within their small holes.... Some even burrowed holes in the ground under their houses, with trap doors, and if any one approached would disappear into their burrows like rabbits.[27]

The story of the 16th New York Cavalry is intimately connected with that of John Mosby. The regiment would eventually find momentary glory in the capture and killing of John Wilkes Booth by Capt. Edward Doherty, Sgt. Boston Corbett, and their small detachment of men from the 16th. However, for most of the regiment's existence, the cavalrymen were hounded by Mosby and his partisan rangers.

Even their superior officers recognized that the New York cavalrymen were simply not up to the task. In early October 1864, General Ulysses S. Grant requested permission to pull forces from the Shenandoah Valley in support of the "Siege of Petersburg." In responding, General Halleck expressed concern about the impact this would have on the security of the countryside between Washington and the valley. He was particularly concerned about Mosby, warning Grant that it would be necessary to "completely clean out Mosby's gang of robbers who have so long infested that district of country."

In Halleck's opinion, General Sheridan's cavalry would be needed to deal with Mosby before being sent out of the valley. He came to this conclusion, he wrote to Grant, because the "the two small regiments [the 13th and 16th New York] under General Augur [then commanding 22nd Corps] have been so often cut up by Mosby's band that they are cowed and useless for that purpose."[28]

ONE

A Regiment Is Formed

At the outset of the Civil War, New York was the richest and most populous state of the Union. Among the first to respond to the call for volunteers after the fall of Fort Sumter, New Yorkers were justly proud of their contributions to the Union cause. After the war, with a bit of hyperbole, the State Board of Military Record declared:

> From every quarter came applications, strongly endorsed for authority to raise men.... The officer drew his sabre, and the private shouldered his musket. Upward, from the Hudson to the Lakes, a martial tide swelled, and rolled to the front of battle. And there was behind, always, the great ocean of loyal popular encouragement. While parents were giving their sons, and wives their husbands, to the cause, it seemed but little for our patriotic citizens to fling their worldly wealth upon the common altar. Cities and counties, villages and hamlets, vied with one another as to which should be foremost in contributing to their country. Finance committees, military aid committees, soldiers' relief societies, sprung up everywhere.[1]

On April 16, 1861, the New York State legislature authorized the initial organization of 38 regiments of volunteers for two-years service. By the end of the war, New York had provided over a half million men for the regular and volunteer forces, some 400,000 of whom were in the "general volunteer service," State Militia, and National Guard, including: 27 cavalry regiments and 10 companies; 15 artillery regiments and 37 companies; 248 infantry regiments and 10 companies; three engineer regiments; and eight companies of sharpshooters. The 16th New York Cavalry was the sixteenth volunteer cavalry regiment organized in the state and one of eight New York cavalry regiments mustered into Federal service between January and December 1863.[2]

Although the 16th had 12 companies, at full strength a typical regiment had 10 companies with a total of 1,025 men:

Field and Staff	Company Formation
1 Colonel	1 Captain
1 Lieutenant Colonel	1 1st Lieutenant
1 Major	1 2nd Lieutenant
1 Adjutant (Lieutenant)	1 1st Sergeant
1 Quartermaster (Lieutenant)	4 Sergeants
1 Surgeon (Major)	8 Corporals
2 Asst. Surgeons	2 Musicians
1 Chaplain	1 Wagoner
1 Sergeant-Major	82 Privates
1 Quartermaster-Sergeant	
1 Commissary-Sergeant	
1 Hospital Steward	
2 Principal Musicians[3]	

Regiments in the Civil War were not formally subdivided into battalions, made up of companies and with a battalion command structure, as they are today. Nonetheless, when several companies—usually four—were grouped together for an operation, under command of a major or senior captain, they often were referred to as battalions. Thus, the first four companies of the 16th that deployed from Plattsburgh to Washington, D.C., in June 1863 under Maj. Morris Hazzard were identified as a battalion in official and informal reporting.

New Yorkers recruited into the 16th New York were armed with Sharps carbines, a breech-loading, single-shot, rifle-barreled weapon that was eight inches shorter and a pound lighter than its namesake, the Sharps rifle. Like the rifle, the Sharps carbine used a paper or linen cartridge, which was fairly easy to load, even on horseback. This gave the cavalryman an advantage, in terms of rate of fire, over infantry equipped with muzzle-loaded muskets, although carbines had a shorter range than rifle-muskets.[4]

Most men in the 16th also were equipped with Colt "six-shot, single-action, percussion" revolvers. Although the loading process was somewhat cumbersome and time-consuming, once loaded the revolver enabled the cavalryman to get off six quick—albeit not very accurate—shots in succession.[5]

While many Union cavalrymen, especially officers, were photographed with sabers, the saber-equipped mass cavalry charge was a rarity, especially for the 16th New York. The New Yorkers, instead, would be employed primarily in the more traditional cavalry roles of patrolling, scouting, reconnaissance and intelligence gathering, and serving as a screening force for the infantry and artillery, while manning the outer defensive lines around Washington.

Sprague Light Cavalry

On January 17, 1863, Spencer H. Olmstead received authority to recruit the "Sprague Light Cavalry," named after New York's State Adjutant General. A native New Yorker and staunch Baptist, Olmstead had been elected pastor of the First Baptist Church in Boonville, Missouri, in 1858; served as pastor of the Huntsville Baptist Church in Randolph County, Missouri, in 1859; and as pastor of the Parkville (Missouri) Baptist Church in 1860 and 1861.[6]

Because of his pro–Union views, Olmstead and his family were forced to leave Missouri in late September 1861. At the time, he was pastor of the Platte City Baptist church that had been established in 1850. Following the surrender of Union troops on September 20 to pro–Southern Missouri State Guard members in Lexington, secessionists in the area had been emboldened, according to Olmstead. He also believed that Union volunteers from an Ohio regiment had alienated the local population by plundering the inhabitants in St. Joseph and the surrounding country "to a shameful extent."

Having spoken out in favor of the Union, Olmstead believed his family was no longer safe, and they fled to Chicago. Arriving there, he reported that his former town was convulsed by "anarchy and confusion, and lawlessness, and everybody in that region has given up the idea of saving any property that is convertible or destructible."[7] Leaving Chicago, Olmstead and his family made their way back to New York State.

Beyond these accounts, not much is known of Spencer Olmstead. According to the *Plattsburgh Republican*, he had had a "military education" in his earlier years and felt it "his duty to temporarily lay down the spiritual and take up 'carnal weapons.'"[8] However, his military background remains a mystery. On September 2, 1862, an S. H. Olmstead was mustered in as a private in Company C, 3rd New York Cavalry, at Austerlitz, southeast of Albany.[9] By the following January, this "young man of unusual fitness for the service to which he has been assigned" was in Plattsburgh making arrangements for raising a new cavalry regiment. The barracks for new recruits were ready, and a local recruiting office opened on January 24, 1863.[10]

Plattsburgh was selected as a major post for organizing volunteer regiments (the 16th and 118th Infantry, as well as the 16th Cavalry) largely due to the efforts and influence of Lot Chamberlain, a steamer captain on Lake Champlain, who was elected Sheriff of Clinton County in 1853 and appointed Paymaster of U.S. Volunteers in 1864. Chamberlain served as commissary for all the regiments organized at Plattsburgh.[11] By late March, men were enrolling in the regiment state-wide, with recruiting offices open in New York City, Buffalo "and other important points" and "quite a number of men have already been sent into camp."[12]

During the spring and summer of 1863, recruiting broadsides for the

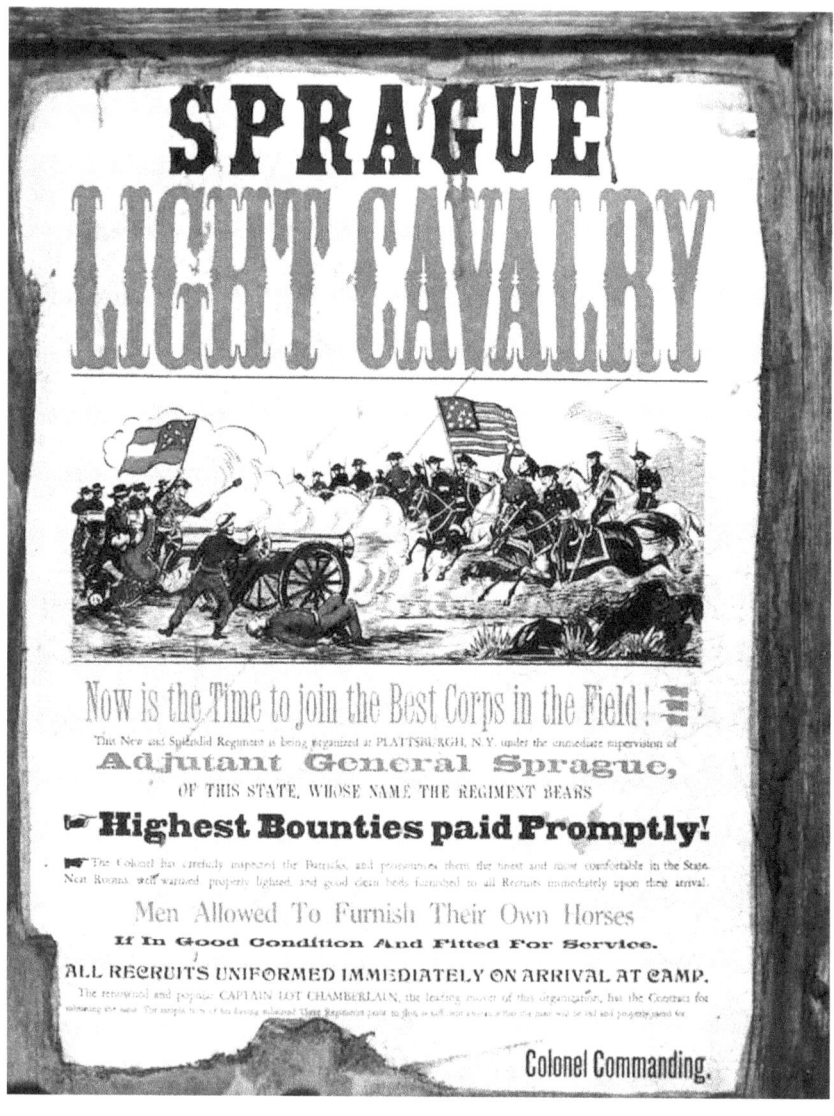

Recruiting poster for the Sprague Light Cavalry (from the collections of the Clinton County Historical Association).

regiment were printed in New York City, showing a body of uniformed Union cavalry, with drawn sabers and plumes in their hats, attacking a battery of Confederate cannon. The posters proclaimed in large letters, "Now is the Time to Join the Best Corps in the Field."

The regiment eventually drew volunteers from Syracuse, Rochester, Albany, Massena, Mooers, Champlain, Troy, Buffalo, Yonkers, Mount Pleasant, White Plains, Brooklyn, Schohaire, Greenburgh, and New York City as well as Plattsburgh. Advertisements placed in local papers offered "extraordinary inducements" for recruits to take part in a "great national drama."

> Complimentary. National Theatre. Great Attractions! Admit the bearer and his friends to a front seat to view the great National Drama now being daily performed, Stoneman in Richmond and The Union Preserved! Performers wanted to take part in this truly exciting National Drama. Salaries liberal. One hundred and fifteen dollars paid in advance, and engagements warranted to last for three years. For further particulars apply to Lieut. John Pettit, tent in front of the Court House, Rochester, N.Y. The reason why. Because, upon being mustered into the regiment, you receive a State bounty of $75 and a U.S. Bounty of $25. Because at the same time you will receive One Month's Pay in advance, making $113. Because you are at once into the service, with pay, rations, and relief for your families. Because you will have the best Horse and Arms, and wear the Handsomest Dress in the Army. Because, upon being discharged, you receive another Bounty of $75. Because you would like to see Richmond and the Elephant,[13] and be commanded by tried and capable officers. Because there is no use hanging around home ignobly, when Capt. McPherson is ready to take you to see the "Great Show" on the banks of the Rappahannock and Rio Grande [sic] Rivers. Now is your chance to change this Check for $175 and Clothing at the Show Tent in front of the Court House, Rochester, N.Y.[14]

Capt. James McPherson (courtesy Steven G. Miller).

Capt. James A. McPherson, the son of a Livingston County farmer, was recruiting for Company G. In September 1862, he had enlisted as a private in New York's 26th Independent Light

Artillery Battery, also known as Barnes' Rifle Battery. New York State records indicate he was commissioned a 1st Lieutenant on November 29, 1862, but was "not mustered" at that rank when the unit entered into Federal service at New Orleans on February 25, 1863.[15]

In New Orleans, McPherson had served as Assistant Quartermaster for the Department of the Gulf until Union forces occupied Port Hudson in early July 1863. Soon after, "desiring more active service," he was mustered out and returned home to New York. He mustered in as captain of Company G, 16th New York Cavalry, on August 13, 1863. As an assistant quartermaster in an artillery unit, McPherson had no cavalry or combat experience, but he had worn the uniform, was an educated man, and had leadership potential.[16]

Meanwhile, by early April, the *Plattsburgh Republican* was reporting that the new regiment, forming at "Camp Norton" in Plattsburgh, was beginning to "give evidence of life and energy." Olmstead had been away establishing recruiting stations, and recruits had begun to arrive "from a distance."[17]

Camp Norton was situated on the banks of Lake Champlain at Plattsburgh Barracks, which dated back to the War of 1812. On May 2, 1861, a group of local citizens met in the Plattsburgh sheriff's office and appointed a committee to "draft a petition to the Governor to make the Plattsburgh Barracks a rendezvous for the mustering and drilling of volunteers." By October, the barracks, now under the command of Col. James Fairman, were fully functioning and declared in "superior order."[18]

The *Republican* highlighted the positive qualities brought to the regiment by some of its newly appointed officers, including:

Camp Norton at Plattsburgh, New York (from the collections of the Clinton County Historical Association).

- Adjutant Henry M. Gaylord, a "splendid fellow" who had seen "honorable service" and bore wounds "received in fighting his country's battles."
- Quartermaster Albert Ladue, a local businessman, "whose soul is in the work before him," and who already had achieved popularity serving as County Sheriff.
- Post Surgeon Dr. J. Platt Foote, the "leading physician of this place," who would serve the new recruits until they left for Washington.[19]

Henry Gaylord, age 33 and formerly a member of Buffalo's 74th Militia, had initially volunteered with the 21st New York Infantry, known as the "First Buffalo Regiment." He had mustered in as captain of Company B in May 1861 and moved with the regiment to Washington, D.C., in June. Assigned to the Army of the Potomac, Gaylord's regiment wintered at newly established Fort Buffalo near Annandale and then moved to Centerville in March 1862. Prior to the Second Battle of Bull Run in late August 1862, the regiment was involved in "various marches, countermarches and minor encounters with the enemy."[20]

Capt. Gaylord never saw major combat with the 21st Infantry. He resigned his commission on August 9, 1862, and returned home. On February 13, 1863, he signed on again, this time as 1st Lieutenant and Adjutant of the 16th New York Cavalry, then still known as the Sprague Light Cavalry.[21]

Capt. Nathan H. Mooney of Company A, on the other hand, had seen combat. With a "common-school and academic education," he had started his own produce business at the age of seventeen. When the war broke out, he enlisted as a private in Plattsburgh's 96th New York Infantry (Macomb's Regiment). Within three months he was promoted to 1st lieutenant. After moving to Washington, the regiment joined McClellan's Army of the Potomac in April 1862 at Fortress Monroe and took part in the siege of Yorktown and Battle of Williamsburg. Mooney's health failed in May 1862, and he was discharged for disability in September. Recovering over the winter, he enlisted in the 16th New York Cavalry in March 1863.

1st Lt. Albert Ladue was 46 years old and married with three children when he was mustered in on March 9, 1863, as regimental quartermaster. He had no prior experience. By September, he had moved to New York City and opened a recruiting station for the third battalion of the regiment that was mustering men at New Dorp on Staten Island.[22]

While Albert Ladue came into the 16th with no military experience, 1st

Lt. George H. Anderson, Co. A, like his company commander Mooney, had seen the defenses of Washington as a private in the 118th New York Infantry. Organized at Plattsburgh in the summer of 1862, Anderson's regiment left New York for the capitol city in September. Anderson served there until May 1863 when he was discharged to accept a promotion to 1st lieutenant in the 16th.[23] In April, George wrote his father from Washington that his transfer and promotion had been approved and that he was not sorry to "change my position from a pack mule to ride a horse."[24]

Another newly enrolled lieutenant who had seen "honorable service" was Charles Frederick Moore, one of five sons of Amasa Corbin Moore of Clinton County, New York, and a grandson of General Benjamin Moore who had commanded the New York Militia at the Battle of Plattsburgh in 1814. The Moores were an established Plattsburgh area family, dating back to Judge Pliny Moore, who founded the town of Champlain at the end of the Revolutionary War.[25] In May 1861, Charles and his older brother Pliny had volunteered in the 16th New York Infantry. Pliny was mustered in as a 2nd lieutenant and Charles as quartermaster-sergeant.[26]

Charles was not happy as quartermaster-sergeant or with the decision of the regimental commander, Col. Thomas Davies, to assign one of his own family members as quartermaster-lieutenant, "a country farmer that knows nothing at all of the business or military life." Apparently, Charles's brother Pliny, although a second lieutenant, was unable to help him. Writing to another brother, Amasa Richard Moore, in November 1861, Charles expressed his determination to resign from the 16th Infantry if he could secure an acceptable position in a new regiment (the 96th Infantry) being raised near Plattsburgh by Lot Chamberlain.[27] The new position was

Lt. Albert Ladue (courtesy Steven G. Miller).

not offered, and Charles remained with the 16th Infantry until February 1862, when he was discharged "for disability." On June 19, 1863, he was mustered in as a 2nd lieutenant in Co. A, 16th New York Cavalry.[28]

One of the regiment's other newly appointed first lieutenants, Henry R. Barber of Co. A, never made it to Plattsburgh. Formerly a sergeant in the 118th Infantry Regiment (also organized at Plattsburgh), he fell ill as he prepared to join his new unit, and "so rapid were the ravages of the disease that he survived the attack but six days."[29]

Regimental Commissary, 1st Lt. Albert B. Wilbur, responsible for procuring and supplying food for the regiment, was highly educated but had no prior military or "commercial" experience. A native of Connecticut, whose family had moved to Menia, New York, northwest of Poughkeepsie, Wilbur graduated from Yale University in 1858. Initially, he taught school in New Haven, but in the late summer of 1859 accepted a teaching post as Assistant Principal of the Riddicksville Seminary, northeast of Murfreesboro, NC. He left his beloved future wife, Sophie H. Morgan, whom he had met while at Yale, behind in New Haven.[30]

On April 22, 1861, Wilbur—the only "union man" in town—was visited by the local sheriff, who presented him with an ultimatum from the state governor to enroll in the Confederate forces on or before April 27 "for the purpose of going to take Washington." Late that night a local friend also visited him, advising Wilbur to "take the oath of allegiance to N. Ca. & the Southern Con-

Lt. Charles F. Moore (courtesy Alice T. Miner Museum, Chazy, NY).

federacy." The following night, Wilbur noted in his diary that "men in disguise" had surrounded his house. He left town two days later and was back in New Haven, calling on Sophie Morgan:

> We met in silence and talked in silence for a while. Dangers all passed and together again. It seems like some delusive dream born to fade out into a dark reality. But 'tisn't—I'm here, really here, thank God.[31]

The following July, Wilbur received a Master of Arts degree from Yale, and in August he began teaching at the Artisan St. School, a small private school for African American children that was supported financially by Mary Lucas Hillhouse, the daughter of a New Haven lawyer and real estate developer.[32] He apparently remained at the school until he enlisted in the 16th New York Cavalry in Washington, D.C., on December 2, 1863. He was commissioned as 1st Lieutenant and Regimental Commissary, with rank from November 10. Sophie Morgan would continue to appear regularly in Albert Wilbur's diary throughout the war.

On June 20, 1863, Col. Olmstead appointed the Rev. Hinton Summerfield Loyd of Waterford, New York, to be chaplain of the Sprague Light Cavalry.[33] Loyd had graduated from Madison University's (now Colgate) seminary in 1858. Ordained a Baptist minister in December 1858, he had first served as a missionary pastor and then with Baptist congregations in Peekskill and Waterford. He was mustered in as chaplain on November 23, 1863.[34]

Regimental Surgeon, Dr. Joseph M. Homiston, then 33 years old, enrolled October 9, 1863, at Albany and was mustered in the following day. An 1850 graduate

Chaplain Hinton S. Loyd, after the war (A1024 Hinton Summerfield Loyd Papers, Special Collections and University Archives, Colgate University Libraries).

of Yale College, he had studied medicine in New Haven and, in 1854, established a medical practice in Brooklyn. Homiston had volunteered for military service early in the war and was commissioned as surgeon of the 14th New York Militia, a Brooklyn unit, in February 1861. In May of that year, the Fourteenth was mustered into Federal service as the 84th New York Infantry. Captured at the First Battle of Bull Run, because he and his fellow medical officers "preferred to remain [on the field] rather than abandon their charge [the wounded]," he had been confined for six months in Richmond—at Libby Prison—and in Charlottesville.[35]

In October 1862, after his release, Homiston resigned from the 84th New York, but some six months later, on April 2, 1863, he re-enlisted in Albany and four days later was mustered into the Westchester Light Infantry, which, along with a number of other units, was consolidated into the 178th New York Infantry. After serving as an inspector for the Army of the Potomac, he volunteered for the 16th New York Cavalry.[36]

One of the recruits who enlisted in Company M at New York City on April 17, 1863, was sixteen-year old George Westinghouse. Born in Central Bridge, New York, near Schenectady and Albany, he was the son of a farm machinery manufacturer. He had served briefly in the 12th New York State Militia before volunteering for the 16th New York Cavalry. Working in his father's machine shop prior to the war, George had already demonstrated engineering talent. He would soon be promoted to corporal and, after the war, would found the Westinghouse Corporation.[37]

Another New York City recruit was Louis Abend. Born in Prussia, he had emigrated to New York in 1850 at the age of 18. Initially working as a farmer, he enlisted in the 5th U.S. Cavalry in San Antonio, Texas,

Surgeon Joseph M. Homiston (courtesy Green-Wood Historic Fund Collections).

on September 28, 1857, for a term of five years. He had blue eyes, brown hair, a "fair" complexion, and stood five feet and six inches tall. He was wounded in a skirmish with Confederate troops at Gaines Mill, Virginia, in June 1862, and was discharged as a "musician" at Harper's Ferry on September 28, 1862.[38]

Abend re-enlisted as a "drummer" in Co. A of the 165th Pennsylvania Infantry ("Drafted Militia"), at Camp McClure in Chambersburg, Pennsylvania, and was mustered in on November 4, 1862. The 165th was part of the 7th Corps in the Department of Virginia, serving in southern Virginia and on the Peninsula. Abend was injured when his horse was hit by a cannon ball, and he was cared for by Harriett P. Crowley, company laundress and nurse. Discharged with his regiment in July 1863, he married his nurse at Carlisle, Pennsylvania, the following month.[39]

Pvt. Louis Abend, Co. H (courtesy Wayne Diercks).

By early 1864, Louis and his bride had made their way to New York City, where he enlisted again on January 22, 1864, this time for three years in Co. H of the 16th New York Cavalry. Harriett followed him to northern Virginia and lived in the encampment of the 16th, most likely continuing to work as a laundress and nurse. Abend's enlistment papers identified him as a "butcher" by trade with auburn hair and a "sallow complexion."[40]

As a drummer and member of the regimental band, Abend was probably not directly involved in close combat. However, he played his drum at President Lincoln's second inauguration and in the President's funeral procession. Following the war, he and his wife moved to Zumbrota,

Minnesota, where he and Jacob Fredrich, a bugler from the 16th, went into farming. His drum is now on display at the Zumbrota Area Historical Society Museum in Minnesota.[41]

Another experienced recruit, enrolled in Co. F by Capt. John J. Schlaefer on May 27, 1863, was Francis (Frank) T. Hagadorn. Francis already had seen some rough duty. In August 1862, then sixteen, he and his nineteen-year old brother William had enlisted in the 125th New York Infantry in their home town of Schaghticoke, north of Albany, Francis as a musician and William as a private. On September 15, 1862, their entire regiment surrendered at Harpers Ferry, was paroled and sent to a parole camp in Chicago, Illinois. William and the rest of the regiment returned to Virginia in December, but Francis remained in Chicago, hospitalized. He was discharged for disability in April 1863, and returned to Troy.[42]

The only job Francis could find, at a local store, paid a mere $1.50 a week for "opening and closing the store, sweeping it out daily, running errands and waiting on customers." Since he was paying $5 a week for board, he "tried daily to get work but could not and was generally told to go to enlist as my country need [sic] more men."[43]

On June 15, 1863, Pvt. Francis Hagadorn and his fellow 16th New York Cavalry recruits left Troy by train for White Hall at the southern end of Lake Champlain, where they boarded the steamer "United States" and sailed up the lake to Plattsburgh. The following morning, after a breakfast of hash, coffee, bread and butter, the new arrivals received a

The Abend Drum (courtesy Wayne Diercks).

medical examination. Francis, as bugler, was first in line. Later in the day, they were sent to the quartermaster and each man was given a jacket, blouse, pair of pants, overcoat, cap, two shirts, two pairs of drawers, two pairs of socks and a pair of shoes.[44]

Among the last recruits from Plattsburgh were three brothers—Edward, James and John Kenelty—sons of John Patrick Kenelty, an Irishman and farmer from Clinton County. All three enlisted for one year in Co. A on September 1, 1864. By this time, several companies of the regiment were already assigned to the defenses of Washington. Edward, the oldest at 25, was married to the sister of a fellow Co. A enlistee, Edmund J. Pickett, and had three children. Twenty-one year old James and nineteen-year old John were not married. The three brothers had seven other siblings, including three older brothers.[45]

Despite assurances of "Highest Bounties paid Promptly" and barracks that were the "finest and most comfortable in the State" with "neat rooms, well warmed, properly lighted, and good clean beds furnished to all Recruits immediately upon their arrival," the process of filling out the regiment was not without difficulties. Under the headline "Important Military Arrest" in May 1863, for example, the *New York Times* reported that John Abendorff, one of the new regiment's captains, had been arrested by the Provost Martial General for conspiring to form a "band of guerrillas."

> Some days since, Provost-Marshal-General NUGENT received information of a conspiracy which was being inaugurated in the Sprague Light Cavalry, and giving the matter careful attention, he procured sufficient evidence to convict the guilty parties, who were at once arrested, and are now in a fair way to receive merited punishment. It appears that Capt. JOHN ABENDORFF, of the above mentioned regiment, devised the scheme of forming a band of guerrillas out of the above command, who were to be ready on their arrival at camp to skedaddle, and commence a career of robbery and bloodshed indiscriminately on friend or foe. The Captain's principal confederate was Sergeant BUCKLER, who was stationed at the camp at Plattsburgh, N.Y. A letter was secured, written by Capt. ABENDORFF, in which was written a cypher alphabet, with the key of explanation, informing the Sergeant that thereafter all communications must be in this cypher. Capt. A. was at once arrested and sent to Fort Lafayette, at which quarters his Sergeant is about to join him. As the men who joined the organization claim they did so for the purpose of exposing it, they are, at present, only detained under arrest in camp.[46]

A month later, the press was reporting a near mutiny at the Sprague Light Cavalry's Plattsburgh camp.

> Four or five hundred men, recruited for the "Sprague Light Cavalry," and rendezvoused at Plattsburgh, were last week ordered to move from that point to Harrisburg. But a portion of the battalion refused to obey orders until they received their full bounty. From their proximity to Canada, affording the disaffected unusual facilities for

desertion, it was not deemed prudent to pay the bounty until some more interior point was reached. A flat refusal to march was the result. When informed of this inexcusable insubordination, Gov. Seymour promptly ordered a hundred and fifty picked men from the 34th (quartered at the barracks in this city [Albany]), under command of Capt. Corcoran, to proceed to Plattsburgh to compel obedience.... They reached Plattsburgh Sunday morning, before daylight, surrounded the barracks of the mutineers, took possession of the cannon on the ground and of all the available arms, and were prepared to make prisoners of all the disaffected before they knew what was going on.

When the mutineers saw the position of things, they blustered a little, but finally quietly succumbed; agreed to behave themselves, came down with the detachment, and are now on their way to the seat of war.[47]

There were other incidents during the recruiting and training period, both curious and detrimental:

- On June 10, thirty-one year-old Pvt. William W. Conger, who had enlisted at Cadyville and was mustered in as farrier in Co. A, died of an accidental musket wound. Conger, a blacksmith by trade, left a wife and several children.[48]
- On June 20, Pvt. Hagadorn and a number of other men who had breakfasted on hash became extremely ill, vomiting and suffering severe stomach pain. They were moved from their bunks to the regimental hospital and given mustard plasters to help ease their stomach pain. In the end, the regimental doctor determined that the hash had contained arsenic. The perpetrator was not found.[49]
- On August 6, William Nichols, a twenty-three-year-old bugler who had enlisted as a private at Oswego in early June, was found dead in a grocery store's outhouse on the east side of the Saranac River. According to a local newspaper, "he came into the premises unbeknown to the proprietor, and was first discovered by Sergt. Craizo [*sic*, probably Quartermaster-Sergeant Benjamin Craozia], who was in search of him." The reporter learned from the coroner's inquest that Nichols had died from a broken neck, "by falling and striking his head against a narrow partition, forcing his neck into a position even with his feet ... and not being able to extricate himself."[50]

The regiment, like many others, also was plagued by early desertions. In mid–June, some 12–15 deserters from the Sprague Cavalry and other regiments in confinement at Plattsburgh were sent to Governor's Island in New York Harbor "in charge of Lieut. Petit" of Company A.[51] These men were just the tip of the iceberg, and some deserted more than once:

JONES, ALPHEUS—Age, 36 years. Enlisted, January 18, 1863, at Syracuse; mustered in as private, Co. A, February 17, 1863, to serve three years; deserted, March 6, 1863, and April 10, 1863, at Plattsburgh, N. Y; dishonorably discharged, July 8, 1863, at Fort Columbus, New York Harbor.

LAWRENCE, RALPH J.—Age, 24 years. Enlisted, March 9, 1863, at New York City; mustered in as private, Co. A, April 9, 1863, to serve three years; deserted, June 1, 1863, at New York City; returned and again deserted, October 29, 1863, place not stated.

MILLAR, ABRAHAM.—Age, 42 years. Enlisted, February 13, 1863, at Plattsburgh, and there deserted, March 23, 1863; mustered in as private, Co. A, April 8, 1863, to serve three years; sent to Governor's Island for safe-keeping; again deserted, June 25, 1863, place not stated.

SHIELDS, JOHN.—Age, 21 years. Enlisted, July 3, 1863, at Buffalo; mustered in as private, Co. E, July 30, 1863, to serve three years; returned to Thirteenth New York Cavalry, as deserter, August 31, 1863, at Staten Island, N.Y.; not taken up on rolls; again deserted, November 1, 1863, at Vienna, Va.; appears in Co. C, Twenty-first New York Cavalry, as John Scales.[52]

A number of men deserted soon after reporting to Camp Norton and collecting their bonuses. Just outside of camp, between the camp and nearby woods, there was a large whortleberry patch where, according to Pvt. Hagadorn, the men would "meet women and other friends who use [sic] to help the men to desert, by bringing them citizens clothes." In an attempt to stem the tide, officers placed sentries outside the camp fence.[53]

The sentry posts apparently were not terribly effective as a preventative measure. On July 13, Hagadorn wrote that "Sergeant Thomas Coulton (who had been reduced to the ranks [private] for being drunk while on duty), James Grace (or 'Hash' as the boys nicknamed him, for eating so much hash), John LaFeaver, Dennis and George Brown, deserted from the Hospital, about midnight." LaFeaver and one of the Browns were caught the next day.[54]

Pvt. Albert G. Martin, of Co. B, who chose to stay, expressed some of the same doubts and feelings of regret that most likely drove many of his fellow recruits to desert. Writing home soon after he enlisted in early May, he begged for his parents' forgiveness:

> I truly repent for going away and leaving you to do all the work and bear up the trouble. I am not sick of the service but as soon as I can get out of it honorable I will come home and will stay with you as long as —— and be so good I always will stay with you and help you and make your Old Days as comfortable as I can. Mother and Father, Forgive me for what I have done and I will always be a good boy to you and obey your command and my prayer is that I may be spared to come home and comfort you both in your Old Days and that you both may be spared and blessed and find happy days yet, and I feel that God has and will answer my prayer. Mother you look sad in your likeness. Cheer up and live for my sake. If I have done wrong I am trying to do better.[55]

Martin, a Canadian citizen whose family had moved from Ontario earlier in 1863, ran off to Plattsburgh to enlist in May. He stuck with his decision, despite his parents' concerns and despite a rash of desertions that decimated his company within two months after it was mustered in. As he wrote to his mother, "When we left N.Y. there was 100 in our company, and now there is about 48—they have deserted but I hear that there is a great many of them caught. I [know] that some of them has enlisted three times before and runaway with the bounty."[56]

"Bounty jumping" was quite common on both sides during the war. The enlistee would collect his bonus, desert, and move on to a new recruiting site and begin the process all over again, often under a new, assumed name.

Sadly, Martin would not return home to take care of his parents in their old age as he promised. On October 1, 1863, he was captured in a skirmish with Confederate troops in Lewinsville, Virginia (now McLean) and imprisoned at Belle Isle, in the middle of the James River in Richmond. In early November, he wrote his parents from prison telling them he was well and expected to be exchanged or paroled soon. He encouraged them not to worry, asking them not to be "uneasy about me nor troubled if you don't get a letter from me right away, for sometimes I can't get a chance to write when I want. Now don't give yourself any trouble about me. I will assure you I will come out all right after awhile, and don't be alarmed but what I will keep in good cheer." He died at Belle Isle "in hospital" on February 24, 1864.[57]

Petty crime also was rampant in the camp. On July 14, 1863, for example, the "office boy" was pulled from the Guard House and forced to walk around the parade ground carrying a log of wood and a placard on his back with "thief" written on it. He had been caught "trying to sell Lieut. Farnsworth's revolver," and had also stolen a box of cigars from the lieutenant, as well as a shawl and $15 from a Mrs. Kelly. Two days later, Pvt. Hagadorn was robbed of $1.50—"all of my money"—on his way from supper to his barracks.[58]

An Amalgamation

The full regiment that finally emerged as the 16th New York Cavalry in October 1863 was a cobbled-together unit containing companies recruited for the Washington Light Cavalry and the 20th Veterans Infantry, as well as the Sprague Light Cavalry. The former two units had failed to fully organize and, as a result, on October 14, 1863, these two were formally consolidated with the Sprague Light Cavalry, which was renamed the 16th Regiment of Cavalry.

Washington Light Cavalry. On July 27, 1863, "Colonel" William W. Hammell (also shown as Hammill in some documents) had received authority to recruit the Washington Light Cavalry. Hammell, originally Captain of Co. F in the 9th New York Infantry Regiment (Hawkins Zouaves), had been wounded in April 1862 at the Battle of South Mills, North Carolina. He was mustered out with the rest of his regiment in May 1863 at New York City and began recruiting for the new unit in late July. An August 1863 *New York Herald* summary of regiments recruiting in New York City and Brooklyn listed the "Washington Light" as a new regiment, under Hammell, with its headquarters at "Mercer House."[59]

Among the men that Hammell enlisted in New York City was a "large fellow who was standing on a corner." When Hammell asked him why he wanted to enroll, the young man answered that "God told him to." The recruit who was inspired by God was Boston Corbett, a seriously mentally troubled hat maker who would gain fame in April 1865 as the man who shot and killed President Lincoln's assassin, John Wilkes Booth.

Ultimately, Hammell was able to fill only two companies, and in October, companies A and B became companies L and M of the 16th. Once Corbett and the other Washington Light Cavalry recruits were consolidated into the 16th New York, Hammell was discharged.[60]

20th Regiment of Veteran Infantry. On July 29, 1863, "Colonel" Engleberth Schnepf (also carried as Schnepp) received authority to reorganize the United Turner Rifles (20th Infantry Regiment) as the 20th Regiment of Veteran Infantry. The men of the United Turner Rifles, who fought at Antietam, Fredericksburg and Chancellorsville, had been discharged and mustered out on June 1, 1863, at the end of their two-year term of service. Schnepf, who originally mustered in as Major of the Turner Rifles in May 1861, had been promoted to lieutenant colonel in April 1862. He was mustered out with the rest of the regiment. In August, Schnepf's headquarters was located in New York City at 225 Grand Street. His attempt to reorganize the unit failed, and those who had enlisted were transferred to the 16th in October.[61]

16th New York Cavalry

The newly formed 16th New York Cavalry consisted of twelve companies:

Company	Muster Date	At	Men From[62]
A	June 19	Plattsburgh	Plattsburgh, Syracuse, Canton, Massena, Mooers, New York City, Altona, & Champlain
B	June 19	Plattsburgh	Buffalo
C	June 19	Plattsburgh	Buffalo, Albany, & New York City
D	June 19	Plattsburgh	Buffalo
E	August 13	Plattsburgh	Plattsburgh, Buffalo, & Massena
F	August 1	Plattsburgh	Plattsburgh, Troy, Ogdensburg, Canton, & Albany
G	August 13	Plattsburgh	Rochester, Plattsburgh, Oswego, Albion, New York City, Barrie & Buffalo
H	August 13	Plattsburgh	Plattsburgh & New York City
I	September 2	Staten Island	New York City, Buffalo, & Plattsburgh
K	September 22	Staten Island	New York City, Yonkers, Mt. Pleasant, Greenburgh, Troy, Yonkers, Buffalo, Albion, Avon & Rochester
L	October 18	Staten Island	New York City, Buffalo, Brooklyn, Greenburgh, White Plains, Arcade, Schoharie, Middleburgh & Cobleskill
M	September 5	Staten Island	New York City & Greenburgh

The Regimental Standard carried by the 16th featured the coat of arms of the United States with 13 gold stars and a red ribbon with the regiment's numerical designation. The shield positioned on the eagle's breast included New York's state motto, "Excelsior." The "flank marker" flags carried by the regiment featured painted inscriptions and a red shield on both sides. "N.Y.S.V." (New York State Volunteers) and "CAVALRY" were in mirror images on the reverse side of each flag.[63]

The First Battalion Departs for Washington

By late June 1863, the first battalion (companies A, B, C and D) of the Sprague Light Cavalry, stationed at the U.S. Barracks (Camp Norton) in Plattsburgh and commanded by Maj. Morris Hazzard, was filled out and under "marching orders for the seat of war" (Washington). Pvt. Hagadorn wrote in his diary on June 21 that when the boat with Maj. Hazzard and the four companies on board passed the camp "we cheered each other."[64]

On July 5, 2nd Lt. Charles F. Moore of Co. A wrote his mother from Washington that they first had been ordered to Fort Stevens which defended the approaches to Washington along the 7th Street Pike (now Georgia Avenue). Soon they returned to the city and were camped some three and a half miles from the "long bridge" (14th Street bridge) and a mile and a half from Alexandria. Five days later, he wrote that they had moved again, this time to Frederick City, Maryland. There, they joined the Cavalry Division helping to cover the Union Army's flank following the battle of Gettysburg as it pursued Robert E. Lee's Confederate forces back through Maryland and into Virginia:

16th New York Volunteer Cavalry Flank Marker (courtesy New York State Military Museum and Veterans Research Center, Saratoga Springs, NY).

> We were ordered to move from Washington the day following my mailage [*sic*] of my last letter [July 6]. We moved about noon marched 25 miles that night & camped. Maj Hazzard was in command of the 3rd Brigade and Col. Johnston commanded the [Cavalry] Division which gave me the Major rank again. Arrived in Frederick City about 3 p.m. on the 7th. The 8th the Division was broken together with the Brigades. Col. Johnston ordered back to bring all remaining cavalry. Wanted me to return with him but I thought it a good time to get rid of the Q'Master Department [he had been appointed Brigade Quartermaster] and told him I would prefer returning to my Company which he has allowed me to do. So now we are here waiting orders as an independent Battalion. We were ordered out to do picket duty yesterday for the city. There has been a great many troops past us on there [*sic*] way to the front which is but a short distance from us. They have been engaged today as we have heard firing quite distinctly here. The Major went out about ten miles and witnessed a cavalry engagement. I fear we will not have a chance to participate for the simple reason that we are

not far enough advanced as yet in drill. But we are anxious, very, to try our hand and hope that chance may offer. We have the rebel army tight now as we have a force driving them down the [Potomac] river, a force at their flank, and a force here to meet them. Then they cannot cross the river because it is so very high.

Over 2,000 have passed us on their way north. This has been the HD [Head] Quarters of Gen. Mead & Gen. Pleasanton but they both took the field yesterday. I saw Gen. Slocum a half a dozen times yesterday. The roads about the city have been full of troops, canon [sic], government wagons, etc. The wounded are being brought into Middletown.[65]

Maj. Morris Hazzard (seated) and Capt. Mooney (U.S. Army Heritage and Education Center).

On July 29, Moore would write again from Alexandria, having moved as rear guard of a column of Union forces from Frederick, through Berlin and Salem, Virginia, and over to Bull Run battlefield to Washington, arriving "all worn out. Horses & men, as we have marched since we started about 400 miles, which for raw men and horses is an uncommonly long march." He reported hearing all sorts of rumors about his still-incomplete regiment including, on the one hand, that it was "all broken up," and on the other that its second battalion was being equipped in Washington and would "join us in the field."

What Lt. Moore did not know was that by August 1, after four months of recruiting, the regiment had a second battalion "on the eave [sic] of departure," and a third "in the process of enlistment." The regimental headquarters was now located at 428 Broadway in New York City, with four additional recruiting stations in the city. A local report noted that half of the men recruited for the regiment were veterans, having served out prior enlistments.[66]

On July 18, Pvt. Hagadorn of Co. F wrote of rumors that the 2nd Battalion would be leaving within a week to "join the 1st Battalion at Frederick City." He expected to receive ten dollars before leaving Camp Norton. To discourage desertions, the balance due would be paid once they reached Albany: "they fear we will desert if paid in full now, as we were only 22 miles from Canada."[67]

On August 17, the Second Battalion (Companies E, F, G and H) with 342 men left Plattsburgh for New York City, arriving at Camp Sprague "below Vanderbilt Landing," near the town of Stapleton on Staten Island's east shore, the following day.[68] The infantry units in the camp performed guard duty while the cavalry was given "Provost" (military police) duty. Apparently the infantrymen and cavalrymen had very little sense of being engaged in a common cause. According to Hagadorn, some of the infantrymen were jealous of the cavalry troops and decided to take out their frustrations:

> One day when most of the Cavalry were out of camp, the Infantry attacked our barrack where only the sick and their attendants were. They threw bottle, stone and everything that they could at us [Hagadorn was among the sick] in our bunks. A company of Cavalry came in camp just in time to protect us. Our officers tried to make peace and beg us not to draw our sabers, but go back to our barrack. One of the riotous infantrymen crept up behind our Major [Horton] and hit him on the head. The Major stopped telling us to retire and ordered us to draw saber, to use the flat side, and to charge. This we did in such good style that we caught the ringleaders and dispersed the rest. The ringleaders were put into the Guard House, this stopt [sic] the riot.[69]

This was not the only incident at Camp Sprague. A week before Hagadorn's battalion arrived, the camp had suffered a massive fire, thought by some to have been set by "some soldier or soldiers of secesh [secessionist] or Copperhead [northern Democrats who opposed the war] sympathies, who had smuggled themselves into the ranks." The hospital was saved, but "all of the southwest side and half of the south buildings"—more than half the barracks—were destroyed, as were the post library and quartermaster's stores, although their contents were saved. For temporary quarters, "some spacious tents" were erected and were "much coveted by the troops to sleep in during the intense heat." Both the sleeping tents and remaining barracks were placed under double guard "night and day."[70]

On September 3, 1863, while Pvt. Hagadorn was on two-month "recruiting duty" in New York because of illness, the 2nd Battalion left Staten Island for Washington. The Quartermaster Department and some of the commissioning officers remained at Camp Sprague. The officers would escort groups of new recruits to Washington after they were mustered in and fitted out. Hagadorn was discharged "for disability" on October 2 but stayed in camp for another two weeks until he received his final pay. He would re-enlist in February 1864, this time with the 13th Connecticut Infantry, from which he would be mustered out at the end of the war at Fort Pulaski, Georgia.[71]

Camp Stoneman

Arriving in Washington, the 2nd Battalion was initially sent to Camp Stoneman, part of the Cavalry Depot at Giesboro Point, today's Joint Base Bolling-Anacostia, on the Anacostia River across from Washington. Established in August 1863 on the property of George Washington Young, the city's largest slave owner, the depot was one of six built by the Cavalry Bureau to supply horses to Union forces. Camp Stoneman, named after Maj. Gen. George Stoneman, Chief of the Cavalry Bureau, was established adjacent to the depot "to house cavalry troopers as they awaited remounts."[72]

Established July 28, 1863, the Cavalry Bureau was charged with the "organization and equipment" of Federal cavalry forces and to "provide for their mounts and remounts." The cavalry depot at Giesboro Point was designed to accommodate from 10,000 to 12,000 horses "sick and well." At the time, there were more than 16,000 "unserviceable" horses near Washington, most of which, it was believed, "with proper care and treatment, could again become fit for service."[73]

Newly formed cavalry units were held at Camp Stoneman's Camp of Instruction, where they received additional cavalry training beyond the basic drills they had learned at enlistment camps. Writing about his experiences years later, QM-Sgt. Cyrus G. Shepard of Co. F described one of the cavalry drills conducted at Camp Stoneman during which he rode on what apparently was not one of the cavalry's finest horses, but rather "one of those tall, raw-boned, hard-trotting animals that no man could ride easily or even decently."

> One of the evolutions for practice was leaping our horses over a huge log erected for the purpose several feet above the ground, and I had a disastrous time when my turn came to undertake this performance. Putting spurs to my charger, I rode pell-mell for

the log, but, not understanding how to induce my steed to leap over, he came down stiff on all fours before the log. I went over the log all right, but the horse did not.[74]

Shepard and his fellow cavalrymen also were issued Colt revolvers, Sharp's carbines and cavalry sabers at Camp Stoneman. They were "drilled regularly twice a day in the use of these weapons and in horsemanship." According to Shepard, their issue from the "culinary department" consisted of a single tin cup that was used "for all purposes—to bring water in and to drink water from; to make coffee in and drink coffee from; to make bean soup in and to eat bean soup from." Their daily rations consisted of six hard tack biscuits or a loaf of bread, "a portion of coffee, one of salt pork or beef, with beans or peas to make soup."[75]

By the time he left Camp Stoneman, each man also had secured a nickname. QM-Sgt. Shepard, being one of the youngest in his company and from the town of Malone, became "Malone Baby." Another man with an abnormally large head and feet so large that his boots had to be special-ordered, became "Top and Bottom."[76]

The 2nd Battalion remained at Camp Stoneman for about eight weeks. On October 29, 1863, Col. J. B. McIntosh, commanding the Cavalry Depot, ordered the commanding officer of the 16th New York Cavalry to "send without delay the men of the 2nd Battalion now in your camp to join their companies at Vienna, Va." The following day, the Depot's Assistant Inspector General was ordered to muster the companies of the 16th "now in the depot" for pay on the morning of October 31.[77]

Meanwhile recruiting to fill out the third battalion (the regiment's final four companies) had continued, with new recruits sent to Camp Sprague on Staten Island. Co. I, in particular, recruited heavily in New York City, and Regimental Quartermaster, Lt. Albert Ladue, manned a recruiting office there.[78] Companies I, K, and L left Staten Island in September, and Co. M departed October 23. All four reported initially to the Camp of Instruction at Camp Stoneman. While there, in addition to training, they also performed duties as required by the Cavalry Depot's commanding officer.

- On October 17, Capt. Otto Kleinschmidt of Co. I, who was also Acting Battalion Major, was ordered to take 150 mounted men detailed from the 18th New York Cavalry, pick up 500 "lead horses" from the corral and "proceed to Fairfax Court House (which point you will reach by 3 p.m. if practicable) when you will turn them over to the QM of the Cav Corps."
- On November 8, Co. L commander Capt. Lawrence Leahy, a

veteran who had been wounded and cited for bravery as a lieutenant with the 9th New York Infantry (Zouaves) at Antietam, was ordered to take command of 100 men, probably new recruits, of the 3rd Division, Cavalry Corps, Army of the Potomac, and travel by steamer to Alexandria to pick up 100 horses. Marching by way of Annandale and Fairfax Court House, he was to turn over the horses and men to the 3rd Division.[79]

In early November, Pvt. Edwin Noonan of Co. L wrote his parents that the camp at Giesboro Point was situated on "fine open hilly country," with plenty of good spring water a half-mile away. Their rations were "even better than on Staten Island," with fresh beef three times a week, along with pork, bean soup, potatoes, and "good bread" from a government bakery in Washington. He was quartered in a four-man canvas tent with "log house" walls calked with clay that hardened like cement. "We make a fireplace and use a barrel for a chimney, which makes it very comfortable."[80]

Noonan described Capt. Leahy as "both a gentleman and a soldier, nothing proud or disdaining about him and never rests until he sees every one of his men cared for." Noonan wasn't sure whether they would winter at Camp Stoneman, but thought they'd be there for at least another month. Capt. James Fleming of Co. M was more certain, writing home on November 7 that he was "in a camp of instruction and very likely to remain here all winter, about 4 miles outside of Washington. I am very well satisfied as the position is a very good

Capt. Lawrence Leahy (U.S. Army Heritage and Education Center).

one and I believe as things appear just now there will be very little more fighting."[81]

Fleming was wrong on both counts. The battalion would leave for Vienna, Virginia, in early December, and the regiment would see a great deal of action. Born in Belfast, Ireland around 1834, Fleming had arrived in New York with his family in 1837. With the outbreak of the Civil War, he enrolled as a 2nd lieutenant in May 1861 with the 9th New York Infantry (Zouaves). Fleming already had seen a good deal of action, including the Battle of Antietam. He had mustered out with his company in May 1863 but re-enrolled that July as a 1st lieutenant and quarter-master with the Washington Light Cavalry. When it was consolidated with the 16th New York Cavalry, he was appointed Captain of Co. M.[82]

Fleming wrote home that he was very pleased to be with a cavalry unit, since he would "have no more long marches upon foot. A Capt. is allowed 4 horses which I expect will carry me over what distance I may be required to go." Fleming closed his November letter with the promise that he might well surprise friends in County Antrim "some early morning by taking a walk through the streets of Larne as I have never given up that idea of coming home again." He would not make good on that promise. On August 8, 1864, Capt. James H. Fleming was killed in action at Fairfax Station.

While the men of companies L and M were pleased with their officers, Co. I was a troubled unit, due to a fractious relationship between Capt. Otto Kleinschmidt and 1st Lt. Joseph N. Schultz. Kleinschmidt was a veteran, having served as an adjutant and first lieutenant in the 41st New York Infantry from June 1861 until discharged for disability on October 31, 1862. Schultz had no prior military experience or service. The two did not get along from the very beginning, Schultz apparently considering the "damn Dutchman" beneath him in station and believing that he, rather than Kleinschmidt, should be in command.

Kleinschidt brought Shultz up on charges twice. On the first occasion, Schultz was charged with conduct unbecoming an officer and gentleman for calling Kleinschmidt a "God damn son of a bitch" on or about October 24, 1863. A court-martial in November found Schultz guilty and sentenced him to be dismissed from the service of the United States on November 30. Since court-martial sentences were subject to review, however, he continued to serve in his company. In May 1864, Schultz got off on a technicality, the Judge Advocate General ruling that it did not appear that the court or its Judge Advocate (prosecutor) had been sworn in: "this being a fatal irregularity, the sentence is inoperative." Schultz was reinstated, ex post facto.[83]

On November 28, 1863, the commanding officer at the Camp of Instruction was ordered to requisition enough horses "to finish mounting the 15th and 16th New York Cavalry regiments" and to forward an ordnance requisition to the Cavalry Depot Ordnance Officer for the 16th. Once those two actions were completed, the 3rd Battalion, 16th New York, departed Camp Stoneman for Vienna, Virginia, on December 5.[84]

In the meantime, however, Lt. Schultz again had been brought up on charges by Kleinschmidt, this time accusing him of "mutiny" while they were still at the Camp of Instruction. There were two specific accusations, the first being that during the month of November 1863 Schultz had, on several occasions, incited the men of Co. I against their captain, telling them that he, Schultz, would soon have Kleinschmidt out of the company, that he would then take command, and that they must obey him and not Kleinschmidt. The second accusation was that on or about December 4, Schultz had countermanded Kleinschmidt's order that the company blacksmith brand some horses assigned to the company, telling the blacksmith that he would be "God damned" if he would let him brand the horses, and that if he did he would "swing him ... higher than he ever was in his life." Schultz was accused of persisting "in this rebellious conduct until put under arrest by his commanding officer." A court-martial held in late January 1864 found Schultz not guilty of both charges, but he was transferred to Co. L on January 24. He would last until October 1864 when he was dismissed for reasons unknown.[85]

While the 2nd and 3rd Battalions were forming and then training at Giesboro Point, the regiment's first battalion, under Maj. Hazzard and now part of the cavalry force commanded by Colonel Charles Russell Lowell, Jr., of the 2nd Massachusetts Cavalry, had been earning its spurs. On August 12, 1863, Albert Martin wrote his parents that his company had left its Washington encampment three days earlier and marched by way of Alexandria and Fairfax to a new camp about a quarter mile from Centreville. They expected to remain there until the area could be cleared of Mosby and his men:

> I suppose there [sic] correct name would be Guerillies [sic] or Highway Robbers, they wait there [sic] chance to come across a baggage train of ours that isn't guarded very well and then capture them and they plunder a great many of the shops. There [sic] leader's name is Mosby. They are scattered all through the State and they know every foot path and by-road in the part but still there has been a good many of them captured and more is captured most every day. There is forty of our men out scouting today for Mosby and his band and I was on guard and could not go with them. Our Colonel said on Dress Parade last night that any man that would capture Mosby dead or alive he would give them a major's pay for there [sic] term of enlistment which is $80 a month. These Guerillies go some times in union dress and some time in citizens.

> I was talking with some soldiers today and they said they was out after the Guerillies before we came here and was eating there [*sic*] breakfast one morning and the Guerillies fired on them and after a short fight they licked them taking eight prisoners and they finished there [*sic*] breakfast and then they took the prisoners and tied them to the trees and shot them on the spot. They don't alway [*sic*] shoot the prisoners but do some times for they deserve it. They ain't fighting for the South, only for plunder."[86]

Indeed, Mosby and his men had been busy. On August 10 they had come down Little River Turnpike, spent the night near Gum Springs, then the next day continued on through the Ox Road junction toward Flint Hill. Avoiding Union pickets, they passed through Vienna and captured one sutler's train near Gooding's tavern and a second about a mile further east. Plundering the wagons and taking all the horses and mules, Mosby and his men started back through Vienna toward Hunter's Mill. There they split forces, half going towards Dranesville and the others toward Chantilly and Gum Springs. In his official account for General J. E. B. Stuart, Mosby reported that he and his men had captured 19 wagons and 25 prisoners, secured the teams and "a considerable portion of the most valuable stores, consisting of saddles, bridles, harness, etc."[87]

In response, Col. Lowell proposed to establish a regular escort of 30 to 50 men along the road from Centreville to Alexandria at certain "irregular" hours and require all sutlers "and stray wagons" to move with these escorts. He also suggested adopting a "more systematic method" for encouraging local civilians to provide information on Mosby's activity, and asked if there were any funds on which he could draw to offer rewards for "valuable and reliable information."[88]

On August 18, 1863, Martin's company was sent out to Lewinsville looking for Mosby's men, as part of a larger force commanded by Lowell that had marched from Centreville to Dranesville in search of Col. Elijah White's 35th Virginia Cavalry (another so-called guerrilla outfit). Martin's detachment of New Yorkers was split off from the main force and sent to check on an alleged enemy camp. It returned from Lewinsville the next day having found nothing.[89]

Three days later, Lt. Moore wrote from his camp near Centreville that he and Col. Lowell had just returned from a "little scout" of 50 or 60 miles, along with 500 other cavalrymen from his battalion, the 13th New York Cavalry, and the 2nd Massachusetts, chasing after Mosby and White:

> We were after White but could not find him. I was on picket about a week since with 40 men on the road that Mosby takes these wagons and had about 4 miles of the road to patrol. Knowing that I was to be relieved I had my horses saddled, made up my mind that I would have a scout (knowing full well I could not be relieved until I was found); just got my men up in good shape when a rider came, full speed stating that

Mosby was down about two and a half or three miles, and had taken some wagons (sutler). We started on a run. Before this 5 of my men & a Sergt. had driven 14 rebels from the wagons & they went back & brought from both [sic] 85 reinforcements. Well we soon arrived at the place, dashed into the woods (as only Cavalry can), ran across the wagons, passed them, pressed the rebels so they had to let loose the sutlers & their horses and hide in the brush where cavalry could not possibly go. Hunted through 5 miles of woods 5 hours. Recaptured sutlers, horses, & one of my own horses which I lost & they got. They did not take anything but the sutlers, money, & watches. Saying they had not time to stay for anything else. Got back on the road near my camp and found my relief waiting for me about 4 hours. Should like to have stayed longer, think that perhaps I might have caught Mosby, what say you to that? He told a sutler he has captured since [then] that he had about as close a run Saturday as he had had.[90]

Lt. Moore's company and the rest of Maj. Hazzard's battalion would continue to engage in scouting, patrol and picket duty under Colonel Lowell throughout August, September and early October. On August 24, Moore and his company again narrowly missed Mosby, who had attacked a contingent of troops from the 13th New York Cavalry watering a "train" of Union horses at Billy Gooding's Tavern on Little River Turnpike in Annandale. Upon learning of the raid, Moore mounted up his 30 men, rode to Gooding's Tavern, and found the party of men who had been attacked. As Moore related to his mother, he was determined to recapture the horses even though he was outnumbered:

> Went on down the road and got back some thirty of the horses, found that they [Mosby's men] had taken a small road off the main road, but being picketed [guarded by Union troops] on the main road could not leave it any distance, and therefore returned to the scene of the conflict some moments before. Among the horses I got our Rebel Captain's horse with full equipment which I now retain for my own use as his were much better than mine.[91]

Ironically, for the second time in less than a week, Moore missed his chance to capture Mosby. Only after the engagement and his report to Col. Lowell would he learn that Mosby had been wounded: "If I had only have known that he was wounded, I would have taken my men from the road (run the risk of a court martial), and would have had him if it took every man I had to do it with."

On September 2, Pvt. Martin of Co. B wrote from Fort Ethan Allen, "about six miles above Washington on the Virginia side right by the Chain Bridge," that his company, along with Co. D, had been relocated from Centreville to undertake picket duty "against some bushwhackers." He enjoyed picket duty since "we have easier time then [sic] when we are to camp they have us out scouting and racing and roaming around and we don't get any peace night or day."[92]

QM-Sgt. Shepard, on the other hand, considered picket duty "hazardous in the extreme" and "one of the greatest hardships of cavalry service," since the cavalry pickets were far outside their camps and closest to the advancing enemy: "a trooper on picket duty was not only exposed because of his position on horseback, but, necessarily, to be able to maintain a good lookout, he must occupy an exposed position, or at least much more so than an infantryman."[93]

Shepard described his first experience of serving on picket duty at night on Little River Turnpike near Germantown as "exceedingly trying":

> The night was dark, and I could not see many feet along the turnpike, and not at all through the trees on the other side. The suspense soon became almost unbearable as I sat gazing out into the darkness, fearing every minute to hear the dreaded sound of an approaching foe. Hearing the barking of a dog at an adjacent farmhouse was some relief, but with it came the thought that it might mean the gathering there of guerrillas who were soon to sweep down upon my post. The minutes crept slowly on, and the suspense and strain increased. Soldiering on the outposts of the Union in Virginia, a lone cavalryman, at dead of night ... brought with it visions of that comfortable bed in the old house in northern New York where I might have been if I only had not gone a soldiering. Waiting and watching, the first two hours pass at least, and no angel of mercy ever accomplished a more blessed mission than did the officer of the guard when he came at midnight and relieved me of my responsible position.[94]

On September 17, the *Philadelphia Press* reported that General Corcoran (who had commanded the 69th New York Regiment at the First Battle of Bull Run) had just visited the Bull Run battlefield, "under a strong escort of Major Hazard's 16th New York Cavalry." The *Press* found Corcoran's description of the battle, where he had been taken prisoner, interesting but was most taken by "the fact that the bodies of the slain were so exposed as to taint the atmosphere. Skulls lie thickly about, as does accoutrements, etc."[95]

In early October, Col. Lowell proposed establishing an "outer ring of defenses around Washington," using the existing cavalry camps at Muddy Branch, Fairfax Court House and Centreville as well as a new camp at Vienna, Virginia, northeast of Centreville. Vienna was close to Washington and some six miles down the road from Lewinsville. It was in a good position to cover Potomac River fords and Fairfax and Loudoun counties. In addition, he recommended setting up picket posts at Germantown, Lewinsville and Annandale.

> Patrols every two to four hours between these posts and the other cavalry camps would keep the roads invariably full of soldiers, and vedettes [mounted sentries] at night would guard the main roads. Lowell proposed blocking the smaller roads with felled trees. He wanted the patrols also to serve as escorts for sutler and other supply wagons.[96]

Maj. Gen. Heintzelman accepted Lowell's recommendations and directed the cavalry brigade to establish its headquarters at Vienna. One battalion of the 2nd Massachusetts was kept across the river in Maryland "covering the Potomac crossings up to Falling Waters." The rest of the regiment moved to Vienna along with seven companies of the newly formed 13th New York Cavalry and the four companies of the 16th commanded by Maj. Hazzard.[97]

Troubles Ahead?

By the time all twelve companies came together in Vienna as the 16th New York Cavalry, the regiment already had taken casualties. Co. B had been involved in a skirmish at Lewinsville in early October, with two enlisted men killed, another two wounded, and ten missing. The circumstances and outcome of the Lewinsville skirmish should have been a red flag, particularly regarding the quality and leadership abilities of the regiment's cadre of inexperienced junior officers. The story of William Jeremiah Keays, the officer in charge on that day in Lewinsville, underscores the operational impact of the lack of formal military training and leadership experience of many of the regiment's lieutenants and captains.

Lt. Keays had no prior military experience or training, but he was "a natural leader of men and he was well educated."[98] He was immediately made a lieutenant and acting captain. On October 2, 1863, his cavalry detachment of 40 men was bivouacked as part of the security force—which also included a detachment of 17 infantrymen—at Camp Beckwith, a "contraband farm" for escaped slaves

Family photograph of Lt. William Keays after the war (courtesy Rod MacDonald).

in Lewinsville. The camp had been established on two farms owned by secessionists, and the former slaves were housed in abandoned buildings on the properties. There they raised their families and grew crops. As of June 30, 1863, Camp Beckwith had 72 residents.[99]

The small infantry detachment was responsible for protecting the "government farm" and maintained a camp guard around the house that was used as a headquarters and for "lodging the men employed on the farm." Lt. Keays's cavalry detachment was to "scout the country, cover the camp of infantry, and to notify them of any advance of the enemy."[100]

During the night of October 2, Keays and his men, encamped in and around the main house at Camp Beckwith, were attacked by troops of Lt. Col. Elijah V. White's 35th Battalion of Virginia Cavalry, a partisan unit similar to Mosby's, from Loudoun County. Twenty of Keays's men were killed, wounded or captured. Four of those captured died at the infamous Andersonville prison in Georgia. According to an investigating officer dispatched under orders from Maj. Gen. Heintzelman, Lt. Keays had incorrectly placed his pickets—or sentries—too close to the camp, and there was insufficient time for them to warn of White's attack. The officer's report concluded:

> In my opinion had the pickets been properly posted (even the same number of men used by Lieutenant Keays would have been sufficient), this surprise could not have occurred, and the men in camp would have been formed certainly in time to have made some resistance, if not sufficiently strong to drive the enemy entirely away, which I think they could have done had they been prepared to receive them. For this I consider Lieutenant W. J. Keays, Company B, Sixteenth New York Cavalry, entirely to blame.[101]

Heintzelman accepted the report and forwarded it up the chain of command on October 5 with a recommendation that Keays be tried by court martial or summarily dismissed. Three days later General-in-Chief Henry Halleck recommended, and Secretary of War Edwin Stanton approved, Keays's dismissal. Keays, however, appealed to the President, through the Secretary of War, for reinstatement, stating that the force under him was "too small to allow him to establish an effective picket guard, that he was enabled to establish three picket posts only, whereas it was required for the protection of the camp in the night that pickets should have been posted at not less than six different points." He also maintained that he took "unusual precautions" against surprise.[102]

Lt. Keays had the full support of the officers of his regiment. Lt. Col. Olmstead characterized him as "a gentleman of high standing, talented, and strictly upright and moral" and was convinced "that if the President

One—A Regiment Is Formed 45

Typical picket post, near Lewinsville, Virginia (Library of Congress).

were duly advised of all the circumstances in the case he would restore Lieutenant Keays to his command." The field officers of the regiment agreed with Olmstead, declaring that Keays was "prompt and efficient in the performance of his duties, and was regarded by them all as eminently qualified for and adapted to the service in which he was engaged; that they could cite instances in which he has exhibited his gallantry in a manner highly creditable to himself and honorable to his regiment."[103] Keays apparently also was well liked by his enlisted men. According to Pvt. Albert Martin, he was "a very common and a nice man."[104]

Keays's battalion commander, Maj. Hazzard, also recommended that he be reinstated, noting that his "connection with my Battalion has been flattering to himself and beneficial to his Company. He always has been prompt, thorough and effective, strictly temperate and considered a competent officer and good soldier." In the end, the Judge Advocate General recommended reinstatement, and the President concurred. On December 31, 1863, Keays was reinstated.[105]

William Keays exemplified a problem that plagued many volunteer units. In the 16th, only a few of the company officers had much, if any, training or experience. Its new Colonel, Henry M. Lazelle, was a West Point graduate. Col. Nelson Sweitzer, Lazelle's replacement in 1864, also was a West Pointer, as was Lt. Col. George Hollister. However, Hollister would be dismissed for conduct unbecoming an officer and a gentleman in 1864. Other senior staff officers, like Lt. Col. John Nicholson and Maj. George Bosworth had significant experience.

- Nicholson had initially enrolled in May 1861 at Buffalo as a 2nd lieutenant in the 21st New York Infantry and transferred to the 100th New York Infantry in September 1861 as a captain. He was discharged from the 100th in March 1863, having fought in General McClellan's Peninsula Campaign and taken heavy losses at Fair Oaks. Two months after his discharge, he volunteered with the 16th.[106]
- Bosworth, who had served several months in early 1861 as an enlisted man with New York's 8th Militia, first enrolled as a major in the 81st New York Infantry in October 1861. The regiment left New York in March 1862 and also served in the Peninsula Campaign. Bosworth was discharged "for disability" on July 17, 1862, at Harrisons Landing, McClellan's headquarters on the James River. He mustered in as a major in the 16th on January 9, 1864, after the regiment had encamped in Vienna.[107]

The individual companies of the 16th, on the other hand, had a mix of experienced and completely green captains and lieutenants. Most had little time or opportunity for training beyond the drills and exercises at Camp Norton, Camp Sprague or Camp Stoneman. Instead, expertise and experience were gained on the ground. Many of those who were veterans had served previously as enlisted men or sergeants. While they had operational experience and some had faced combat, few had leadership experience.

- Seven of the twelve original company captains had led men in combat. Captains Leahy (Co. L) and Fleming (Co. M), who had served as officers in the 9th New York Infantry (Zouaves), had seen major combat at Antietam, where Leahy had been cited for gallantry. Captains Mooney (Co. A), Gaylord (Co. K), Schlaefer (Co. F), Morse (Co. E), and Mickles (Co. B) had seen some action as junior officers with McClellan's Army in the Peninsula. Capt. Kleinschmidt (Co. I) had been a company lieutenant and regimental adjutant at 2nd Bull Run, but his unit had been held in reserve. Four captains had no prior experience.

- Few lieutenants had prior service as officers, and only two of these (Lt. Gail and Lt. Maroney of Co. M) had seen combat. Most of those other original lieutenants with some combat experience had formerly served as privates. Five had served as corporals or sergeants: Dow of Co. D, Moore of Co. E, Moody of Co. H, Hildebrand of Co. I, and Cannon of Co. L. Of some two dozen lieutenants who mustered in between the spring and fall of 1863, nine had no military experience.

As a combination of three partially formed regiments, the 16th also lacked the unit cohesion and personal loyalty (officers to men and men to officers) that was the major strength of most volunteer units recruited from specific geographic areas. With diverse companies, recruited from throughout the state of New York—major cities and smaller towns and villages—the regiment had no real common geographic identity beyond the State of New York.

Col. Lazelle, himself a recently promoted captain in the regular army with no experience above the company level, faced the immediate challenge of commanding a regiment that lacked strong junior leadership and that was inadequately prepared for the mission given to it. He had not participated in the officer selection process and had little or no time to observe basic unit training and weed out weak performers. With additional time for training and vetting—particularly at company level, since many of its operations were company-size actions—the regiment might have avoided the problems that would plague it over the next year and a half.

The New Colonel

Most likely because many "colonels" organizing volunteer regiments lacked military training and command experience, State Adjutant General John Sprague sought out seasoned officers to lead New York's regiments. Capt. Henry M. Lazelle, U.S. Army, an 1855 West Point graduate with whom Sprague had served in the 8th U.S. Infantry out in Texas prior to the war, also was looking for a volunteer command. In 1861, Sprague and Lazelle had been caught up in the surrender of Federal forces in Texas by pro–Southern Union General David Twiggs, when Texas joined the Confederacy.

In January 1861, after an extended leave of absence from the 8th Infantry, Sprague (then a major) had been ordered back to Texas. Upon his arrival in San Antonio in March, he was prevented from rejoining his regiment at Fort Bliss and was arrested by a Committee of Public Safety. On April 23, Sprague was paroled by Confederate authorities and left Texas for New York. There, he became a mustering and disbursing officer in Albany and soon thereafter Adjutant General of the State.

Meanwhile, Lazelle—on parole—had slowly made his way back to Washington from Texas, securing permission finally to leave Richmond, Virginia, by signing a very restrictive parole agreement. Under the parole system, a practice going back to ancient times, a prisoner of war was released "on his honor" not to take up arms again. During the Civil War, the so-called Dix-Hill Cartel, signed in July 1862, codified a process for exchanging prisoners and releasing them from their parole restrictions once exchanged.

Eventually exchanged for a Confederate officer, Lazelle had been assigned to the Commissariat of Prisoners where he was responsible for inspecting Federal prison facilities and parole camps. He also had served as Union agent for a major prisoner exchange in Vicksburg, Mississippi.

In an early February 1862 letter to Sprague, Lazelle—anxious to leave staff duty and secure a volunteer command—had recounted "a very satisfactory interview" with a Lt. Col. Hall at Fort Marcy regarding a potential assignment in command of another one of New York's forming regiments. For reasons unknown, Lazelle was not selected for this

Col. Henry M. Lazelle, circa 1882 (author's collection).

regiment. Rather, on September 17, 1863, he accepted appointment as Colonel of the 16th New York Cavalry. He noted, however, that he would be assuming command "with hesitancy and a want of confidence—the Cavalry is not my forte—even if I have one—but one thing is certain, so long as I retain command of it I shall do my duty so far as I know and can learn it to the extent of my capacity—and I hope you will not have occasion to feel that your confidence in me has been misplaced even though you ask me to manage men, *and horses*" (emphasis original).[108]

Lazelle was not necessarily displaying a sense of false modesty. He had ranked near the bottom of his class in cavalry tactics and horsemanship when he graduated from West Point, and his name had been absent on the list of graduates "especially recommended for promotion in the mounted corps." He had only limited "combat experience," mostly chasing Indians in Texas and New Mexico. As a junior officer, he also was not familiar with the complexities of managing and leading a regiment, much less a newly formed one with raw recruits and a number of inexperienced company officers. Thus, he must have known he faced some major leadership challenges.[109]

Two

Colonel Lazelle Joins His Regiment

Col. Henry M. Lazelle, U.S. Volunteers, joined his regiment on October 23, 1863, at Vienna, then the terminus of the Alexandria, Loudoun and Hampshire Railroad line from Alexandria.[1] The Independent Cavalry Brigade now had three full regiments in Vienna. Col. Charles R. Lowell of the 2nd Massachusetts commanded the brigade. When he was in the field, that responsibility fell to Lazelle since he was senior to the 13th New York Cavalry's Col. Henry S. Gansevoort.

The rail line to Vienna had once extended out into Loudoun County. Because it was one of only two strategic routes (the C&O Canal being the other) for any large-scale movement of personnel and supplies westward out of Washington, Robert E. Lee had ordered the destruction of all bridges on the railroad on May 24, 1861, just one day after Virginians voted to secede from the Union. Hence, Vienna became a railhead (terminating point) supplying the encampment there, as well as troops camped along Washington's outer defensive line, running from Prospect Hill, off Georgetown Pike, and roughly following Chain Bridge Road through Fairfax Court House and down to Fairfax Station.[2]

According to Charles Humphreys, Chaplain of the 2nd Massachusetts, the encampment of his regiment and the brigade headquarters on Josiah Bowman's 240-acre Ayr Hill property, overlooking Vienna's railroad station, was:

> ... surrounded with a heavy abatis [defensive barricade] of felled trees branching outwards to guard against sudden attacks of guerrillas. Here we spent the winter of '63 to '64, and made ourselves as comfortable as we could, with board floors in our wall-tents, and with brick fireplaces, and with chimneys made of mud and sticks. Our chimneys were of necessity so shallow that on windy days the smoke would be forced in gusts down the flue into our tents, and I have often been driven out into the storm

for self-preservation—though doubtless if I had stayed in I would have been preserved, but only as a smoked and dried specimen of suffering humanity. Still we had a great deal of satisfaction in our fireplaces, and when the nights were cold and clear, the logs blazed brightly, our tents often resounded with laughter and song and all went merry as a marriage-bell."³

Top: Cavalry Brigade Headquarters on Ayr Hill, Vienna, Virginia. *Bottom:* Abram Lydecker's store was used for officer housing and possibly a hospital (Library of Congress).

Col. Lowell and his new wife, Josephine, had more pleasant quarters in Bowman's "little house" on the hill: "We have all the luxuries and some of the necessaries. Housekeeping is under difficulties, but is a success. It's a great thing, *pendant thiver* [sic], to have a Brigade in a fancy Department, and to have your wife out to command it."[4]

The brigade also took over a general store with an upstairs residence near the station on Church Street, using it for officer housing and possibly as a hospital. Built by Abram and Susan Lydecker in 1859, the store had served as a polling place in 1861 for Virginia's secession vote, in which Vienna voters had cast their ballots 77 to 44 against secession. Sometime in late 1861 or early 1862, when Confederate troops were occupying Vienna, Lydecker had been arrested as a northern sympathizer and incarcerated at Castle Godwin Prison in Richmond. His building remained in either Confederate or Union hands throughout the war.[5]

Following the war, Lydecker returned to Vienna, bought a 104-acre farm outside of town, and continued to operate his store. In 1872, his daughter and son-in-law, Anderson Freeman, moved to Vienna. Freeman took over the store around 1874. After selling the Vienna store, Abram Lydecker opened a new store and mill nearby at Hunter's Mill Station.[6]

Upon arriving as a full regiment in Vienna, Lazelle and the men of the Sixteenth set up camp about a half mile away from the Bowman tract on another hill—also overlooking the railroad station—on property owned by Moses A. Commins. He had purchased land west of the station and built a foundry and plow factory near the intersection of today's Lawyers Road and Maple Avenue. A strong Union supporter, Commins had feared "rebel molestation" after the Battle of Bull Run, and had left his property and opened a foundry in Washington, D.C.[7]

When the 16th New York occupied the Commins property, the troops cut down timber to erect buildings and fortifications. Lazelle and his wife moved into the Commins house in December. As compensation for using the property, Lazelle signed a notice of "safeguard" on November 8, 1863, protecting the property and stating that "all officers and soldiers belonging to the Army of the United States are therefore commanded to respect this safeguard and to afford if necessary protection to the person, family or property of Moses A. Commins as the case may be." In March 1864, Commins signed an "Article of Agreement," that cancelled all of his claims for damages "except that portion of hard wood timber that actually may have been cut by the 16th N.Y. Vol. Cav. Regt.—the temporary buildings erected for use of the Regt. to be left on the premises of Commins for his benefit."[8]

At some point, the defenses of Vienna also may have included—or at least the Army may have contemplated—three "block houses" built in a triangular pattern around the village and station. An unsigned, undated sketch in the records of the Office of the Chief of Engineers, depicts their locations: one several hundred yards northwest of the railroad station and close to the railroad tracks; another several hundred yards east of the Bowman house and near the road from Lewinsville; and the third several hundred yards southwest of the Commins house and near the road out to Flint Hill.[9]

One postwar discussion of the use of "block-houses" as defensive structures described them as "usually erected of logs, one and two stories high" with the face of the upper story at "an angle of forty-five degrees to the face of the first story, thus concentrating a direct fire upon an enemy approaching from any point of the compass." Each, according to this account, could hold about a company of men.[10] Although, they could well have been constructed, there is no known photographic or written evidence on the actual existence of the block-houses depicted in the sketch.

At the time the 16th New York moved into its quarters on the Commins property, the 22nd Army Corps' cavalry brigade (with the 2nd Massachusetts and 13th and 16th New York regiments under Col. Lowell's command) was formally attached to Brig. Gen. Michael Corcoran's division, headquartered at Fairfax Court House and subordinate to Brig. Gen. Gustavus De Russy's Defenses South of the Potomac. Three months later, Brig. Gen. Robert O. Tyler would replace Corcoran. And, in May 1864, Tyler's Division would be discontinued and Col. Lowell's cavalry brigade would become truly "independent."[11]

Within days of moving to Vienna, men of the Sixteenth were out on patrol and picket duty and under the watchful eyes of Confederate Ranger John S. Mosby. On October 19, 1863, Mosby had reported to General J.E.B. Stuart that there were three regiments of Union cavalry at Vienna and that he planned to attack a cavalry camp (probably associated with the Vienna brigade) at Falls Church the next evening. His intention, he wrote Stuart, was "to detain the troops that are occupying Fairfax, by annoying their communications and preventing them from operating in front."[12]

Culling the Herd

Upon joining his new regiment, Col. Lazelle must have realized that he was saddled with a less than ideal collection of junior officers. According

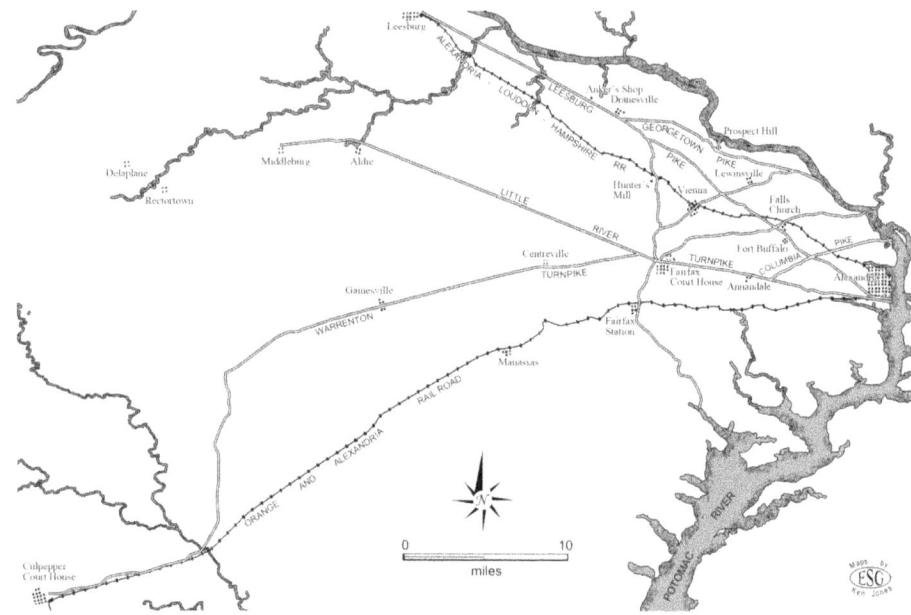

Northern Virginia, 1863–1864.

to 2nd Lt. Charles Moore, Lazelle almost immediately began to weed out weaker, less effective officers as well as those with serious character flaws. Among the first to go was Capt. Ronald McNichol, Co. K, who was dismissed on October 23, and replaced by Henry M. Gaylord, who at least had had some experience with the 21st New York Infantry.

Lt. Col. Spencer Olmstead, who had organized the Sprague Light Cavalry, was dishonorably dismissed on November 21, 1863, by direction of the President, for "receiving both transportation in kind and travelling expenses, for the same journey, and for the unauthorized and improper use of transportation blanks, furnished by the Quartermaster General of the State of New York." He was replaced by West Point graduate George S. Hollister, who had served in New Mexico prior to the Civil War and was mustered in as Lieutenant Colonel of the Sixteenth on December 30, 1863. According to his muster roll records, Olmstead eventually was able to have his dishonorable discharge modified to simple dismissal.[13]

Next to go was Maj. Morris Hazzard who had aggressively argued that Lt. Keays should be reinstated. Hazzard was dishonorably dismissed "by direction of the President," on November 27, 1863, for "habitual intemperance and neglect of duty."[14]

By the middle of December, 2nd Lt. Moore was convinced that Col.

Lazelle was targeting volunteers "to get regular officers in and then transfer the men to the regular army there, making himself a Colonel in the regulars instead of captain…. I have no doubt at any dislike he takes to an officer he will or has used that way [an examination board] of getting rid of them." Writing to his parents, Moore vowed that he did not want to "remain in such a place, or with such a Man" and told them he was seriously considering resigning. He decided, however, to wait "at least until some of those other regulars come, and see what they are." In the end, no "regulars" arrived, and Moore remained with the regiment, was promoted to first lieutenant of Co. C in September 1864, and later brevetted to captain.[15]

Winter Operations

Throughout the late fall and winter of 1863–64 Union and Confederate forces saw little major action in either the eastern or western theaters. That does not mean, however, that troops slept the winter away in camp. On the contrary, the Union cavalrymen in Vienna were almost constantly on picket duty or in the saddle, either reacting to Mosby's raids or scouting throughout northern Virginia:

- On one such scout that fall, some 200 men, commanded by Maj. Nicholson, were ordered to "march by way of Aldie and Upperville, examine the passes, return, and report with all possible dispatch." The following morning, after bivouacking overnight near Arcola, they were fired on by a group of Confederates while crossing Goose Creek. Having superior numbers and firepower, they overwhelmed the rebels who eventually turned and ran. After the skirmish, "a few of us went down the hill and out on the plain where the rebels had been. We found and buried three dead men, and brought in three wounded prisoners." Eventually they reached Snicker's Gap on the Blue Ridge, but "no signs of any considerable force of Confederate could be discovered," so they returned to camp by way of Warrenton, Centreville and Fairfax Court House.[16]
- On November 17, Col. Lowell reported that a sergeant and two men of the 13th New York, on picket duty at Germantown, had been captured the day before by rebel troops wearing Union uniforms: "1 man in our uniform approached the vedette [mounted listening post] on the road, and while his attention was directed

to a pretended pass, between 20 and 30 men in Union overcoats rushed out of the wood and captured the sergeant and 2 men, leaving a third wounded on the field."[17] Wearing Union uniforms as disguises was a common practice of Mosby and his men. It also was not uncommon for Confederate soldiers found wearing Union uniforms to be shot on the spot as spies by their Union captors.

- The following day, Lowell dispatched a 100-man scouting party out toward the Blue Ridge searching for guerrillas. Four days later, along with 100 of his own men and 50 from the 16th New York, Lowell met up with the scouting party between Middleburg and Rectors Crossroads. He split the force into three parties, one moving north toward Philomont in western Loudoun County and another southward through White Plains, the Manassas Gap Railroad and across Bull Run Mountain at Hopewell Gap. Lowell and the rest of his troops moved southward beyond Aldie. The operation was a success, capturing 18 "uniformed soldiers, who claimed to be Mosby's men"; seven "notorious smugglers and horse-thieves"; 35 horses; 13 sets of horse equipment; 25 revolvers; and 30 army blankets.[18]
- On December 9, Mosby and 30 men attacked another vedette manned by a corporal and five privates. Two Union men and five horses were captured. Simultaneously with this attack, another group of Mosby's men attacked the Lewinsville Station.
- The next day, a group of rebels attacked a picket post at Langley, capturing Pvt. James Randall of the 2nd Massachusetts.
- On December 13, some 20 guerrillas attacked a picket at Germantown, mortally wounding two men and capturing five horses.[19]
- On December 21, 20 to 30 mounted and dismounted "guerrillas" attacked a picket post manned by a corporal and five privates near Hunter's Mill, taking four horses and wounding two men. One of the wounded men was "shot a second time through the body by a guerrilla" after he surrendered and gave up his pistol. Soon after, 10 to 15 men fired on a Union officer and escort on the road to Fairfax Court House and two Union escorts were wounded.[20]
- On December 28, Mosby's men captured three pickets near Hunter's Mill. In response, Col. Lowell led a large body of men from all three regiments out Little River Turnpike to Mount

Zion Church. One detachment was sent as far as Hopewell Gap in the Bull Run Mountains. Several separate scouting parties captured two rebel officers and 17 privates, including ten of Mosby's men, along with ten "citizens" and one rebel forage contractor.[21]
- On January 4, Mosby reported to General J.E.B. Stuart that during the month of December, he and his men had captured "100 horses and mules and about 100 prisoners. A considerable number of the enemy have also been killed and wounded."[22]
- On January 6, guerrillas attacked a picket post at Flint Hill.
- On January 14, guerrillas slipped by the stable guard in Vienna and stole 15 horses.
- On January 27, Lowell was ordered to send a squadron of cavalry (two companies) to scour the country from Vienna, through Centerville, to Bull Run bridge in hopes of intercepting rebel cavalry reported to be in the neighborhood of Sangster's Station, near the current town of Clifton.[23]
- The next day, guerrillas captured a pair of four-horse teams and their drivers near Annandale; two guerrillas were spotted near Fairfax Station; and "several parties were reported to have been seen between Fairfax Station and Devereux." In response, Col. Lowell dispatched two scouting parties, one to Annandale and another out through Centreville to Bull Run. The Bull Run scouting party learned that Mosby and 60 men had passed by Bull Run bridge earlier, and it found "a few scattering rebels near Centreville," but otherwise everything was quiet.[24]

Ambush at Anker's Shop

In early February 1864, General Stuart noted that Mosby's "sleepless vigilance and unceasing activity have done the enemy great damage. He keeps a large force of the enemy's cavalry continually employed in Fairfax in the vain effort to suppress his inroads. His exploits are not surpassed in daring and enterprise by those of *petite guerre* in any age. Unswerving devotion to duty, self-abnegation, and unflinching courage, with a quick perception and appreciation of the opportunity, are the characteristics of this officer."[25]

One such "appreciation of opportunity" came on February 21, when Mosby learned that a scouting party composed of troops from the 2nd

Massachusetts and 16th New York had been seen at Rector's Crossroads (today's Atoka in Fauquier County). Mosby started in pursuit with 160 men. Upon reaching Middleburg, he discovered the Union cavalrymen had gone toward Leesburg. Reconnoitering around Leesburg, Mosby soon discovered the men from Vienna had encamped along the pike near Dranesville.[26]

Early the following morning, Mosby moved his troops out to the pike about two miles from Dranesville, on the property of Samuel Ankers, a farmer, blacksmith and horse breeder, "at a point offering fine natural advantages for surprising an enemy." Distributing his companies so they could attack "their front, flank and rear simultaneously," he lay in wait.

> Soon the concerted signal—a volley from the carbineers under [Capt.] Montjoy—announced the time for attack. With a terrific yell, Chapman, Hunter, and Williams, with their brave commands, dashed on the unsuspecting Yankees. Surprised and confounded, with no time to form, they made but feeble resistance, and were perfectly overwhelmed by the shock of the charge. They fled in every direction in the wildest confusion.[27]

In his report on the action, Brig. Gen. Robert O. Tyler, commanding Tyler's Division (Defenses South of the Potomac) headquartered at Fairfax Court House, confirmed that it, indeed, had been a major rout. The detachment of 125 men from the 2nd Massachusetts and 25 from the 16th New York, commanded by Capt. J. Sewell Read of the 2nd Massachusetts, had "fought well" but were finally "driven toward the Potomac near Muddy Branch." In all ten men, including Capt. Read, were killed and seven wounded. About 60 of the detachment were as yet unaccounted for.[28]

The night of February 22, Union cavalrymen were sent out in pursuit of Mosby and his men as far as Goose Creek. They returned the next morning with eight Union bodies and seven wounded troopers. Some 70 men were still unaccounted for, and Mosby was said to have quickly moved out toward Snicker's Gap in the Blue Ridge on the border of Loudoun and Clarke counties.[29]

On February 25, in response to the attack on Read's troops, Col. Lazelle ordered a larger force out to Dranesville: 200 each from the 2nd Massachusetts and 16th New York, and 125 from the 13th New York. On the way up the pike, a few rebel cavalrymen were spotted on the hills near Dranesville, but no large party of rebels was found. The force moved on to Belmont, Middleburg, Aldie, Farmwell Station, Gum Springs and Centerville, picking up various tidbits of information about Mosby's movements before returning to Vienna shortly after midnight.[30]

Mosby's attack on February 22, now known as the Second Battle of Dranesville or the Ambush at Anker's Shop, was a classic example of an ambush or "ambuscade," relying on good intelligence, a keen understanding of the enemy, and surprise. These surprise attacks were "the greatest fear of small Civil War cavalry detachments marching along contested roads." Often, they were their greatest undoing.[31]

As emphasized by James Williamson, who served with him, Mosby also had the classic advantages of the insurgent over the regular military:

> While the enemy were compelled to guard their lines, Mosby had none. When a body of troops was sent in search of him it was a very easy matter to keep out of their way if in heavy force, or cut off and attack any detachments from the main body and harass them on their march; or, by ignoring their presence altogether, compel them to return to protect their own camps. It would have been folly for our little band to have met and fought every force sent against us. The enemy's resources being so much greater than ours, the contest would have been too unequal and it would have simply been a question of time as to when we would be utterly destroyed or driven out of the country.[32]

On February 29, the 16th New York mounted its final operation for the month. Responding to reports that Mosby and five of his men had been seen near Chichester Mills, on Pohick Creek near today's town of Burke, 200 men under command of Maj. Nicholson, were sent out to "scour the country from Annandale to the Occoquan, by Wolf Run Shoals," then between Bull Run and Centreville, and on to Gum Springs, Frying Pan and Dranesville. The quest was for naught.[33]

Condemned to Andersonville

Six of the 13 men from the 16th New York captured by Mosby at Anker's Shop on February 22 were sent to the infamous Andersonville Prison in Georgia. All six died before the year was out:

- Pvt. Grafe H. Eldrichsburg, Co. K: initially sent to Richmond and then on to Andersonville, died September 16, 1864, at Savannah, Georgia.
- Pvt. George Howe, Co. M: died October 1, 1864, at Andersonville, of diarrhea.
- Pvt. Godfrey Pontius, Co. K: died August 2, 1864, at Andersonville, of scurvy.
- Pvt. Anton Rose, Co. L: died October 3, 1864, at Andersonville, of scurvy.
- Pvt. August Torbeck, Co. L: died July 20, 1864, at Andersonville, of scurvy.

- Pvt. Lawrence Williams, Co. L: died August 26, 1864, at Andersonville, of scurvy.

By the end of the war, a total of 54 men of the 16th New York would be sent to Andersonville Prison. Twenty-eight would die there, most of scurvy or severe diarrhea, the latter most likely from contaminated drinking water. Co. L would have the greatest number of deaths at Andersonville—ten between January and November 1864.[34]

Justice for a Deserter

Two weeks before the ambush at Anker's shop, the troops of the cavalry brigade had assembled on Ayr Hill to witness the execution of a Union deserter. On January 24, while on picket duty at Lewinsville, Pvt. William E. Ormsby of Co. E, 2nd Massachusetts, had deserted his post—taking with him two horses and six pistols—to join up with Mosby's Rangers. Ormsby, a native New Yorker, had enlisted in San Francisco and was mustered in with the rest of the 2nd Massachusetts' California contingent at Readville, Massachusetts. He had just turned 21 when he was sworn in and was described as five feet three and a half inches tall, with a fair complexion, blue eyes, and brown hair.[35]

Col. Lowell sent 60 troops of the 2nd Massachusetts after Ormsby, and they encountered him on February 5, when he and eight of Mosby's Rangers attacked them at Aldie Mill. Ormsby was captured, and Lowell quickly convened a drumhead court martial the following day. In his defense, Ormsby maintained he had no intention of joining up with Mosby. Rather he simply wanted to go home to see his parents in New York. He claimed he had been drunk on the day he was captured in Aldie and was not voluntarily accompanying Mosby's men.[36]

Despite his plea of innocence, Ormsby was found guilty of "desertion to the enemy" and sentenced to die by firing squad.[37] As QM-Sgt. Cyrus G. Shepard noted years later, "deserters to the enemy were always shot when the traitor could be secured. In this case, the traitor deserted while doing the important duty of a picket, thus leaving the door unguarded and the camp liable to surprise."[38]

This was Pvt. Ormsby's second court-martial in less than two months. On December 16, 1863, he had been charged with selling, losing, or otherwise criminally disposing of a "valuable government horse," entrusted to him by his company commander, while on leave to visit his brother in

Alexandria. He returned with "a worthless animal entirely unfit for service giving a reason that he 'had made a swap' with a negro man near Falls Church." Ormsby was found guilty and sentenced to forfeit $6.50 of his monthly pay for four months.[39]

Most likely to discourage other desertions, Lowell ordered that all Union troops in camp at Vienna witness Ormsby's execution. At 11 a.m. on Sunday, February 7, the brigade was "drawn up in a hollow square, with the rear rank 'open order,' and the doomed man, seated on a rough pine box which was to be his coffin, in a cart, was driven around the square, while the band played the death march, and then down the center where his grave had been dug."[40]

According to Samuel J. Corbett, a soldier from the 2nd Massachusetts, "just before his eyes were bandaged, he stepped up before the firing party, placed his hand upon his heart, and said, 'Boys, I hope you will fire well.' He was then seated upon his coffin, his eyes bandaged; the word was given to the firing party, and William E. Ormsby was in eternity." Valorous Dearborn, another soldier from the Second, noted that Ormsby "bore it bravely. He died at half past twelve with two bullets in his left breast."[41] The Adjutant of the 2nd Massachusetts later reported that Ormsby was buried on the spot of his execution.[42]

After the war, the bodies of men who had been hastily buried at Union encampments and battle sites were collected and re-interred in the newly established Arlington National Cemetery. Ormsby's body was among them. Ironically, he is buried in Section 13, not far from the Confederate Monument, at grave number 12860.

While the outcome of the Ormsby case was unique, both armies faced high levels of desertion, particularly among volunteers. Some simply couldn't resist the urge to return home, rest up, and take care of family affairs. They would then return to their old unit or volunteer for a new one. Others would leave as soon as they received their enlistment bonus, wait for a bit, and then join another unit for another bonus.

By January 1, 1864, less than three months after the regiment had formally mustered into the Federal service, some 560 men of the 16th New York, out of a total of over 2,200 who had enlisted, had deserted. The State Adjutant General identified some 300 as simply "deserted, as shown on descriptive list of deserters, dated January 1, 1864." For another 230, the Adjutant General identified specific dates and, in many cases, locations of desertion. Over half of these occurred between June and October 1863 as the regiment was forming and starting to engage in combat operations in northern Virginia. Many of the men may well have been "bounty jumpers."

At least two switched sides, twice. On June 25, 1864, Pvt. Martin Bishop, of Co. E, who had enlisted as an 18-year-old in June 1863 at Buffalo, was captured near Centreville. Sent to Andersonville Prison, Bishop accepted an offer of freedom and joined the Confederate Army. He was then captured once more, this time by Union forces at Egypt Station, Mississippi, in December 1864, and sent to the military prison at Alton, Illinois, where he re-enlisted on April 14, 1865, in the 5th U.S. Infantry.

Four days after Bishop was captured, Pvt. Richard Allison, a 22-year-old from Buffalo assigned to Co. D, was captured at "Boggs Station" (not further identified) on June 29, 1864. He enlisted in 10th Tennessee Infantry, CSA, while being held prisoner at Andersonville, and he too was recaptured at Egypt Station and confined at Alton Illinois Military Prison. He also re-enlisted April 14 in the 5th U.S. Infantry.

The vast majority of desertions, as was common, occurred within days or weeks of the soldier's enlistment and mustering in. In many cases, troops deserted as soon as bounties were paid. In other cases, reality set in as their training began, and fear drove them away. Whatever the reason behind the many decisions to run, the number of desertions in the Sixteenth dropped off significantly in 1864 (64 men) and was down to a trickle as the war ended in 1865 (45).[43]

Three

The Spring 1864 Campaign

Early in March 1864, President Lincoln appointed Ulysses S. Grant "General-in-Chief" of the Union Army and promoted him to Lieutenant General. In his new role as commander of all the armies, Grant first visited Maj. Gen. George Meade, commanding the Army of the Potomac, on March 10. The following day, Grant left Washington for Nashville, Tennessee, to meet with Maj. Gen. Sherman, who would replace him as commander in the west.[1]

In February, the President had called for an additional 200,000 volunteers and in March another 200,000. In Virginia and the Army of the Potomac, eyes were looking south toward Richmond once again. For Mosby and his men, the "vast bodies of troops moving around in all directions" were a welcome challenge and opportunity:

> Small parties of our men, either with Mosby himself, or under command of some of our officers or trusty men, were constantly engaged in scouting for the purpose of gathering information or cutting off communication and destroying supplies in the rear of the advancing armies, thus annoying and crippling them in their movements and compelling them to send back men from the front to protect the rear. As soon as we discovered a weak point, advantage was taken of it, and as a consequence the line would be strengthened. If this was done by weakening another place, we soon ascertained that fact and would swoop down on it like a hawk on a chicken yard.[2]

For the men of the 16th New York Cavalry, the spring of 1864 was largely taken up with improving Washington's outer defenses in northern Virginia and mounting scouts and reconnaissance patrols in response to alleged sightings of Confederates or in the aftermath of actual attacks. One such operation in March was typical of many that would follow that spring.

On March 19, a "large scouting party" of men from the 16th New York and 2nd Massachusetts, under Maj. Nicholson of the Sixteenth, was sent out to "scout the country toward Leesburg." A portion of the detachment returned the following day with two prisoners belonging to Gen.

J.E.B. Stuart's cavalry and eleven "supposed to belong to Mosby's and White's commands."³

On April 4, in response to a report that some guerrillas had been seen "in the vicinity of our lines,"⁴ another large scouting party of some 200 men from the Second and the Sixteenth, commanded by Maj. Douglas Frazar of the 13th New York, moved out on a three day march in the midst of horrible weather: "The boys put on a woeful look—but it's no use—we are soldiers & a wet skin—no fire—a heel on the soft mud—or an all night ride are all to be expected if not desired. The boys started off with good spirits in their hearts but no whiskey in their canteens."⁵

After marching for six hours, the combined command arrived in Chantilly. Leaving the men of the 2nd Massachusetts there at the Stuart farm, Frazar continued on with the New York troopers to Centreville. The next day the two groups reunited at Centreville and made themselves "as comfortable as possible in the Old Tavern (horses and all), a desperate nightmare." The combined command returned to Vienna, empty-handed, April 6.⁶

On April 14, another combined scouting party of 50 men from the Sixteenth, under Capt. John J. Schlaefer of Co. F, and another 50 from the Second, under Capt. Rumery, left camp under command of Maj. William Forbes of the Second. Departing shortly after noon, the command moved out past Hunter's Mill arriving near Middleburg after midnight. Continuing through the night, they marched through Aldie and arrived at Mount Zion Church around three in the morning. After feeding their horses and cooking breakfast, "we resumed our march, taking the back road from Aldie to Centreville. Here things became exciting and the boys had their fun, if charging over fences through fields and brush can be called

Capt. John Schlaefer (author's collection).

fun." They returned to camp after noon on the 15th, "horses and men nearly fagged out."⁷

Along the way, they captured a corporal and five privates from Mosby's battalion, or as Valorus Dearborn wrote: "six Johnnies were made to ask quarters of the blue bellied Yankees." According to the official report, the prisoners belonged to a party of Mosby's men "whose intention was undoubtedly to destroy bridges, from the fact that one of the party taken had a canteen of turpentine on his person."⁸

The Capture of Capt. Nathan H. Mooney

In January 1864, the 1st Battalion (companies A, B, C and D) of the 16th New York had been detached from the regiment in Vienna and sent to Fairfax Court House to serve as General Tyler's guard. On April 16, Capt. Mooney of Co. A, along with an orderly, set out for Washington. Less than a mile into the trip they were captured by men of the 15th Virginia Cavalry. Placed under guard of a man named Davis, Mooney took his first opportunity to escape and attacked his guard. It was for naught as the other guards quickly came to the rescue. Davis was so enraged that "he swore vengeance on the captain, and told him to say his prayers, and, so saying, put his gun to the captain's heart and fired, but the gun failed to go off, and the captain was saved by the kindly aid of the other guards."⁹

Mooney first was sent to Libby Prison in Richmond. The local paper reported his arrival there on April 16.¹⁰ He remained in Richmond until May 7, 1864, when he was moved to Danville, North Carolina, and on to Macon and Savannah, Georgia, and finally to Charleston, South Carolina. On the day he left Libby Prison, the *Plattsburgh Republican* reported that Mooney had written friends that he was "taken between Vienna and Richmond, losing his horse, equipage and two hundred dollars in money. He is, however, cheerful and expresses hope of soon being exchanged."¹¹

While incarcerated in Charleston, Mooney and his fellow Union prisoners came under fire from Union guns when, on September 18, 1864, 180 shells were lobbed into the city. In October, he was moved once more to Columbia, South Carolina. On November 3, he and five others escaped, but Mooney and two of his fellow escapees "found it advisable to return."¹²

On November 28, Mooney again escaped. Traveling some 350 miles over 27 nights, hiding during the day and being fed "by the colored people," he made it to within 20 miles of Union lines when he was again captured. In late January 1865, he was moved to Charlotte, North Carolina, where he escaped a third time. Alas he was "doomed again to disappointment, being captured by bloodhounds." His Confederate captors must have had enough of Capt. Nathan Mooney, however. As soon as he was returned to Charlotte, he was paroled.[13]

Around four o'clock in the morning on April 23, Mosby and 30 of his men attacked a picket post near Hunter's Mill, manned by men from the 16th New York. Mosby "dismounted his men, leaving a few in charge of the horses, and charged on foot."[14] The New York men were taken by complete surprise "with a loss of 9 horses and 3 men captured and 1 man wounded. No resistance was made by the pickets, only three shots being fired."[15] Mosby sent the prisoners and horses back to Fauquier under Lt. W.H. Hunter, while he and the rest of his men went off in another direction.[16]

Learning of the attack, Col. Lowell, commanding the brigade at Vienna, sent out a detachment from the 2nd Massachusetts that caught up with Hunter and his Confederates near Aldie and "chased them up the [Little River] pike through the town, the rebels scattering in all directions." Lt. Hunter was taken prisoner and two Union horses retaken, but the rest of the rebel party escaped, taking with them the captured men of the Sixteenth.[17] At least one of those captured, Pvt. Levi St. Dennis of Co. F, was sent to Andersonville Prison where he died of scurvy on October 4, 1864.[18]

More Court Martials

On April 25, 1864, Capt. Schlaefer of Co. F was arraigned by court-martial on four charges dating as far back as August 15, 1863, when his company was quartered at Camp Sprague on Staten Island. The charges brought against him by Col. Lazelle—apparently looking for legitimate reasons to get rid of him—included neglect of duty to the prejudice of good order and military discipline; conduct to the prejudice of good order and military discipline; conduct unbecoming an officer and a gentleman; and disobedience of an order. His specific misdeeds included:

- At Camp Sprague, he took a five-day leave without first arranging for his company to receive clothing and eating utensils and refused to allow his sergeant to procure them in the city.
- While part of his company was stationed at Falls Church, he spent much of his time in Washington and neglected his duty and his company. He also failed to place a "sufficient and suitable" guard over a barrel of government whiskey, and through his

Three—The Spring 1864 Campaign

neglect the guard got "crazy drunk and went into Falls Church, Va., creating great disturbance." Schlaefer knew of this but failed to report it.
- In October 1863, he issued his 34 men a 40-gallon barrel of whiskey at times when some of his men were drunk "and should not have been provided with rations of whiskey." Whiskey issues also were not made regularly, according to Army regulations, but "very irregularly."
- On one of his trips from camp in Falls Church to Washington, he took a shotgun from a civilian who was hunting for small game. A few days later he directed his company first sergeant, Henry Field, to send the gun to Washington to be forwarded to his home in Troy, New York.
- On November 14, 1863, he refused an order from his commanding officer through his adjutant to detail a private for daily duty. Again on November 23, he disobeyed an order from his commanding officer "relating to some refuse rubbish in the rear of his company tents and relative to some timber lying against the stable stockade of his company."[19]

Maj. Gen. Christopher C. Augur (Library of Congress).

Schlaefer ultimately was found "not guilty" on all charges except "conduct unbecoming an officer and a gentleman" for absconding with the shotgun, even though the gun was returned to its owner in December 1863 before the trial. His sentence—to be dismissed from the service of the United States, effective June 1, 1864—was approved by Maj. Gen. Christopher C. Augur, now commanding 22nd Corps and the Department of Washington.

On April 30, Regimental

Commissary Albert B. Wilber wrote in his diary that 2nd Lt. Michael H. Maroney of Co. M also had been dismissed "without trial for living with a woman as his wife who is not his wife."[20] Maroney had previously enrolled as a lieutenant with the 155th New York Infantry in the fall of 1862 but resigned February 6, 1863, at Suffolk, Virginia. He had mustered in with Co. M of the 16th on October 19, 1863, and was dishonorably dismissed April 23, 1864 "for conduct unbecoming an officer and gentleman." Maroney was an Irishman, born in Tipperary, who, like many others, had identified his occupation as "soldier" when he first enlisted.[21]

"Success" at Upperville

On April 28, 1864, Col. Lowell led a combined force of cavalrymen from the 2nd Massachusetts and 16th New York on a major operation to search houses, "gobble up Mosby," and obtain wool from John Holland's mill near the present town of Delaplane. The cavalry moved first through Leesburg and then on to Middleburg, where they were joined by infantry from Tyler's Division, and "together they scoured the country around for three or four days."[22]

After moving through Leesburg, Upperville, Paris, Bloomfield, Union, and Rectortown, Lowell reported on May 1 that they had encountered "no force by Mosby" and had returned with arms and contraband goods, 21 of Mosby's men and two blockade runners, along with 20 to 25 horses. They also brought back a portion of the wool at the mill and "supplied the command pretty well with tobacco," but it was "impossible to get teams to haul the remainder of the wool."[23]

According to Mosby Ranger James Williamson, Mosby's men were so vastly outnumbered by the Union force that they "could not risk an open field fight, but by hovering around their camps, making sudden dashes and firing on them, we kept them [the Union cavalry] from straggling and doing more damage. Some sharp skirmishes took place at times, in which quite a number were lost on both sides."[24]

The final tally of Union cavalry losses in the operation were one sergeant killed, one man taken prisoner, and two wounded in the 2nd Massachusetts; and two privates killed and three taken prisoner in the 16th New York. According to Lowell, one of those killed and all of the Union men captured "were straggling away from the command improperly."[25] Nonetheless, Maj. Gen. Augur, reporting back to Army Headquarters, declared victory:

This is the third successful operation of Colonel Lowell within the last month, embracing in all a capture of about 50 of Mosby's men, between 30 and 40 horses and equipments [*sic*], and a good deal of other property. I desire to commend in strong terms the zeal and ability displayed by Colonel Lowell in these various expeditions.[26]

The Horrors of the Wilderness

Several days after the deadly Battle of the Wilderness in Spotsylvania, west of Fredericksburg, May 5–7—an inconclusive battle with nearly 30,000 casualties—a long train of ambulances was sent out from Washington and northern Virginia to gather up the Union wounded "who were being temporarily stored in barns and farm houses near the battlefield." QM-Sgt. Cyrus Shepard and a small detachment of men from the Sixteenth were dispatched as part of the escort troops. Years later, the horror of what they found on the battlefield—including vast numbers of unburied bodies—as they loaded up the wounded was still etched vividly in Shepard's mind:

> Often I have prayed that visions of those upturned faces, blacken and distorted, of the staring, glazed eyeballs, of the stiffened, outstretched hands, seemingly still grasping for support, those rigid forms wrapped in blue and gray, that had fought their last battle and now lay side by side in that great charnel field, might be blotted forever from my recollection.... We saw in one place where the men in line of battle had taken off their knapsacks and laid them in a long row, evidently to be prepared to make a charge upon one of these earthworks of the Confederates, some little distance in front. These knapsacks remained almost undisturbed, while the men lay, some in heaps, some here and there in front of the fortifications they had charged upon. At this point the Union dead lay thickest. I believe I could have dismounted and walked a distance as great as two city blocks and never once have stepped upon the ground, walking on dead bodies all the way.[27]

Shepard and his fellow cavalrymen loaded the wounded into ambulances and started back toward Alexandria, "where the nearest help and hospital service could be procured."[28] General Grant's Army had moved on to Spotsylvania Court House in his drive toward Richmond. For most, if not all, of the men on detail that day, the carnage must have been shocking, unlike anything they had seen or imagined while manning the defenses of Washington.

General Augur Reorganizes

In mid–May, Maj. Gen. Augur ordered changes in the disposition of Union forces covering northern Virginia. Lowell was ordered to move his brigade headquarters and one of his three regiments from Vienna to Fairfax Court House (today's City of Fairfax), where they would be joined by a battalion of Pennsylvania infantry and the 17th New York Artillery Battery, already stationed there. Lowell decided the 16th New York would make the move.[29]

On May 14, in the midst of the move to Fairfax Court House, Col. Lazelle was ordered to send a squadron of cavalry to scout the country "toward the fords on the Rappahannock below Rappahannock Station" to determine whether any Confederate cavalry were in the area or for indications of Confederate intentions to make raids on the road toward Belle Plain. The commander of the squadron was instructed to "treat guerrillas who may be met with the utmost rigor." On May 17, Capt. Philo D. Mickles of Co. B, telegraphed his report from Belle Plain: "Mosby has concentrated, and I met his force in considerable numbers this p.m., three miles from here, toward Stafford Court-House. Davis, the guide, wounded by them, and ordered to remain here to-morrow and scout with a force from here."[30]

Alexander G. "Yankee" Davis was born in Litchfield, Connecticut, but had moved to Fairfax County by 1850. Living on the road between Fairfax and Aldie, about a mile from Mt. Zion Church, Davis was a successful farmer at the outbreak of the war. A staunch Unionist but too old to serve in the Army, he volunteered his services as a civilian scout and was assigned to Col. Lowell's cavalry brigade.[31] Davis remained in Virginia after the war but eventually moved to Mount Airy, Maryland, where he applied for a Civil War pension in 1890 and died in 1901.

Another civilian scout who worked closely with the cavalry brigade was Charles "Charlie" Binns, a former

Charlie Binns, circa 1890 (Thomas Balch Library, Special Collections, Charles E. Binns Vertical File).

member of Mosby's command who, according to Ranger Williamson, "while on a drunken frolic" had engaged in some "acts of rascality for which Mosby ordered his arrest. In order to escape punishment he knew he deserved and which he feared Mosby would inflict, he deserted and fled to the Federal camp in Fairfax."[32]

Binns, who came from an influential Loudoun County family, had moved to Fairfax County in 1854, married his cousin's widow, and voted in favor of secession in May 1861. Warned in June 1863 that he was about to be arrested for his Confederate sympathies, he fled to Middleburg with four other men and joined up with Mosby.[33]

The "rascality" that drove Charlie away from Mosby apparently was more serious than Williamson suggested in his account. According to Binns family descendants, he killed another one of Mosby's men "in a drunken brawl." In any case, he "presented himself at the camp of the Second Massachusetts Cavalry on November 17, 1863, and offered his services to the United States government."[34] On January 18, 1864, the Chief of Staff of 22nd Corps authorized Col. Lowell to "employ Charles Binns as a scout with compensation at the rate of one Ration and $50 per month to date from November 17, 1863."[35] Binns was involved in a number of scouts out of Vienna, including the affair at Anker's Shop. During that disastrous encounter with Mosby, Charlie's horse was shot out from under him and "his right knee was lacerated and badly injured."[36]

Binns remained "in Federal service" with the cavalry brigade until April 27, 1864, when "his employment as scout and guide ceased, his services being no longer required."[37] In early May 1864, before leaving Vienna for Fairfax Court House, Col. Lazelle gave Binns a personal letter to help him through Union lines:

> I take pleasure in recommending to your favorable consideration Mr. Chas. Binns of Virginia. He has for the past five months served the United States most zealously as a guide and has rendered invaluable service in this manner to the troops of this command and to this Cavalry Brigade. He is a gentleman and in my estimation one who can be depended upon for good and faithful performance of such duty as he may be employed in. His arduous and dangerous service always at peril of life demonstrated this. He leaves this region of the country as Mosby the Guerilla [sic] has offered $5,000 for his life or person and a commission in his [Mosby's] command.[38]

More Moves

Preparing for the move to Fairfax Court House, Lt. Albert Wilbur, now serving as Brigade Quartermaster, spent Sunday, May 15, "tearing down Stables and other camp structures," and was busy the following day "helping move the 16th." The Chaplain and Col. Lazelle "and his lady" moved to Fairfax Court House on the 17th. Wilbur was somewhat nostalgic on the regiment's last evening in Vienna:

> Took a walk about nine o'clock p.m. with the Chaplain around the camp, following the line of abattis. It was our last walk together at Vienna for tomorrow he is to move with the regt. It is an unusually lovely night. The moon sheds a soft light from her half-filled horn. Clouds of varied and fanciful form float through the upper blue, and gentle breezes waft to us the fragrance of summer flowers. This is so much like the evenings of "other days" when Sophie [his fiancée] walked with her hand on my arm, that I can't help feeling a little sad and wishing for the return of those happy hours.[39]

By early June, other moves had been ordered, and the cavalry brigade was now spread out over Fairfax County: the 13th New York remained at Vienna and the 16th New York at Fairfax Court House; the 1st Battalion of the 2nd Massachusetts remained at Muddy Branch, Maryland, and the 2nd and 3rd battalions had moved to Falls Church.[40] Although there still was a Federal presence in Vienna, Mosby was emboldened by the departure of the 16th New York and 2nd Massachusetts. As Capt. Wilber noted in his diary:

> Since we left Vienna a number of citizens there have been arrested by Mosby and sent to Richmond because of their unionism. We have sent out several scouting parties to arrest Secesh [sic] citizens and bring them in as hostages. A Dr. Powell and several others have been secured. They took it rather hard, but can't help themselves. Their treatment here is far more lenient than it ought to be.[41]

The Lt. Tuck Affair

On the evening of June 23, "a small squad" of Confederate Capt. James C. Kincheloe's partisans intercepted a four-man 16th New York patrol from Fairfax Court House, capturing two. The two who escaped capture "brought word to Annandale," and the following morning Col. Lazelle dispatched 40 men, commanded by 1st Lt. Matthew Tuck of Co. K, in search of the rebels. Tuck, an Englishman and veteran of the Crimean War with the Grenadier Guards, had deserted in Canada when the British command would not allow him to marry a Canadian woman. He and his new wife left Canada in 1862, and he enlisted in the 16th New York at Rochester. He was initially mustered in as first sergeant of Co. G but promoted to first lieutenant of Co. K in February 1864.[42]

Finding no signs of the rebels, Tuck and his men stopped around 11:00 a.m. on June 24, about a mile and a half beyond Centreville, to feed themselves and their horses beside a field with newly cut hay. Upon learning of Tuck's patrol, Mosby, who had passed through Centreville shortly after Tuck and his men, dispatched about 60 of his men. Locals later reported that Tuck's horses "were unbitted, some of the men in cherry trees on the other side of the road, some asleep; there was one man on picket sitting on a fence, but in a very poorly chosen position."[43]

Mosby's attack was devastating. The man on picket was shot, and Lt. Tuck later reported that his men were "demoralized and panic-stricken, scattering in all directions." A couple of his men who were having breakfast in a nearby house and "saw Mosby's men going past" were the only ones who returned fire. Lt. Tuck returned to camp, alone, around 2:00 p.m. Meanwhile, having received additional intelligence that morning about Mosby's presence in the area, Col. Lazelle had sent out a much larger party of 150 men, under Maj. Nicholson, to support Tuck's patrol.

When Tuck returned, Lazelle immediately ordered him out again with another 15 men to catch up with Maj. Nicholson and follow Mosby's trail as far as Aldie. Lazelle then sent another party of 100 men and horse-drawn wagons, under Maj. Forbes of the 2nd Massachusetts, to the original ambush site "to pick up stragglers and horses and any wounded men that may be there." They were then to join Nicholson's group if Mosby was thought to have more than 60 men. As of 6:00 p.m. on the 24th, none of the original patrol except for Lt. Tuck had returned to camp.

On June 25, Col. Lowell reported up the line that Maj. Forbes had brought back three wounded men, "two dangerously," and that another five had returned to camp on foot. He believed all the horses and the rest of the men and arms had been captured. Estimates of Mosby's numbers ranged from 200 to 900:

> The strength of Mosby's column [200] was estimated by Dr. Hart and Mr. Mellon (good Union men), both of whom saw it pass; and another citizen says Lieut. Frank Fox told him as he passed they had about 200. Major Nicholson with his 150 men returned with Major Forbes, and reached Centreville yesterday p.m. Got the impression that Mosby was from 400 to 900 strong and remained there, sending party to camp to report what he had learned.[44]

In large part due to Lt. Tuck's neglect in setting up pickets to ensure the security of his men while they rested, Mosby left Centreville with 31 prisoners and 38 horses.[45] Twenty-four were sent to Andersonville Prison, among them Pvt. Boston Corbett, who had been reduced in rank from sergeant in February 1864. Eight died there, most of them from scurvy. One opted to enlist in the 10th Tennessee Infantry to avoid further incarceration and was later captured by Union forces. Another escaped from Macon,

Georgia, and returned north. The rest, including Corbett, survived Andersonville and eventually were exchanged and returned to the 16th New York.[46]

Lt. Tuck was neither held accountable for the disaster in Centreville nor reprimanded. Indeed, he was promoted to captain on July 30, "with rank from June 16," and took command of Co. I on August 4, 1864, after Capt. Otto Kleinschmidt was cashiered. Tuck, it seems, was considered "a valuable scout and later led a number of patrols that earned him Colonel Lazelle's approbation."[47]

Four

July–August 1864
More Challenges, More Losses

The summer months of 1864 would prove to be transformative for northern Virginia and the Independent Cavalry Brigade. Driving factors impacting directly on the 2nd Massachusetts and indirectly, but significantly, on the 16th New York were the advance of Confederate General Jubal Early's Army of the Valley toward Washington in July—with the aim of relieving pressure on General Lee's besieged Army in Petersburg—and the opening of Union General Sheridan's Shenandoah Valley campaign in August.

By July 6, Early's Army had crossed the Potomac near Harper's Ferry and was in western Maryland moving toward Washington. General Grant, concluding that Early intended to attack the capital city, ordered Maj. Gen. James Ricketts' 3rd Division of VI Corps and all dismounted cavalry at City Point on the James River to move north to Baltimore and then west to the Monocacy River by July 8 to bolster General Wallace's VII Corps with an additional 5,800 men.

At the so-called Battle of Monocacy south of Frederick, Maryland, on July 9, Wallace was able to hold the Confederates for 24 hours. Outnumbered, Wallace's Union forces eventually withdrew toward Baltimore and Washington. General Early resumed his march on the capitol the morning of July 10, reaching Rockville that evening.[1]

On July 11, Early's Confederates reached the outskirts of Washington near Silver Spring, where Washington's outer defensive fortifications were manned by a hastily formed collection of Home Guards, clerks, and convalescent troops. During the night, however, Union reinforcements arrived:

... veteran units from the Union VI Corps disembarked from troop transports and marched north through the streets of Washington to bolster the defenses. On July 12,

Early was finally in position to make a strong demonstration, which was repulsed by the veteran Union troops. In the afternoon, VI Corps units sortied against the Confederate skirmishers, driving them back from their advanced positions in front of Forts Stevens and DeRussy. President Lincoln watched the action from Fort Stevens and came under fire from Confederate sharpshooters. Recognizing that the Union Capital was now defended by veterans, Early abandoned any thought of taking the city. Early withdrew during the night, marching toward White's Ford on the Potomac, ending his invasion of Maryland. "We didn't take Washington," Early told his staff officers, "but we scared Abe Lincoln like Hell."[2]

When Wallace met Early's forces on the Monocacy River on July 9, Col. Lowell's 2nd Massachusetts was covering the lower approaches to the Potomac. Mosby had moved much of his command east of the Blue Ridge to support Early's movement to the Maryland Heights.[3]

On July 10, Maj. Gen. Augur ordered Col. Lowell to bring his regiment to Washington to bolster defenses at Tennally-town. Lowell quickly complied, turning over command of the brigade to Col. Lazelle and leaving some men behind to load the regiment's supplies. By the end of the next day, the 2nd Massachusetts was spread between the Potomac and Fort Stevens, less than five miles north of the Capitol out the 7th Street Pike (now Georgia Avenue).

This was the last time the New York cavalrymen would see their New England and California compatriots. In August, the 2nd Massachusetts was reassigned to the Cavalry Corps of Maj. Gen. Sheridan's Army of the Shenandoah. With the departure of the 2nd Massachusetts, Maj. Gen. Augur's report on the Department of Washington for the month of July showed the Cavalry Brigade, now under Col. Lazelle's command, with 29 officers and 422 men "present for duty." Given the amount of territory the brigade had to cover and its operational responsibilities, the numbers were very low.[4]

On July 12, with Fort Stevens under fire, Maj. Gen. Augur was doubly concerned about the ever-present potential threat from the south. Having received reports of enemy activity near the defensive lines manned by the 13th and 16th New York, he ordered Col. Lazelle to keep his scouts "well out toward the gaps and toward Manassas" and to notify him if he should "learn of the enemy's advance in force." Lazelle responded that, in light of the departure of the 2nd Massachusetts and the low strength of the two remaining regiments, he was making adjustments in the brigade's defenses:

> In view of the present emergencies I have abandoned the design of Colonel Lowell of leaving two companies at Annandale, and also at Cross' Farm (intermediate between this point [Falls Church] and Annandale). There is a dismounted company at Lewinsville in a stockade. At present I picket to that point and one mile beyond. I

propose to call in the men at Lewinsville, and patrol the country north to that point and beyond in the same manner as I have now adopted south of this place to Annandale. There are in the two regiments now here a large number of men (about one company) who are almost without arms; recruits and men who have lost their arms by disaster, etc. They are and will be of little use here. Should you approve it I will send them in to report for the defense. I propose to remove all baggage, with the exception of one wagon to a regiment, to a point inside the Alexandria pickets, and with the whole force remaining to remain on this line or farther out. I have sent 200 men to the front (in the direction of the gaps) and toward the fords of the Potomac in three different parties—two of 50 and one of 100.

Augur approved Lazelle's proposal but asked that Lazelle "keep the vicinity of Annandale well watched by frequent scouts."[5]

The following day, Col. Lazelle moved the brigade (and 16th regimental) headquarters to the vicinity of Fort Buffalo, about a half-mile southeast of Falls Church and near the present-day Seven Corners. Built in 1862 between Taylors and Perkins hills, the stockade, along with Fort Ramsay on adjacent Upton's Hill, was one of the Falls Church area's more substantial fortifications with earthworks and gun emplacements.[6] Albert Wilbur wrote home that from the new camp "we have a fine view of the surrounding country for miles in every direction." The only downside was "a want of water."[7] Capt. James Fleming of Co. M had an even more positive report on the regiment's new camp:

> The country around here abounds with all sorts of fruits. All you have to do is pull and eat as there is a great variety and you have only to take your choice [the camp was surrounded by farms and orchards]. The country around is beautiful. We are camped upon a hill and have a splendid view for miles around. We are in sight of Alexandria and a little further to the rear is Washington and to the left is Georgetown.... We get to purchase from the farmers around anything in the way of eatables but have to pay very high for them.... We have not as much marching on foot as when in the infantry, but we have some very long marches upon horseback to perform sometimes.[8]

As Col. Lazelle and the 16th New York moved to Fort Buffalo, General Early moved his army back toward the Potomac River and Leesburg. On July 13, General Grant ordered the 6th and 19th Corps out in pursuit. Throughout the next seven days, Early's force engaged in numerous skirmishes with Federal troops in Poolesville, Purcellville, near Berryville, and at Ashby's Gap. By July 16, he was headed back into the northern Shenandoah.[9]

Meanwhile, the men of the 16th New York were out on patrols almost daily "with a view of ascertaining the whereabouts of the enemy, and, as far as possible, his intentions," scouting out toward Goose Creek, Bristoe Station and Thoroughfare Gap, to Rappahannock Station and beyond, and, closer in, out to Centreville and Manassas.[10]

On July 15, Lazelle sent a scouting party out under 1st Lt. Tuck to gather information on the status of trains running on the Orange and Alexandria Railroad. Tuck reached Rappahannock Station the evening of the 16th and found "no trains were running there," but learned from "more than twenty different parties" that trains were running to the Rapidan and that Confederates were repairing the Rapidan bridge to extend the usable track. Tuck had also learned that rebel troops were waiting at Rapidan and that two or three companies of cavalry were at Culpeper. Lazelle was effusive in his praise for Lt. Tuck's performance on this mission:

> I would respectfully mention the conduct of Lieutenant Tuck as worthy of great praise. He has passed over a great extent of country, has been frequently surrounded by the enemy, has obtained satisfactory information, and has brought his party to camp without the loss of a man. I trust it may in some part atone for a misfortune to a former party under his charge [the ill-fated encounter with Mosby near Centreville on June 24].[11]

Another Court Martial

While the defenses of Washington were preparing for the feared attack from Jubal Early's troops, Lt. Col. George S. Hollister of the 16th New York was brought before a court-martial, presided over by Col. Henry S. Gansevoort, commander of the 13th New York. The two charges against him—"conduct unbecoming an officer and a gentleman" and "conduct prejudicial to good order and military discipline"—were not unusual. The specifications were grievously offensive to 19th century sensibilities:

- That he sexually assaulted Capt. Washburn while he was asleep at Fort Ethan Allen, Virginia, around January 20, 1864, while a guest in his quarters and sharing his bed. Capt. Washburn repeatedly told him to stop.
- That he kept approaching Washburn in this manner on several other occasions at posts in Annandale, Fairfax Court House and Vienna in February and June 1864.
- That he made similar assaults on Lt. William Farrell on several occasions in January 1864 in Vienna.
- That he allowed for a period of three months the "notorious circulation throughout the Regiment ... and the Cavalry Brigade, of stories of his scandalous conduct to the effect as detailed in the foregoing specifications."
- That on June 10, 1864, he rode out with officers and an enlisted

escort to a house in Annandale where he sexually assaulted a girl.
- That he associated and drank with an enlisted man, "knowing him to be an enlisted man," and sergeant major of the regiment between March 20 and April 10, 1864.
- That on diverse occasions, he drank and caroused in the presence of enlisted men in his quarters and with junior lieutenants of the regiment, on several occasions until near morning and with "much noisy uproar," at Vienna for a month from the middle of February 1864 and at Annandale on or about June 9, 1864.[12]

This was not the first time Hollister had been brought up on charges for inappropriate behavior. Prior to the war, while serving as a lieutenant with the 7th Infantry at Fort Union in New Mexico, he had been charged with diverting wagon trains to haul and deliver soldiers to disreputable Mexican women. He was found not guilty.[13]

This time, however the charges and specifications were much more serious. Col. Gansevoort convened the court on July 1 and heard conflicting testimony from officers and enlisted members of the Sixteenth, both to Hollister's character and to the veracity of the charges and honesty of those making them. After ten days of testimony, the court adjourned "to meet again" on July 13. It never did. There was a final notation in the file: "Camp, Cav. Det., 13th NY Vols. Cav. Tennallytown, Md., Aug. 23rd, 1864. There has since the above date no quorum present & no business transacted by the court," signed by Col. Gansevoort and Capt. C.H. Hatch, 13th NY Cav., Judge Advocate.

Hollister would remain with the regiment until he was dishonorably dismissed three months later "by direction of the President for conduct" under War Department Special Orders No. 337, October 7, 1864. After an appeal orchestrated by his widowed mother, who used his deceased father's old political connections in writing to Secretary of State William Seward, among others, these orders were revoked in January 1866, and he was "honorably mustered out of the Volunteer service," effective the same date.[14]

Reorganizing the Defensive Line

By July 18, the brigade headquarters and staff were again back at Falls Church, and on the 23rd Col. Lowell and the 2nd Massachusetts were back in camp at Vienna, the threat to Washington having receded with Early's withdrawal. The Sixteenth's Albert Wilbur was pleased that Lowell was back in command of the brigade, noting that "Colonel Lowell is to remain in command of this brigade. Good!"

His pleasure would not last long. Three days later Lowell and the 2nd Massachusetts were again ordered to report to the 6th Corps at Rockville to join in the rescue of Brig. Gen. George Crook's infantry and cavalry forces which had been soundly defeated by Early's men near Winchester. Lowell's regiment was sent up to the Monocacy River near Rockville, Maryland. They would not return to Fairfax County.[15]

The Massachusetts cavalrymen would serve valiantly in the Shenandoah Valley and later in the final battles at Petersburg and Appomattox Courthouse. Col. Lowell, however, would not accompany his regiment south to Richmond. He was mortally wounded on October 19, 1864, during a Union counterattack at the Battle of Cedar Creek near Strasburg.

Prior to the very temporary return of the 2nd Massachusetts to Vienna, Col. Lazelle had submitted a lengthy proposal to Lt. Col. J. H. Taylor, Chief of Staff and Assistant Adjutant General of 22nd Corps, for restructuring the cavalry brigade's defensive deployments. As of July 19, the two New York regiments were temporarily deployed on "the hills in the vicinity of old Fort Buffalo." With only two regiments to maintain a defensive line in Fairfax County and engage in scouting operations to observe enemy movements "so far as his operations might extend to this side of the [Blue Ridge] mountains," Lazelle proposed a series of adjustments that would enable him to cover both requirements with his reduced numbers.

- Three companies (one mounted and two un-mounted) would be placed in a "defensible stockade" near Lewinsville between the Georgetown and Leesburg-Alexandria pikes, "in a position to guard them."
- Another three companies (one mounted and two un-mounted) would be placed in a stockade at Annandale "in a position to control the Little River pike."
- The remaining force would remain near Falls Church "in a defensible camp" controlling Falls Church village, railroad, etc." Lazelle believed neither the temporary camp near Fort Buffalo nor the former camp of the 13th New York and 2nd Massachusetts "in the valley near here" were well enough suited for the defense.
- The mounted companies at the three locations could then "patrol constantly" between Annandale and Falls Church, and between Lewinsville and Falls Church, "on the pikes."[16]

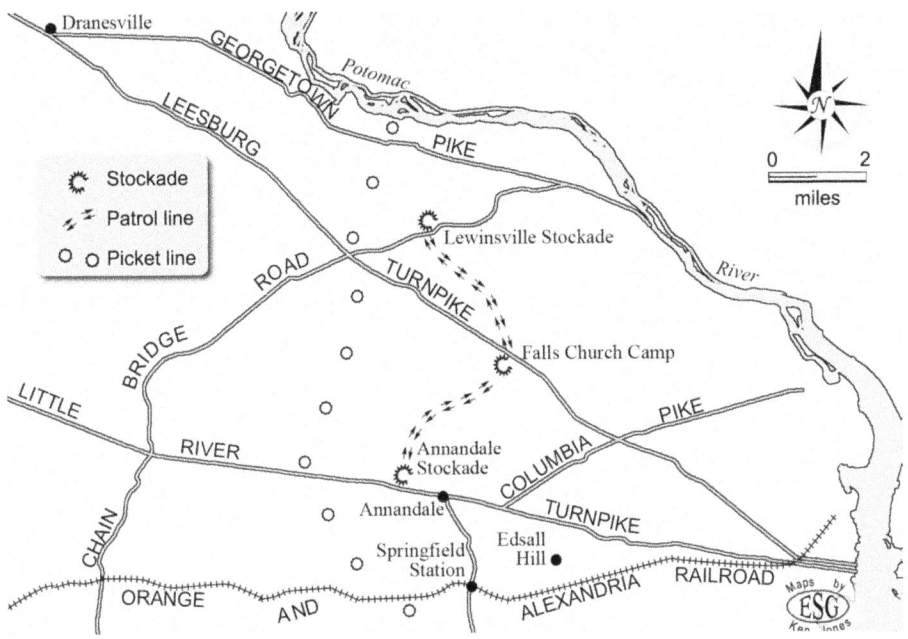

Lazelle's Proposed Deployment, July 1864.

Lazelle also was determined to "prevent the constant annoyance arising from small parties of guerrillas (from two to fifteen in number) passing through our lines, hovering about us, snatching up a patrol or picket here and there by ambuscade, etc." So he also proposed using the dismounted troops at the three camps to establish a "secret picket line of from two to three miles out in ambuscade, sending men in parties of from six to twelve, with two days' rations, posting them in the night and concealing them, always changing their positions each time of posting, and with orders to interfere with no persons but guerrillas." With no more than about 100 men, he believed, he could establish an effective defense from the Potomac in the north to Braddock Road near Annandale, and "on all the roads and paths leading toward our lines."[17]

Harkening back to his days fighting Apaches on the Texas frontier, Lazelle believed there were only two options to deal effectively with "this wily and almost intangible enemy." One approach, the "occupation of his whole country by a commanding force in every district," was simply impossible with the two regiments "whose immediate [available for duty] strength is not over 300." The other was "to fight him after his own manner with the force which we have." Using the picket lines he was proposing, Lazelle believed, he could successfully deal with the small parties Mosby was sending into Federal lines to "operate against our pickets, or patrol, or small escorts."

> It is my belief that by adopting the tactics of the enemy, by selecting and setting aside from men of this command a sufficient number as scouts and guides, retaining them on that duty, and sending out mounted parties under their guidance to desirable forest covers, always moving by night, until information by which a surprise or ambuscade of the enemy could be accomplished, that very much success could be gained which our present system of acting as regular cavalry, and almost always openly, could never enable us to obtain, inasmuch as our enemy can always count our numbers and ascertain our precise locality, and fight or run as he thinks proper, or use the forest to conceal him.[18]

Lazelle concluded his proposal with a request that the dismounted troops at each stockade come from 22nd Corps infantry units, since the "separation of the man from his horse" would be harmful to the New York cavalry companies. In the end, his request for infantry troops was denied, and he was forced to disperse his cavalry troops. Eventually, he also moved his headquarters and Falls Church contingent to Fort Buffalo.

By June 28 Lazelle could report that three of his cavalry companies had been sent to Annandale and two to Lewinsville. Both of these sites were "protected by a strong enveloping abatis." Lewinsville had a stockade inside of its abatis, and a similar stockade was under construction at Annandale. In addition:

> A continuous line of pickets, with reserves at two intermediate points, has been established between here [Falls Church] and Annandale, and a line below Annandale to Edsall Hill [8 miles southwest of Alexandria and about a mile and a half from Springfield Station on the Orange and Alexandria railroad]. A line of pickets, with one intermediate reserve, has been established between this point [Falls Church] and Lewinsville, thence above to near the Potomac. It is believed the whole line is sufficiently closed from the Potomac to the Orange and Alexandria road to place all ordinary travel across it within the restrictions required by passes. At six different points west of this line, and from one to four miles beyond it, small dismounted parties are placed to intercept small bodies of guerrillas constantly lurking about it.[19]

Meanwhile, with his remaining cavalrymen, Col. Lazelle continued to send out scouting parties on almost a daily basis, some without incident, others not. A party of ten men from the 13th New York returning from a three-day scout to Culpeper and Manassas on July 21 was ambushed between Sangster's Station (near Clifton) and Fairfax Station by 50–60 Confederates, with five men taken prisoner. Five days later, an uneventful scout returning from the Rapidan River reported that trains were running to Culpeper Court House and that there were some 200 Confederate cavalry there and another three companies at the Rapidan Station. The

Federal cavalrymen captured a scout from the 6th Virginia Cavalry who reported a concentration of Confederate General Ewell's Corps just west of Manassas Gap.[20]

On July 29, based on "returned scouts and parties whom I consider reliable," Lazelle reported that Mosby was west of the Blue Ridge and Leesburg with a piece of artillery, but that there were no troops around Aldie except for a few "strolling guerrillas," and no troops at all at Culpeper or along the Orange and Alexandria tracks. General Early's headquarters was reported 15 miles north of Manassas Gap at Millwood, east of the Blue Ridge, where the rebels had several mills in operation, "grinding up wheat and grain."[21]

A day later Maj. Gen. Augur ordered Lazelle to take measures "to obtain daily information" and report back from the country toward the Rappahannock and "well up to the Blue Ridge." If he was unable to gather information, he was to "report cause of failure." Lazelle responded on July 31 that he simply lacked the forces to meet this scouting requirement "except by small parties." Four companies, each, from the 13th and 16th New York were on "detached service." One company of the Thirteenth was at Fort Ethan Allen overlooking the Potomac near Chain Bridge, another in Washington, and two at the Lewinsville stockade. One company of the Sixteenth was in Alexandria and three manned the stockade at Annandale. The remaining "present for duty" strength of the two regiments in camp near Fort Buffalo was 522 men. Of these, "128 are daily required for grand guard and picket duty on our extended line, and 128 more to relieve this guard." That left 266 men for scouting, "taking everything in camp." Lazelle judged that a scouting party of less than 300 men could not "with hope of entire success, go beyond the Bull Run Mountains at this time, in consideration of even Mosby's organization," and this would leave none available for scouting toward the Rappahannock.[22]

Sheridan Moves to the Valley

On August 7, 1864, General Grant placed Maj. Gen. Philip H. Sheridan, then commanding the Army of the Potomac's Cavalry Corps, in command of the new Middle Military Division, encompassing the old Middle Department and the departments of Washington, the Susquehanna, and West Virginia. His principal objective was to take control of the Shenandoah Valley, which would cut General Lee's line of communication to the northeast and deny him access to Virginia's breadbasket.[23]

Col. Mosby and his rangers had two tasks as "the only force operating in the rear of Sheridan's army." His main objective was to "vex and embarrass Sheridan and, if possible, to prevent his advance into the interior of the State." His secondary objective was to prevent the troops manning the defenses of Washington and "guarding the line of the Potomac" from reinforcing Sheridan in the valley. Thus, he planned "frequent attacks on the outposts in Fairfax and demonstrations along the Potomac. His prime targets were the 8th Illinois Cavalry, "the largest and regarded as the finest regiment in the Army of the Potomac," which was stationed at Muddy Branch, and the two New York cavalry regiments in Fairfax County.[24]

Meanwhile, Col. Lazelle had lost his bid for any reduction in the scouting load on his over-stretched cavalry regiments. On an almost daily basis, he was required to send out patrols beyond his ambush and picket lines.

- On August 1, Capt. Lawrence Leahy of Co. L, 16th New York, returned with his detachment from scouting around Aldie and Thoroughfare Gap, reporting that Aldie was "unusually quiet and free from even small parties," while around 100 men from the 6th Virginia Cavalry had been sighted in the vicinity of Thoroughfare Gap. Another scouting party out to Leesburg had reported "no force of any unusual strength" in the town or west to the Blue Ridge. However, Mosby, "with 350 men, 60 head of beef-cattle, and a number of wagons taken in Maryland," had passed above Waterford and moved south on July 31.[25]
- On August 4, Lt. Tuck returned from the Rappahannock with a small patrol reporting that "substantially, matters in the vicinity of the Rapidan and Culpeper Court-House remain in the same state as formerly reported"; that there were about 100 Confederate infantry and cavalry at the Rapidan railroad crossing, "with cavalry pickets out and pickets toward Orange Court-House"; and nearly 200 infantry at Culpeper Court House, with trains moving daily "carrying supplies and forage south." Mosby also had been in the area.[26]
- A 20-man patrol was attacked the evening of August 5 by a large number of rebels. The officer in charge ordered his men to "disperse into the woods." All escaped and "found their way safely into camp," with a loss of three horses. The scouting party reported a force of 500–600 men from Mosby's and White's bat-

talions, "Mosby in command," near Leesburg, engaged in "a considerable amount of plunder."[27]
- On the morning of August 8, a picket post with a corporal and three privates from the 16th New York near Burke's Station, about three miles southeast of Annandale, was surrounded and captured by seven of Mosby's men. The corporal escaped, but the three privates and all four horses were captured. According to Ranger James Williamson, the corporal had gone down to a nearby spring to get a drink and thus avoided capture.[28]
- That same day, another party of Mosby's men moved out to "capture two picket-posts on the old Braddock Road." The Union men manning one of the posts suspected an attack and moved off. The second party was attacked and pursued within three miles of Alexandria. Three men and their horses were captured.[29]

Captain James H. Fleming, R.I.P.

Responding to these attacks, Col. Lazelle sent out two parties of 30 men each, one commanded by Capt. John McMenamin, Co. B, 13th New York, and the other by Capt. James Fleming, Co. M, 16th New York. Anticipating the Federal response, Mosby moved out with 38 men from his encampment near Centreville. While riding "through the pines," Mosby and his men were fired upon by the men of the 13th New York who were waiting in ambush, wounding two. According to Mosby Ranger Williamson, the Federals then "fled in the direction of Fairfax Station." There, at St. Mary's Church on the Ox Road, they met up with Capt. Fleming and his men. When Mosby, who was following behind McMenamin, came upon the two patrols, the Union cavalrymen were allegedly "resting, eating supper and feeding their horses."[30]

Alerted to Mosby's approach, the Federals "mounted their horses and formed in an open field. Mosby sent his men and charged them. The enemy reserved their fire until he was within forty yards of them. They then opened on him with their carbines. This fire was harmless, being too high. After the first volley, seeing none of their foe fall, they [the Union troops] broke and retreated in great confusion, with Mosby after them."[31]

In his preliminary report, Col. Lazelle could account for 33 men and 39 horses missing. According to James Williamson, Mosby's men captured 27 prisoners and 37 horses. Six Union cavalrymen, including Capt. Fleming, were killed and eight wounded, three from the Sixteenth. Fleming's body was found along the road "stripped of much of its clothing." It was brought back to the cavalry brigade camp at Falls Church and buried in the Falls Church graveyard. Albert Wilbur wrote in his diary that Fleming had been "shot through the back of his head and is already much decomposed."[32]

After the war, Capt. James H. Fleming was reinterred at Arlington National Cemetery. His marker there is one of those in Section 26 that border the large Civil War Unknown plot. In death, he salutes his fellow soldiers.

Col. Lazelle immediately convened a board of investigation to examine and report on the facts of the case and determine who was responsible. In his reports to Maj. Gen. Augur, he pulled no punches, attributing the defeat to "disgraceful mismanagement" and a "misapplication of their weapons." However, he also reminded Augur that the men of his brigade were operating under severe hardship due to the "unusually small number" of men available for duty: "The scouting parties and parties of observation sent out have been small in numbers because of the constant demand upon the men. It is certain that the duty assigned to this command cannot be done effectively with the present force."[33]

Having heard that Mosby's men were outnumbered three-to-one, Albert Wilbur deemed the skirmish at St. Mary's a "disgraceful affair." He seemed to place the blame on Fleming, writing that "censure must be silent for on whose head the blame would fall the clamps of death are resting." There are insufficient details about this encounter to judge whether Wilbur's "censure" was well founded. However, Capt. Fleming's obituary was much more flattering, characterizing him as noble, brave, and generous:

> With an abundance of the native wit and geniality of his country [Ireland], he combined good sound sense and general information. As a friend, he was generous and constant; as an enemy, honorable. Those who knew him longest loved him best, and many a manly tear dropped upon his grave from eyes that had looked upon him but a few short months. In his fall our country has lost a brave defender, a gallant son of her adoption.[34]

Only one of the men of the 16th New York who were captured on August 8, Pvt. Thomas Smith of Co. C, was sent to Andersonville Prison. He survived his incarceration and escaped at Florence, Georgia, on March 12, 1865. Most of the others captured that day were eventually paroled at the Aikens Landing exchange site on the James River, south of Richmond. Two were not so fortunate and died "of disease" in the prison hospital at Danville, Virginia: Pvt. John Miers, Co. E, on December 10, 1864, and Pvt. William Wagner, Co. K, on February 22, 1865. Conditions at Danville—

six large tobacco warehouses converted into bare-bones barracks—were hardly better than at Andersonville, although the men were somewhat protected from the elements. More than 7,000 Union prisoners were held at Danville during the war, and some 1,400 died of diseases such as small pox and dysentery.[35]

Following the attack at St. Mary's Church, Col. Lazelle had patrols out on almost a daily basis. He reported "everything quiet" around Falls Church on August 13, and that a patrol sent out north and west of Leesburg had found "no considerable body of the enemy ... reported in that vicinity." The following day, he reported the sad results of a sergeant from the 16th New York taking matters into his own hands. "Hearing some reports concerning the enemy," the sergeant took three privates out on the Braddock road, "without orders." Riding beyond a 16th New York picket on ambush duty, the sergeant and his men, themselves, were ambushed by nine or ten Confederates. The sergeant was "shot through the head and killed instantly." One private was captured. The other two escaped.[36]

On August 15, Col. Lazelle again reported his concerns to Maj. Gen. Augur over the small number of men in his two regiments. Of the 720 enlisted men present for duty, 100 were "sick and in confinement." Of the 620 actually available, 275 were on "special, extra, or daily duty," leaving less than 350 men to meet all patrolling and scouting requirements levied on the brigade. The next day, he reported to Augur that he would leave for the Rappahannock River the morning of August 17 with about 275 men: "I should have left today, but the failure to get horseshoes in the Sixteenth, and other delays, rendered it necessary to postpone." Setting out with three and a half days' rations and forage, Lazelle and his men returned on August 20 "with one live rebel!" and seven horses from the 15th Virginia Regiment.[37]

More importantly, however, he was able to report—from observation and information obtained from locals—that the Confederates were not attempting to repair or use the railroad above Culpeper Court House; that there were some 2,000 enemy infantry and 500 cavalry at Warrenton and a much larger force of 10,000 cavalry and infantry at Culpeper moving up toward Warrenton; and that the rebels were "using the roads between Warrenton and Chester Gap and Manassas Gap [east and southeast of Front Royal], and passing trains, troops and supplies over them constantly."[38]

The concern at the time, as General Sheridan's troops were pulling back from Cedar Creek toward Winchester in the valley, most likely was whether General Early would be reinforced: "Early's ability at bluff did not help [Sheridan] and Mosby's guerrillas disrupted supply and communication lines, forcing Sheridan to detach sizable contingents to counter that threat. Everyone tended to overestimate the real strength of the Confederates."[39]

While Lazelle's cavalry used active patrolling and scouting to search for signs of enemy activity—the most effective use of cavalry—the intelligence they gathered, more often than not, came from the local population. Some came forward willingly. In other cases, the Union cavalrymen resorted to subterfuge. For example, in a follow-up report on his recent scout, Lazelle noted that the information on rebel use of the Orange and Alexandria Railroad and the force at Culpeper was obtained in Elkton, Virginia, from "several citizens who talked freely to our men, under the impression that they were rebels, as they were disguised."[40]

Often, these reports from locals were widely different. On August 23, for example, three days after Lazelle returned with his information on Confederate activity around Culpeper and Warrenton, a "citizen named J. J. Perk" appeared at brigade picket lines reporting that "as he estimates, 20,000 infantry and 5,000 cavalry" had left Culpeper "last Friday a week" on the Sperryville Road toward Thornton's Gap or "via Warrenton to Chester Gap." He believed the cavalry to be part of Confederate General Fitzhugh Lee's forces and the infantry "part of [General] Longstreet's corps." Based on Perk's "method of estimating the strength of the force," however, Lazelle pegged it at about 10,000 infantry and 3,000 cavalry, which was more consistent with the information his men had developed during their scout.

The problem was that Perk's information pre-dated Lazelle's by a week. Moreover, on August 25, Col. Gansevoort, commanding the 13th New York, returned from a three-day scout, having obtained "positive information" that there were no Confederate forces at either Warrenton or Culpeper and that a force of over 10,000 infantry and cavalry had passed through Warrenton a week earlier. Such were the frustrations of developing timely and accurate order-of-battle information on enemy forces in highly fluid situations.[41]

Attack at Annandale

At 10:20 a.m. on August 24, Lt. Col. Henry H. Wells, Provost Marshal, Defenses South of the Potomac, sent a cryptic message to Maj. Gen. Augur:

> An attack was made at Annandale about 5 o'clock this morning; the force is not known. The rebels were driven off. Major Horton, of Sixteenth New York, is following

rebels up. Mosby was said to be in command, and demanded surrender, which was refused. He had two pieces of cannon, and fired grape and canister. Re-enforcements have been sent from Falls Church.[42]

Mosby had gathered his command at Rectortown the morning of August 23, and 300 reported for duty. Moving off at noon with two pieces of artillery—a 12-pound rifle and Napoleon gun—they crossed the Bull Run mountains around nightfall and continued under cover of darkness to the 16th New York stockade at Annandale. Reaching the camp, they discovered that "the horses had nearly all been sent off and the garrison [cavalry company] was in stockade." The rebels captured or drove in the Union pickets, and the two guns were placed into position. At daybreak on August 24, Mosby sent Capt. Montjoy to demand that the fort surrender.[43]

According to Capt. Joseph Schneider, Co. C, commanding the 16th New York detachment at Annandale, he was first alarmed by three shots fired by his picket—a sergeant and three privates—on the Fairfax Court House road before they were captured by Mosby's men. Almost immediately, Mosby's men "fired about three shells into our camp; then a detachment of about 100 men charged up toward our entrance." The men of the Sixteenth fired a volley, and the rebels "swerved to the south, surrounding the south and east side of our camp."[44]

While Captain Mountjoy advanced under a flag of truce to demand surrender, Mosby moved his artillery pieces to within 300–400 yards of the stockade, one facing the southwest corner and the other trained on the northwest corner. Schneider refused: "A German commands this fort and he will never surrender." Mosby's artillery opened fire "in good earnest, one piece throwing shell, the other grape." After

Capt. Joseph Schneider, after the war (courtesy Robert Snapper).

"nearly a dozen more shots," Mosby sent Lt. Harry Hatcher in under a flag of truce toward the northwest side, "where Captain Mickles [of Co. B] had charge of the defenses."[45]

Mickles yelled at Hatcher to "tell Colonel Mosby I will not surrender, and if he sends that rag up here again I'll shoot it to hell." Hatcher implored him not to do that for "it's the only handkerchief I've got!" With that, Mosby resumed shelling the camp, but to no avail: "the entrance [to the stockade] was strongly defended by the abattis and Annandale being one of the system of works protecting the city of Washington, it was known that reinforcements would be despatched [sic] to the relief of the garrison when the sound of the guns was heard."[46]

Meanwhile, Capt. Schneider had dispatched several orderlies on horseback to alert Col. Lazelle at Falls Church, where "to arms" was sounded and about 150 men were mounted and sent over "to reinforce that command." By the time they arrived in Annandale, however, Mosby had departed. Lazelle's troops followed Mosby some ten miles, determining that he had retreated by way of Fairfax Court House. There they learned that Mosby and his men "had gone through town in great haste, and when outside the town, broke and went [in] different [directions]."[47]

This was one of a handful of reverses that Mosby and his men suffered against the men of the 16th New York Cavalry and their fellow New Yorkers in the Thirteenth. In this case, despite having nearly a two-to-one advantage in manpower, Mosby's force simply was unable to breach a strongly built stockade defended by well-led troops.

The stockade at Annandale, known locally as Fort Schneider, was located on the land of James S. Purdy, a Unionist and one of four in his precinct who had voted against Virginia's Ordinance of Secession. Today, Purdy's farm, then with a little over 300 acres, is the location of the Annandale Campus of the Northern Virginia Community College.[48] The stockade was well enough fortified that the only casualties for the 16th New York were two wounded horses belonging to Co. A. The artillery fire also "deranged some of our quarters and Company C's stable."[49]

Joseph Schneider was one of thousands of German immigrants who volunteered in the Union Army during the war. But, unlike many others, he came into the war with military training and experience. Born in June 1834 at Bensburg, North Rhine–Westphalia, just outside of Cologne, Schneider had attended a military academy in Prussia and passed the officer's examination in 1850. Deciding not to continue on to officer school because he "had become a thorough democrat, opposed to the empires and monarchies and did not want to enter the army," Schneider instead was apprenticed to a tanner for three years.[50]

Completing his apprenticeship, he worked as a tanner until he became eligible for conscription. Learning that his brother and uncle were leaving soon for America, Schneider returned home and joined them, sailing from Antwerp, Belgium and arriving in New York in late September 1854.

Unable to find work as a tanner in New York City, Schneider joined his brother in Clifton Springs, Ontario County, southeast of Rochester, to work the harvest; moved on to Milford, Ohio, near Cincinnati, working as a piano teacher and farm hand; then as a waiter in Emporium City, near Cairo, Ohio; and finally as a journeyman compositor for the local newspaper. In Ohio, Schneider contracted "fever and ague" and was advised to return north. Arriving in Buffalo in July 1857, he found a job as a hotel porter.[51]

In August 1857, Schneider enlisted as a private in the 3rd U.S. Infantry Regiment, serving for five years. With the outbreak of war, he re-enlisted in September 1862, this time for three years as a private in the 1st New York Mounted Rifles. Six months into this assignment he transferred to the 16th New York Cavalry as an officer. Although, like Col. Lazelle, Schneider had been caught up in the surrender of Federal forces in Texas after the State seceded from the Union early in 1861, it appears to be purely coincidental that he ended up with a captain's commission in the 16th New York.[52]

Undeterred by his poor showing at Annandale, Mosby stayed in the area, although his next attack also had mixed results. Early the morning of August 25, the cavalrymen at Falls Church were again roused from their beds. This time Mosby had "gotten between one of our Picket posts & captured some 16 sick horses" that were "contagious" and kept quarantined from the rest of the command's horses. According to Lt. Moore, the horses were virtually worthless as "most could not be cured. If he mixes them among his, they will kill all his horses. Indeed it is a fine joke on him."[53]

On August 26, Col. Lazelle was ordered to prepare the 16th New York for a joint scout with the 8th Illinois Cavalry, which was serving as part of the Provost Guard for Washington, in the direction of Upperville. That same day, on his own, he had dispatched Maj. Horton with 220 men, "all that could be sent of the Sixteenth New York, including one company from Annandale," to thoroughly scout the country between Falls Church, Goose Creek and beyond. In this operation, he was not responding to orders, but rather to "well authenticated" reports that a force of some 100 rebels was in his immediate vicinity "having been seen yesterday immediately east of

Fairfax Court-House, and this morning between this point and Vienna." Mosby and a few of his men also had been reported in Fairfax Court House.[54]

On August 28, while Horton and his 220 men were out on their scout, Lazelle received follow-up orders for Horton's detachment to join the 8th Illinois near Aldie. The Eighth, under command of Maj. John Waite, was to leave Muddy Branch the morning of August 29 and reach Aldie by noon on August 30. The two units, under Waite's overall command, were to move rapidly to Upperville and Middleburg, "surprising any force of guerrillas lurking in that vicinity." Their real objective however, was to destroy the sources from which Mosby was obtaining men, horses and support:

> To this end you will arrest and bring in all males capable of bearing arms or conveying information, between the ages of eighteen and fifty, excepting those mentioned in the inclosed list [sic—the list was not found in the records]; impress all wagons, and bring them in loaded with forage; destroy all crops of hay, oats, corn, and wheat which you cannot bring in, and seize all horses. When horses are taken from Union men, make memoranda to that effect, in order that the horse may be identified or the owners indemnified. Collect all information within reach of the movement of the enemy and embrace it in your report; any which you may regard as of great importance should be sent in by a small party of trusted men. Mosby's headquarters are reported as alternating between the houses of Mr. Blackwell and Mr. Turner, near Upperville.[55]

Lazelle was instructed to inform Maj. Horton that the duration of the scout was "indefinite" and that after the supply of rations for his men and horses were exhausted, they were to "live on the country."[56]

There was only one problem: where was Horton? On August 29, Lazelle had to confess to Maj. Gen. Augur that a party he had sent out to give Horton his new orders had not found him after 24 hours, "though they went as far as Gum Spring." Lazelle immediately sent out another party of 35 men. In desperation, he also sent information to Maj. Waite to take the men he needed from the Annandale stockade and that he would send "rations and forage sufficient for the whole force from here until they can supply themselves."[57]

Lazelle received a curt response from Lt. Col. Taylor, Augur's Chief of Staff, informing him that the general did "not think it advisable to change the instructions already issued." Taylor also informed Lazelle that "your resignation has been suspended." There are no other references in the *Official Records* to Lazelle attempting to resign at this time, although he would resign in mid–October.[58]

On August 30, the search party finally caught up with Maj. Horton and delivered his orders to immediately depart for Gum Springs in hopes of meeting up with Maj. Waite. If Waite and the 8th Illinois were not at

Gum Springs, he was to go on to Aldie. If they were not at Aldie, he was to push on "as long as there remains a probability of overtaking his party with safety to your own." Horton was told he would find Capt. Washburne of the 16th New York at either Gum Springs or Aldie with three days of forage for Horton's command.[59]

Maj. Horton and Maj. Waite did finally meet at Aldie at 6:00 p.m. on August 30, and they returned together to Falls Church the following evening. The 8th Illinois had completed the mission on its own. That night, Albert Wilbur noted in his diary that there had been three attacks on their pickets in the last few hours. Thus ended a tumultuous month for the 16th New York Cavalry.[60]

Five

September–October 1864
More and More Losses

In September and October, while Sheridan and Early "sparred back and forth" in the Shenandoah Valley,[1] Mosby and his rangers continued to be the "only force operating in the rear of Sheridan's army."[2] At the same time, Mosby continued to maintain pressure on the Independent Cavalry Brigade in order to keep it pinned down in Fairfax County.

During the night of August 31, three picket posts—near the brigade headquarters camp near Fort Buffalo, on Braddock Road, and on the road to Falls Church and Annandale—were "attacked simultaneously and driven in." The following morning at 6:30 a.m. another picket about a half mile west of Falls Church was attacked and a vedette was captured. Late in the day on September 1, two separate forces of 20 to 30 men attacked two picket posts between Fort Buffalo and Annandale virtually simultaneously. Five Union cavalrymen were captured. At about the same time, a picket post on Little River Pike "toward Fairfax Court House from Annandale" was attacked. A sergeant was wounded and two privates captured. The two attacks severed communication between the stockade at Annandale and Fort Buffalo.[3]

As a result, Col. Lazelle once again had to thicken his static defenses. He immediately expanded the picket posts all along the line to a corporal and four privates each, "dismounted the entire line" except for a corporal or sergeant at each picket station, and directed each picket "to build a cribwork of fallen trees to intrench [sic] themselves by day" and thus better guard against mounted attackers. At night, a concealed vedette would continue to guard each road and the pickets, also concealed, would be located within 200 yards.

Lazelle also sent out two parties of 50 men each from the 16th New

York "to examine the country in our vicinity" and another 100 to Annandale for a few days so that "a more effective stockade might be completed there." Capt. Schneider, commanding at Annandale, had requested more men in the wake of the attacks, to help complete the stockade's defenses. That same day, Maj. Gen. Augur warned Lazelle of "reliable information" that Mosby was still located close by and was expected to attack again that night. Lazelle subsequently warned the 13th New York captain commanding the stockade at Lewinsville that Mosby was expected to attack that evening with some 100 to 200 men.[4]

On September 3 and 4, Lazelle reported that the scouting parties had turned up little, beyond some 30 rebels seen near the Lewinsville stockade who were chased but quickly scattered into the woods. Despite persistent reports of Mosby's continued presence in the area, all remained quiet for the next week or so.

In reality, Mosby was nowhere near Fairfax, having moved out to Rectortown where, on September 3, he divided his command, sending one squadron off through Ashby's Gap to the country around Berryville and leading the other squadron, with about 90 men, through Snicker's Gap and on to Myer's Ford on the Shenandoah River.[5]

"Hardly the Bold Deed"

Mosby did not return to action in Fairfax County until September 13 when, while reconnoitering the cavalry brigade's quartermaster camp at Falls Church, he "discovered a butcher sleeping beside a beef he had killed. The man was brought out, with his horse, in spite of his vigorous protest against what he thought was a joke played on him by some of the 'funny boys' in camp." Determining that the camp was "poorly guarded," Mosby sent a few men back to steal horses, but they fled once the camp "was alarmed." Mosby ordered all but two of his men to return to Fauquier County. He, Guy Broadwater, and Thomas Love remained in the area.[6]

Two days later, on September 15, a large scouting party from the 13th New York, under command of Col. Gansevoort, was returning to Falls Church from Chantilly when they received reports from scouts that "Mosby had been seen to pass through the [Fairfax] Court-House toward Centreville a short time previous with two men." Gansevoort immediately dispatched a party of five men to attempt to intercept Mosby on the Centreville road. The Union cavalrymen and the three rebels ran into each other on the road and opened fire on each other simultaneously. Two of the Union cavalrymen's horses were killed outright and their riders scattered into the woods. The other three Union men "fled full speed with Love and Broadwater after them until I [Mosby] called them back to my assistance."[7]

In the initial barrage, Mosby had been wounded, one ball shattering the handle of his pistol and another entering his groin. He was able to stay on his horse and ride "with difficulty, until his companions secured a light wagon to carry him off." Love and Broadwater took him to The Plains, "where he was kindly cared for by the family of Major Foster until he could be removed to Lynchburg," where he recuperated at his father's home. He would recover sufficiently to rejoin his command on crutches in Fauquier at the end of the month.[8]

In a later report to Maj. Gen. Augur, Col. Lazelle gave credit to Pvt. Henry Smith of the 13th New York for what Mosby, in his memoirs, characterized as "hardly the bold deed Lazelle described." He also determined, based on reports from a variety of local citizens, that Mosby had been "taken out of our reach into a safe location," most likely in Lynchburg or Richmond.[9]

Success at Rapidan Station—Almost

Meanwhile, a deserter from the 11th Virginia Cavalry had "delivered himself up" to Col. Lazelle and reported on what he had seen as he made his way to Fairfax County from Richmond through Lynchburg, Culpeper and Warrenton. Based on the deserter's report that there were only "small guard" forces in Culpeper and Warrenton and also only a "small guard" at the Rapidan River railroad bridge south of Culpeper Court House, Lazelle had proposed to Augur that the 16th New York undertake a "scout" out to the Rapidan. The mission was approved on September 14, and Lazelle left Fort Buffalo early the morning of September 17 with 275 men from the Sixteenth and 50 from the Thirteenth.[10]

Lazelle and others were aware that the bridge across the Rapidan had recently been rebuilt by the Confederates, "for the double purpose of completing the railway communication from that place with Richmond and affording an easy exit from the Shenandoah valley of all the harvest and plunder collected by [General] Early in his late occupation of that district."[11] Federal authorities also knew that a large warehouse at Rapidan Station "was filled with grain, etc., awaiting transportation."[12] The purpose of the expedition was to destroy the bridge, and thus "cut off railroad communication between General Early in the valley and Richmond,"[13] and to capture or destroy any Confederate stores there.

The initial phase of the operation went off without a hitch. Marching by way of Kelly's Ford on the Rappahannock River near Culpeper Court House and Raccoon Ford on the Rapidan south of Culpeper, Lazelle's command "arrived at the south side of the Rapidan opposite the station before dawn" on September 20. At daylight, they crossed the river and captured 200 horses and mules as well as the Confederate guard force of two officers and 20 men. After cutting away its supports and burning the railroad bridge, "a structure 200 feet long and 40 feet high on trestle-work," they burned the station house, telegraph office, three railroad cars, and "a very large flour mill, running six sets of stones" with "300 barrels of flour and a large quantity of corn and wheat." Before leaving, they also "pulled down the telegraph and destroyed a part of the railroad track."[14]

Completing its work at Rapidan Station, Lazelle's command moved up the railroad tracks, "on three parallel lines,"[15] toward Culpeper to destroy a train of cars further up the track, stopping at Mitchell's Station about two miles south of Culpeper. Although they had faced "light skirmishing" all the way from Rapidan Station, all the information available to him convinced Lazelle that "there was no considerable force to be encountered."[16]

He was wrong. They were about to run into Maj. Gen. Joseph P. Kershaw's division, which had "arrived from the [Shenandoah] valley the night before on his way to Richmond," and who had "posted his troops to receive me in front and on the flanks of the crossroads near Culpeper."[17]

As recounted by QM-Sgt. Cyrus Shepard, who was riding security out on the left flank of the main force, several men in the open ahead of him began firing. He raced back to the main column, where he "found the men drawn up in a line of battle, and looking ahead, I saw a large body of men moving hastily about, forming in line with an evident intention of knowing more about the Yankee cavalrymen who were before them."[18] Indeed, Kershaw's men had allowed the advance element to pass by, and when Lazelle's main columns approached, "a terrific fire was opened by rebel infantry."[19]

As later reported by Col. Lazelle, upon reaching the junction of the Culpeper and Stevensburg roads, he found them "commanded by hills, on which was a simple line of entrenchments with rifle pits in front" and about 200 men and four pieces of artillery. On the left, "obstructing the Stevensburg road" were some 100 cavalry and 300 infantry, with forest cover to their rear. Lazelle decided to move to the base of a "long, high hill" opposite

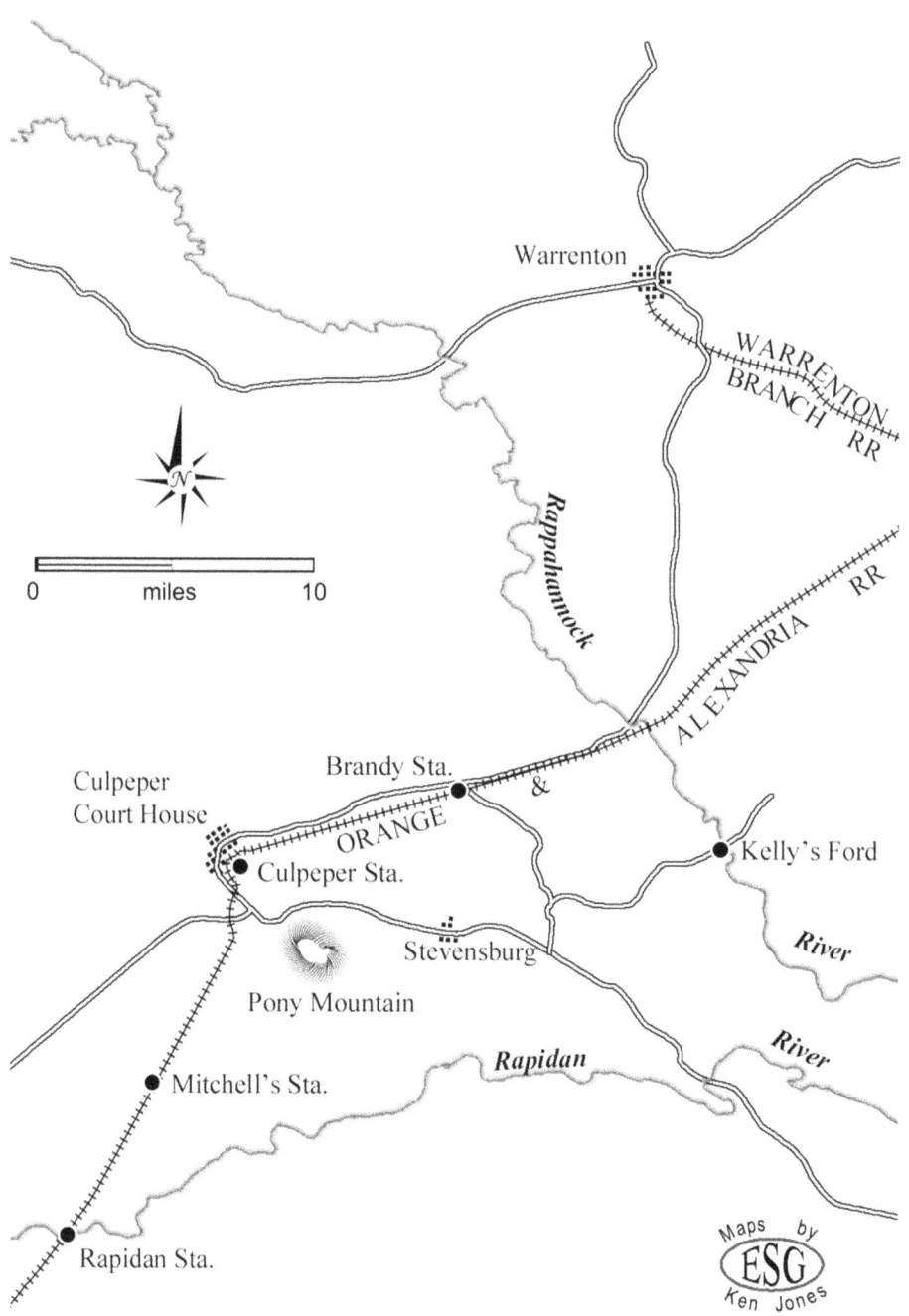

Attack at Culpeper, September 1864.

the Confederate troops, "with a forest above it," hoping to avoid the artillery and infantry, while he threw out a line of skirmishers.[20]

According to QM-Sgt. Shepard, the fire from the Confederate line was intense, with "grape and canister shell and musketry, and for the first time I was in a battle and under fire and heard the music of the bullets as they sang their sickening death-song in the air.... I saw men here and there throw up their arms and fall from their horses."[21]

Lazelle ordered a flank movement, but some 100 men surged ahead, "fled past the column in great disorder," and joined the officers and men of the advance guard, which had been allowed to pass. Instead of halting the surge, rallying the men, and returning to the main body, the advance guard, now with some 150 men, "went directly on at a rapid pace to Stevensburg," and then by way of Kelly's Ford back to Falls Church.[22]

Responding to the fire from Kershaw's troops on the main column, Capt. Leahy of the 16th New York and Capt. Brown of the Thirteenth charged with their commands "in the hope of routing the infantry; but owing to the positions the enemy had taken up, with a swamp to their front, were repulsed with loss. The enemy cavalry seeing this charge repulsed, at once charged on the rear of the column, with the view of cutting off the only road now left for retreat; but were defeated in their main object with heavy loss."[23] Sgt. Volney Mudge of Co. K remembered the action as particularly intense:

> Then how the shells flew as we tore along toward that rebel regiment. What do they mean? That crowd does not form square to resist cavalry, we are surprised they do not open fire. But alas! We soon found out why they seemed so indifferent. Our horses are becoming mired, we cannot advance, there we are—en masse huddled together—then the regiment opens fire—scores of men and horses go down. "Return sabre! Draw revolvers!" are the orders. Major Horton [13th New York] takes command. He says "boys, our colonel wants you to back out of this! As fast as you reach the high ground halt and wait for the rest." Well such a getting back. Lieut. French's horse is shot through the neck and falls, throwing the Lieut. His horse arises and runs to the rear. Capture that horse! Shouts the lieutenant. But we have to leave poor French with nearly a hundred others.[24]

Meanwhile, Lazelle attempted to rally his remaining troops and charge through the lines. As recalled by QM-Sgt. Shepard, Maj. Nicholson rode up and said:

> You see those rebels in front and to the left of us, this big mountain, which is called Piney Mountain, to the right, while back of us are Richmond and Libby Prison. Any direction we may move has trouble for us, but Col. Lazelle has determined to make a break direct through the rebel lines, and cut his way through, if possible and reach the turnpike to their rear, that extends to Kelly's Ford on the Rappahannock.[25]

Lazelle sent a scout up a hill ahead and to the left "to see if the rebels are making a movement to outflank us." The scout was "shot through the body as he sat on his horse on the brow of that hill." The order to "draw sabers" was then given, and the New Yorkers charged the rebel lines:

> As we approached the rebel lines they gave us a volley that emptied some saddles, but instead of forming in hollow squares to receive cavalry, as they should, they kept their line of battle, giving us a volley first from the front and then from the rear rank, and then we were upon them and they broke and scattered in all directions, and we were through their lines almost before we knew it.[26]

Lazelle was able to get his remaining troops into the tree line and break off contact with all "but small parties of the enemy's cavalry." The command reached the turnpike in the rear of the Confederates and turned toward the river, "and all knew that it was a race for Kelly's Ford. If the rebel cavalry should arrive there first and occupy the high ground on the northern side of the river they could easily prevent our crossing and nothing would remain for us but to surrender."[27]

The New Yorkers won the race. They skirmished all the way to Kelly's Ford, and bivouacked on high ground about three miles from the ford. The next day about 40 Confederate cavalry troops harassed the column until it arrived at Bristersburg, 16 miles from Kelly's Ford. The captured Confederate mules were "abandoned" and all but eight of the Confederate prisoners escaped.[28]

The initial reports of the clash between Lazelle's command and Kershaw's division coming into brigade headquarters were devastating. Albert Wilber wrote in his diary on September 20 and 21 that the "rebs" had drawn the Union cavalrymen into a trap and cut the column in half. One column escaped; the other had been captured. Among those reported captured were Lazelle and 14 other officers along with 200 enlisted men. Wilber had little respect for those who had run: "The skedaddlers left one of their number, a beastly drunk, behind unarmed. The party that did not skedaddle found him shot through the heart.... Maj. Bosworth, who has no reputation at all, Capts. Gaylord, Washburn & Baker, who have such a bad one for bravery, were in command [of those who escaped]."[29]

Wilbur also seemed to place blame squarely on Lazelle's shoulders, noting that instead of returning directly to Fort Buffalo, he had diverted to Culpeper Court House, resulting in the loss of "most of the mules, two ambulances, some horses and "the prisoners we had taken."

In the end, these initial loss reports were exaggerated. Although he did lose all of the captured Confederate men and mules, Lazelle reported only eleven of his own men wounded and 22 missing, including his nephew

Lt. George French of Co. K, who was captured and sent to Danville Prison. He would be paroled at Aiken's Landing on the James River in February 1865 and return to the 16th New York. In his report, Lazelle singled out Lt. French and Lt. Doherty (Co. H), along with Captains Mickles (Co. B) and Leahy (Co. L) of the Sixteenth, and Capt. Brown of the Thirteenth, for having "behaved most fearlessly in their efforts to retrieve what was lost."[30]

Of those men captured, for whom there are records, four perished from disease in the Confederate prison at Salisbury, North Carolina: Pvt. William N. McLean, Co. B, on December 8, 1864; Pvt. Jacob Rugen, Co. E, on November 4, 1864; Pvt. William W.S. Stephens, Co. E, on November 26, 1864; and Pvt. William White, Co. E, on November 4, 1864.[31]

Responding to Lazelle's report, Maj. Gen. Augur telegraphed that it appeared to him "that a number of the enlisted men, if not influenced by the example of, at least not checked or rallied by, certain commissioned officers, behaved shamefully." He ordered Lazelle to provide the names of the officers involved.[32]

On Sept. 24, Lazelle reported back that he could not "without much hesitation" present names for censure, since all had "a multiplicity of excuses, some circumstances in which are partially confirmed by reports of others." Nonetheless, he singled out Maj. George Bosworth of the 16th New York, who commanded the advance guard. Having been sent two orders, "one to move to his right to a position to join me and the second to halt," Bosworth had obeyed neither "explicitly" or "only partially, and but for a moment," and, on arriving at Kelly's Ford and finding no enemy, he also did not halt and wait for the rest of the command. Lazelle also singled out lieutenants Henry P. Field (Co. H) and Henry S. Larned (Co. B) of the 16th New York for leaving their companies and going ahead with the advance guard. He concluded his response by noting that in his opinion "the conduct of more than half the officers of this command" was "deserving of the severest censure in not controlling and giving orders to their men."[33]

In the end, Maj. Gen. Augur ordered Col. Lazelle to bring Maj. Bosworth before a general court-martial "at first opportunity that offers."[34] There is nothing in the records to indicate whether or not Bosworth was ultimately tried by court-martial. However, he remained with the Sixteenth through the end of the war, was appointed 1st Lieutenant with the 9th Cavalry in 1867, and was mustered out of the Federal service in January 1871.[35]

Lieutenants Field and Larned were not so fortunate. On October 1, 1864, they were "dishonorably dismissed," by order of the President, for "leaving their companies whilst their commands were in front of the enemy, and neglect of duty, in not controlling and giving proper orders to their men."[36]

Lazelle accepted no blame on his own account. Indeed, in July 1866, he was brevetted to major in the regular Army for "gallant and meritorious service in action near Culpeper, Virginia, to date from September 19, 1864."[37]

Opening Up the Manassas Gap Railroad

While the 16th New York was licking its wounds from the encounter with Kershaw's troops, General Sheridan was moving up the Shenandoah Valley. Writing to General Grant from New Market, Sheridan noted that he was 80 miles from Martinsburg and finding it "exceedingly difficult to supply this army." On September 22, Grant wrote to General of the Army Halleck asking about the feasibility of opening the rail lines from Washington all the way to Strasburg. The Orange and Alexandria line was already open from Alexandria to Manassas Junction, and Halleck responded that he had learned the Manassas Gap Railroad could be "put in running order" to Piedmont, 16 miles from Front Royal, in a matter of days. However, there were problems beyond Piedmont:

> From there to Front Royal all the iron of the track has been carried away, and it will require about a week to replace it. From Front Royal to Strasburg all the bridges, which are very long, have been destroyed and the rails removed; but it is thought that Front Royal will serve all the purpose for the defense of the Valley that Strasburg would, a pontoon bridge being established across the river at that place.[38]

Halleck thought it prudent, however, to send a "competent engineer officer" out to survey both Front Royal and Strasburg, and he directed Maj. Gen. Augur to provide a cavalry escort. Lazelle, tasked with providing the escort, replied on September 23 that he had informed the engineer, who wanted to go all the way to Strasburg along the rail bed, that it would be "extremely hazardous" to send a force of 350 men further than the vicinity of Piedmont, and that he could not spare a larger force "with present dispositions." Augur replied a few hours later that Lazelle should send the escort, making it as strong as he deemed necessary. Augur would compensate the loss from Lazelle's defenses with companies then stationed either at Fort Ethan Allen, Fort Reno, or Alexandria, closing his telegram with a cryptic "Will that be sufficient?"[39]

Col. Lazelle wisely deemed it "sufficient," and reported back to Augur that he would "endeavor to send an escort of 600 men." He asked Augur to provide at least 200 replacements, specifically a company of infantry and three of cavalry, "as it is probable that their united effective strength is not over 150 men."

Augur responded quickly, through his chief of staff, informing Lazelle that since General Sheridan had driven the enemy "entirely south of the Manassas Gap Railroad," an escort of 500 would be sufficient. Lazelle immediately dispatched the 13th New York under Col. Gansevoort, with about 500 men and the engineer. The men of the Sixteenth remained in camp recuperating from their beating at Culpeper Court House.[40]

Meanwhile, Col. Lazelle once again turned his attention to John Mosby and local collaborators. On September 26, he directed Capt. Schneider at the Annandale stockade to send out a dismounted night raiding party, "with a careful officer," to search the house of Mrs. Dickens on the Ravensworth Road, also known as Ossian Hall. She allegedly was having frequent visits from Mosby's and Kincheloe's men. They also were to search two other houses in the area—one belonging to "an Irishman who lives on and takes care of Mr. Moran's place," and the other belonging to Mr. Seaton, "who lives on the Fairfax road." Schneider's men were to confiscate any passes held by people on these properties. Lazelle also authorized Schneider to send out similar night raiders "to search for guerrillas and examine houses at any time when you think it should be done."[41]

On September 29, the 16th New York's brief respite from action came to an end. Maj. Gen. Augur ordered Col Lazelle to take "as strong a force as your command will afford" the following day toward Culpeper Court House once again to determine the nature of "the force occupying Gordonsville and approaches, if any reinforcements have been forwarded from Richmond to [General] Early, and if there is any indication of Early's movement in this direction [toward Washington]." Early had recently clashed with General Sheridan's Army of the Shenandoah, at Winchester and Fisher's Hill. Lazelle departed camp the evening of the 30th with 400 men.[42]

On October 4 and 5 he reported back that there were no Confederate troops around Culpeper Court House except for a small home guard and a few cavalry and scouts, nor were there any troops in or around Gordonsville, except for a "small railroad guard from Gordonsville to Orange Court-House, along the line of the Orange and Alexandria road, and that there is no force occupying Gordonsville, except a provost conscript guard of a few men, a few conscripts, and a portion of a regiment, about 200 men, composing a recruiting camp for disabled horses."[43]

Lazelle doubted the veracity of other reports from several different sources that General Early had been reinforced with 5,000 men and "sent forward with [General] Longstreet, who was to assume command," a doubt he shared with the Honorable John Botts, one of his sources.

John Botts, a strong "Unionist" Virginia judge who lived in Culpeper, was officially neutral but apparently willing to share information regarding his and his family's observations. Writing to his brother on October 6, Lt. Charles Moore reported that he had joined Col. Lazelle "at the residence of John Miner Botts, who together with his family treated us most splendidly. Never have I before known what Southern hospitality was." Moore believed Botts to be "a strong Union man," as well he was.[44]

Botts' and Lazelle's doubts were correct. Longstreet did not return to duty as corps commander until October 17. Lazelle also was able to confirm that Kershaw had left Gordonsville and that the Orange and Alexandria Railroad was "in good order beyond Rappahannock Station to Culpeper."[45]

John Minor Botts and his family at their home in Culpeper, Virginia (Francis T. Miller, *The Photographic History of the Civil War, Vol. 7*, 1902).

Meanwhile, Col. Gansevoort of the 13th New York, temporarily commanding the cavalry brigade at Falls Church, was ordered to send a company of men out to the "Construction Corps" on the Manassas Gap Railroad to act as couriers between the engineers and General Sheridan's headquarters in the valley.[46] Although both General Grant and General Sheridan had concluded that the Valley Campaign was essentially over and that Sheridan could begin moving toward Richmond, Commanding General Halleck remained concerned about the potential for "rebel raids" and, ultimately, the threat to Washington. In his view this meant maintaining a strong garrison around Manassas Gap to "operate on either side of the Blue Ridge," and keeping the rail lines from Alexandria to Front Royal open (both the Orange and Alexandria and the Manassas Gap railroads). Moreover, "In order to keep up communications on this line to Manassas Gap and the Shenandoah Valley, it will be necessary to send South all rebel inhabitants between that line and the Potomac, and also to completely clean out Mosby's gang of robbers who have so long infested that district of country."[47]

On October 5, having discovered that the Federal construction party of infantry and engineers had advanced up the Manassas road, occupying Salem and Rectortown "with trains of cars loaded with railroad material," and "only a single company of cavalry for couriers," Mosby attacked the group at Salem with devastating results. Fifty prisoners, "all their baggage, camp equipage, stores, etc." were captured, and a "considerable number" killed and wounded. The Union force fell back to Rectortown, "with two long trains of cars. The railroad is torn up and bridges burned in their rear, and all communications cut."[48]

The following day, General Augur ordered Col. Lazelle, back in Falls Church, to "collect all your available force (leaving sufficient guard for your post and to patrol your front)," and march to Alexandria along with 200 rounds of ammunition. From there, he was to go by rail "to the front" and meet Augur at Rectortown.[49] Lazelle decided to send Col. Gansevoort in command and at three in the morning instructed Albert Wilbur to go to the brigade arsenal, draw the ammunition and have it at the Alexandria railroad depot by nine. "The orders were obeyed, through much tribulation."[50]

On October 7, Gansevoort left Alexandria for Rectortown with 625 men from the two New York regiments.[51] The following day, Augur was able to report that the railroad was open to Rectortown and telegraph lines strung two miles beyond. The tracks were in poor condition, however: "Heavy trains passing over it have shown that many of the ties are so much decayed as to be unable to hold the spikes, the track consequently spreads and the trains go off."[52]

Security for trains running between Alexandria and Manassas Junction also was a key concern. As noted by the station superintendent at Alexandria, it was impossible to get guards "for even one-third of the number of trains I am running on the Manassas line." At a minimum, he needed 30 men to guard each train and to run them in two- or three-train convoys. "When the road is open for business, I will require at least 540 men per day, 90 men each for six convoys." Given how thinly stretched they were, the 13th and 16th New York Cavalry regiments would not be called upon to perform this additional task.[53]

A week later, on October 15, Gansevoort, with his regiment, two squadrons of the 16th New York, and two companies of the 5th Pennsylvania Artillery, reported a major strike against Mosby. A few days earlier, Mosby had split his command into three groups: one in the Shenandoah Valley, one operating along the Potomac in Maryland, and one in Fairfax. One of his captains had hidden their artillery at "Emory's, a secluded spot on the Cobbler Mountain," near Deleplane in Fauquier County. Sgt. A. G. Babcock and a "few trusty men" were left guarding the artillery.[54]

According to Mosby Ranger James Williamson, John H. Lunzeford, who had served as a guide and helped conceal the battery's worth of equipment, then "deserted and piloted Colonel Gansevoort," who was scouting in the area, to the concealment site. Based on Gansevoort's official report and Augustus P. Greene's recollections, however, Gansevoort's troops actually encountered some of Mosby's men while on "a raid" in the area. A rebel prisoner identified the general location of the artillery, and Gansevoort moved his men "over very intricate roads to a point at the base of the mountains, where a sort of bivouac was surprised and nine members of the battery captured, including Babcock."[55]

Learning little about the precise location of the artillery from the rebel captives, Gansevoort's dismounted cavalry and a company of Pennsylvania artillery "vainly" spent time "skirmishing the mountain." After almost giving up, the cavalrymen were able, "by intimidation," to force a "driver" to lead them to the right trail. The driver, in all likelihood, was Lunzeford, the alleged "deserter."

> By deploying skirmishers and moving up the precipitous side of the mountain, covered with heavy undergrowth for about a mile and a half, and following its summit for some distance, the three-inch ordnance gun, 12-pounder howitzer, and two small mountain howitzers, with limber of caisson, sets of harness and ammunition, were discovered in a dense thicket. These [undoubtedly the guns used in the furtive attack on

the Annandale stockade] were drawn down the stony sides of the mountain to the command below, and thence to Piedmont."[56]

Once back in Piedmont, Gansevoort's troops "dismounted" the artillery pieces and prepared to send them back to Maj. Gen. Augur at Rectortown. Gansevoort asked, however, to keep the small mountain howitzer, which he had repaired and "replenished with ammunition," until he returned to camp in Falls Church. According to Augustus Green, the Federal troops also discovered Mosby's "books and papers and his muster roll, which gave us the name of every man under his command." Some of those men identified in Mosby's papers "used to enter our camp in the disguise of poor farmers, selling different articles, such as butter, eggs and sometimes applejack. And by this means obtaining information they could in regard to our plans."[57]

It did not take long for Mosby and his men to respond. On October 16, his entire command met at Bloomfield, southwest of Roundhill and Purcellville at the foot of the Blue Ridge. Mosby left three companies to "operate along the [Manassas Gap] railroad," and took the other three down to Fairfax "to attack a large wagon train between Burke's Station and Fairfax." Not only were they too late, but the Federals had been warned of the threat, and the wagons had "gone into camp, with a heavy infantry guard." So Mosby and his men camped overnight near Centreville.[58]

The following morning they moved toward Annandale. Once again, Capt. Schneider's stockade was the target. They encountered Schneider's pickets, capturing one, but another escaped. As before, however, the Federals were warned, and Augur's staff quickly dispatched infantry support to both Annandale and Fort Buffalo. Col. Lazelle sent some additional cavalry from Fort Buffalo. As recounted by Mosby Ranger Williamson:

> The cavalry came out. We halted and remained in sight for some time, but as they made no demonstration, Companies A and B advanced toward them, when they hurried inside of their fortifications. Companies A and B then proceeded along the Ox road in the direction of Frying Pan, and then home. General Augur's cavalry had been notified of Mosby's presence in Fairfax, and while Augur's cavalry were being sent to Fairfax in pursuit, Mosby was quietly marching back to Loudoun.[59]

The Murder of the Reverend Read

While Mosby was on his way back to Loudoun, Col. Lazelle completed reinforcing the Annandale stockade with an additional 100 men from the cavalry brigade's heavy artillery detachment at Fort Buffalo. He apparently was satisfied enough with its security to send a third of the 300 infantry reinforcements back to Brig. Gen. DeRussy, commanding the division at Fort Corcoran in Arlington. This left 265 "effective men" of the 13th and 16th New York Cavalry at Falls Church "or in vicinity."[60] What these men did not know was that they were the next target of Mosby's men.

Mosby had left one company under Captain Richard P. Montjoy behind in Fairfax. Montjoy was a Mississippi native who had first fought in the Louisiana infantry[61] and had set "an enviable record as a fighter."[62] His objective was to infiltrate the Falls Church camp at night and capture whatever and whomever he could.

At two in the morning on October 18, Montjoy and his men crept into Falls Church village, stopped at the church, which was serving as a Union hospital, broke into a barn across from the church, and stole five horses. They then started up the Alexandria–Lewinsville pike toward Vienna, where they encountered a picket post manned by a corporal and three privates from the 16th New York. All three men were captured, and a member of the village home guard named Frank Brooks, who attempted to help the Union troopers, was shot and killed.[63]

At about that time, Mosby's men heard a horn blowing in the village. At first they thought "somebody was going out a 'possum hunting," but when they reached the house of the Reverend John D. Read they realized it was a village home guard warning the Union camp. Read and "one of his negro employees" were taken prisoner.[64] The home guard's warning aroused the Union camp, and Mosby's men came under fire, "which in the darkness did no damage. Three or four negro infantry were killed; 6 prisoners and 7 horses were brought out."[65]

Family photograph of the Rev. John D. Read (courtesy Mary Riley Styles Public Library Local History Collection, Falls Church, VA).

The Reverend Read, pastor of the Columbia Baptist Church in Falls Church and an ardent abolitionist, had been forced to move his family to Washington, D.C., early in the war, losing all their possessions. They eventually returned to Falls Church ministering to local whites and blacks and organizing a home guard. Through his contacts, especially the "grapevine" of black families living around the county, he picked up and passed on to the Union headquarters information regarding Mosby's activity. Being considered a "spy," he had been "under surveillance" by Mosby's men.[66]

The Reverend Read and his employee, along with the other captives, were taken away. Read was "brutally murdered in a dense pine wood near Hunter's Mill." Mosby's men also shot his negro companion, "leaving him for dead in the woods." He escaped, however, with a slight wound in the head and "the loss of an ear, blown off by a pistol shot." He later reported that a "reserve party" of some 100 men joined Montjoy's group near Vienna. According to the official report, there was no doubt Read had been murdered: "The surgeon who has made an examination of the body states that the skull at the base of the brain is blown to atoms, and the flesh around the wound is filled with powder, as if the pistol had been placed close to the head."[67]

Initially, the Reverend Read's wife had difficulty getting assistance in retrieving her husband's body, "the Union men not daring to go in search of it."[68] Later in the day, however, "hiring an open wagon, the only vehicle available, she and her daughter, Lottie, drove to Fort Head at Tyson's Corner (where Read's body had recently been moved) and claimed her husband's remains."[69] Chaplain Loyd of the 16th New York conducted the funeral service for the Reverend Read the following day. All of the men of the 16th New York captured by Capt. Montjoy's men on October 18 were confined in southern Virginia and released in February 1865.

Colonel Lazelle Resigns

On the same day that Mosby's men attacked the camp at Falls Church, Lazelle submitted his resignation as colonel of the 16th New York Cavalry and, thus, also as cavalry brigade commander. Lt. Col. J. H. Taylor, Chief of Staff, 22nd Army Corps, telegraphed Maj. Gen. Augur on the 18th that "Lazelle's resignation has been this day accepted." It was forwarded to the Adjutant General of the Army the following day. The official account of the Falls Church attack, also dated October 19, was signed by Maj. James Birdsall of the 13th New York. Since Col. Gansevoort was in the field with his regiment, Birdsall was the senior officer at the brigade headquarters and, thus, now temporarily in command of the brigade.[70]

The exact circumstances and timing of Col. Lazelle's resignation are uncertain, given the reference in late August to his resignation having been "suspended." In his official letter Lazelle provided a number of reasons, all of which suggest it was his decision and that he had not been asked to resign. Most fundamentally, he based his decision on his inability to "advance the interests of the regiment and that of the service," but he stated categorically that "the fault is not mine."

Rather he blamed his own inabilities on two factors. First, that the regiment was an amalgamation of "other regiments partially completed" containing "very many officers without pride, or courage, or honor." Those he had dismissed had been replaced by "executive appointments [by the New York State Governor] in some cases as bad as those dismissed." These bad officers, he maintained, "by long continued worthlessness," had destroyed the fighting spirit and "good which should have been evoked from the men."

Lazelle also made a veiled reference to Lt. Col. George Hollister's court-martial for sexually assaulting members of the regiment as having given the regiment an "unenviable" reputation. Thus, he concluded:

> As I have not been supported, I cannot make the regiment progressive; and my position as Colonel becomes little more than one of pay; and since I took command to advance the service interest, that of the regiment, and my own, I had rather resign it and do the duties of my legitimate grade, than fail, and have the failure known as my own.[71]

In a March 1866 letter to the Army's Board of Adjudication Regarding Military Service History, Lazelle explicitly identified the "disgusting conduct of Lieut. Col. [Hollister] of Regiment" and his inability to recommend or otherwise influence Governor Horatio Seymour in officer appointments to the regiment, as the prime reasons for his resignation.[72]

Still, the timing of his resignation and its ultimate cause are curious. It appears to have been voluntary, most likely the culmination of increasing frustrations. It also apparently had been under review since at least August. Indeed, two days before Lazelle signed his official resignation letter, Maj. Gen. Sheridan had written to New York Governor Seymour from his Middle Military Division headquarters, informing Seymour that the "16th N.Y. Cavalry is without a Col." and requesting that Capt. Nelson B. Sweitzer, 1st U.S. Cavalry, be appointed to the position. Sheridan contended that Sweitzer had "every qualification which could be desired" and had "made himself a handsome military record in every segment of the cavalry corps during the Campaigns of the present year and heretofore."[73]

General Sheridan was not in Col. Lazelle's direct chain-of-command

and would not have known of Lazelle's intent to resign. It is possible, however, that he had been informed, either by Maj. Gen. Augur or General of the Army Halleck, that Lazelle's resignation was going to be accepted and had been asked to recommend a replacement.

On the same day he submitted his resignation, Col. Lazelle took his final action as regimental and brigade commander, signing a letter "to whom it may concern," recommending that Dr. James Hunter—from one of Vienna's founding families and owner of Hunter's Mill—whom he had arrested for entertaining Mosby at his house, be released from confinement:

> On a more recent development of facts connected with the matter, it appears that Mosby was not an invited guest, but a self-imposed one; and that the hospitality was rather obligatory on the part of Dr. Hunter, and was protested against by Mrs. Hunter. It was conceived at the time that Mosby's honor would have forbid such an act; but it seems well established that Dr. Hunter would only have subjected himself to violence, or his property to seizure, had he done otherwise.
>
> Believing that Dr. Hunter on this occasion acted from mistaken motives and has violated no oath of allegiance or fealty to the United States, and that he is strictly honorable in his observance of assurances given by him, I respectfully recommend his release from imprisonment, with the injunction upon him that nothing but uncompromising conduct to the Government of the United States, and of opposition to its enemies, can protect him in his rights of a citizen under the Government.[74]

Dr. James Hunter was released—date uncertain—by the end of the war. He died in February 1867 at the age of 62 and was buried in the family graveyard in Vienna.[75]

Six

A New Colonel and Brigade Reorganization

On November 12, 1864, Nelson Bowman Sweitzer was mustered in as Colonel of the 16th New York. A member of Maj. Gen. Sheridan's West Point class of 1853, Sweitzer was an experienced cavalry officer who had served on "frontier duty" in Oregon and Washington with the 1st Dragoons. In 1861, all Army dragoons were re-designated "cavalry," and the 1st Dragoons became the 1st U.S. Cavalry. Sweitzer was a captain at the time.

From July 1861 to April 1863, Sweitzer had served in the volunteers as aide-de-camp to Maj. Gen. George McClellan, with the rank of lieutenant colonel. He was brevetted to major in the regular Army for gallantry in the Peninsula Campaign. As a lieutenant colonel, he took command of the 1st Cavalry in August 1863, operating in central Virginia, the Richmond Campaign (May–August 1864), and in the Shenandoah Campaign under General Sheridan. He was brevetted to lieutenant colonel in the regular Army on September 19, 1864, "for gallant and meritorious services at the Battle of Winchester."[1]

According to QM-Sgt. Cyrus Shepard, Sweitzer was a "strict disciplinarian," and for those who dared break his rules or Army regulations, "a week in the guard house was an ordinary event," as was extra duty. Shepard also wrote that a favorite punishment of many officers was to have the miscreant carry an empty pork or beef barrel with a hole cut in the top so it could "slip over the head and rest on the shoulders." The trooper would then have to "march up and down in front of the guard house" for the number of hours his sentence required. Shepard maintained that perpetrators of the most serious offenses sometimes were "strung up by the thumbs so that their feet would barely touch the ground."[2]

Six—A New Colonel and Brigade Reorganization

A week after Sweitzer took command of the regiment, the 22nd Corps cavalry brigade was reorganized, substantially augmented with infantry and additional cavalry, and placed under the temporary command of Col. William Gamble, 8th Illinois Cavalry. The new command included the 5th Pennsylvania Heavy Artillery, the 202nd Pennsylvania (Infantry) Volunteers, the 8th Illinois Cavalry, and the 13th and 16th New York Cavalry regiments. On November 29, it was officially designated the 1st Separate Brigade, Department of Washington.³

The newly expanded brigade was expected to cover a defensive line running from the Orange and Alexandria Railroad tracks at Springfield Station, through Fairfax Station, Fairfax Court House, and Vienna, and ending at Prospect Hill on the Leesburg Pike, where the Madeira School is now located. According to the War Department orders:

Col. Nelson B. Sweitzer (U.S. Army Heritage and Education Center).

> The distribution of troops will be as follows: the Two hundred and second to hold the Orange and Alexandria Railroad, headquarters at Fairfax Station; the Fifth Pennsylvania Heavy Artillery to hold the line from the station to Prospect Hill, inclusive, headquarters at Vienna; Thirteenth New York Cavalry, with headquarters at Prospect Hill; Sixteenth New York Cavalry, with headquarters at Vienna; Eighth Illinois Cavalry, with headquarters at Fairfax Court-House.⁴

The existing posts at Annandale and Falls Church, established by Col. Lazelle, were to be maintained: Annandale by a battalion of heavy artillery and a company from the 8th Illinois; Falls Church by a company of heavy artillery and another company from the 8th Illinois. Springfield Station was to be manned by a company of Pennsylvania infantry. Quartermaster and commissary depots were set up at Vienna and Fairfax Station. This scheme freed up the two New York cavalry regiments for scouting and other missions.⁵

On November 26, in advance of sending Sheridan's Sixth Corps, including its valued cavalry, out of the Shenandoah to reinforce General Grant in southern Virginia, General Halleck wrote to Sheridan that it seemed to him that "before any cavalry is sent away, Mosby's band should be broken up, as he is continuously threatening our lines." Sheridan responded that he would soon "commence work on Mosby," laying out his intentions in almost biblical terms:

> I will soon commence on Loudoun County, and let them know there is a God in Israel. Mosby has annoyed me considerably, but the people are beginning to see that he does not injure me a great deal, but causes a loss to them of all they have spent their lives in accumulating.... Those who live at home, in peace and plenty, want the duello [sic] part of this war to go on; but when they have to bear their burden by loss of property and comforts, they will cry for peace.⁶

The following day, Sheridan ordered Maj. Gen. Welsey Merritt and his 1st Cavalry Division to move through Ashby's Gap into the Loudoun Valley "to clear the country of forage and subsistence, so as to prevent the guerrillas from being harbored there in the future, their destruction or capture being well nigh impossible, on account of their intimate knowledge of the mountain region."⁷

Merritt was reinforced with additional cavalry regiments from the Army of the Shenandoah as well as from Washington. On November 29, Maj. Gen. Augur ordered Col. Gamble to send 800 cavalry, under Col. Sweitzer, "to report to General Merritt, near Snickersville, with five days' rations and as much forage as possible. They must procure corn from the country."⁸

Sweitzer left on November 30 with all available men from the 16th New York, reinforced by men from the 13th New York. They returned on December 3.⁹ According to Sheridan, Merritt and his reinforced command "carried out his instruction with his usual sagacity and thoroughness, sweeping widely over each side of his general line of march with flankers, who burned the grain and brought in large herds of cattle, hogs and sheep, which were issued to the troops."¹⁰

While Merritt's campaign left much of the agricultural infrastructure of Loudoun County in ruins, its impact on Mosby and his men, and the threat they posed in the upper Shenandoah, in Sheridan's eyes least, was negligible:

> Mosby's men not only eluded capture, but were able to conceal themselves in the very neighborhood through which the Union cavalry was riding. This bespoke a dangerous force, if not numerically, at least potentially. Before Merritt returned to camp,

Sheridan changed his plans concerning the Sixth Corps. Russell and Ricketts' divisions took to the road, but Getty's remained behind.[11]

A Chaplain's Report

On December 9, 1864, Chaplain Hinton S. Loyd submitted a report on the "general history and moral condition" of the 16th New York Cavalry for the month of November to the Adjutant General of the Army. In it he expressed some concern that the "abandon, characteristic of soldiers subsisting on an enemy's country [because much of the regiment had been providing security and scouting along the Manassas Gap Railroad]," as well as their "deprivation of the religious privileges and restraints proffered in camp," had caused a lapse in the "moral tone" of the regiment.

Now that the regiment was back in Vienna, he hoped that "the discipline and moral influences offered here will soon correct these evils." While the regiment was headquartered in Falls Church, Loyd and the chaplain of the 13th New York alternated holding Sunday services "in the commodious Brigade Hospital," and tried to "elevate and improve the moral condition of the command" by circulating religious tracts, maintaining a free library, and talking with the men.[12]

Meanwhile, the 16th New York was settling into winter quarters in Vienna, described by QM-Sgt. Shepard as "like a harbor to the sailor, like home to the wanderer."[13] By this time the camp was heavily protected: encircled by an abatis rising to a height of 15 to 20 feet and secured outside by a "line of guards who patrolled regularly day and night" and two lines of pickets. Shepard's quarters consisted of a log cabin with canvas roof, and his company's horses were also stabled under cover: "the company street extended the full length of the row of tents and stable." Each company had a cook, "who drew the rations from the commissary and prepared them in bulk for the entire company, and then issued to each man his portion, already cooked." Coffee was the "great beverage of the army," as the local sutler was allowed to sell whiskey only "to commissioned officers or upon their order."[14]

The day-to-day routine in camp was one of relative boredom: reveille at daybreak, followed by "stable call," when the men would fall in for roll call and then be dismissed to feed and groom their horses; then breakfast call. After breakfast, the normal routine was sick call, guard mount, drill, water call, supper call, and taps. For the "deadbeats and lazy soldiers," sick call was the highlight of the day—the time for them to "assemble with those who were really sick, to try to impose on the surgeon, and by the place of sickness to get excused from duty." Shepard remembered one soldier who:

> ... seemed to have all the diseases known, until finally his last and the surgeon's patience were both exhausted, and as he appeared one morning, the doctor greeted him with "what is the matter with you this morning?" "Oh, doctor, it hurts me so to breathe" was the reply. "Confound you," said the doctor, "then stop breathing."[15]

The boredom of camp routine was regularly broken throughout the winter by patrols and scouts. On December 9, 1864, the 16th New York in Vienna and the other elements of the command at Prospect Hill, Fairfax Court House and Fairfax Station were ordered to mount daily patrols in "the country in front of the line from Wolf Run Shoals [on the Occoquan River] to the Potomac River, connecting with each other," in order to "thoroughly examine the country to a distance of eight or ten miles outside our lines, collect and report all the information that can be obtained in regard to the enemy."[16]

The regiments of the separate brigade also faced regular demands to support Union operations on the fringes of their area of responsibility. On December 19, for example, General Sheridan sent two cavalry divisions from the Shenandoah through Chester Gap near Front Royal to "capture some herds of cattle that are being collected near Bloomfield and Union." Col. Gamble was ordered to send 1,000 cavalrymen, including 300 from the 16th New York, to White Plains, and from there to Middleburg and Aldie, "to bring in all sheep, cattle (except milk cows), hogs, and horses that can be gathered up on the route from beyond Thoroughfare Gap," and turn them over to Union authorities in Washington.[17]

The following day, Lt. Charles Moore wrote his mother that "our Colonel (16th NY) yesterday made a very narrow escape; he was going from Vienna to Wash. in an ambulance with Capt. Gaylord & two employees of the Sutler Department with an escort of some 6 men, when they were attacked by Gurillas [sic] to the number of 40. The Colonel & Capt. made their escape by jumping from the ambulance & taking to the woods."[18] In all, four of Sweitzer's men were captured, three were wounded, and they lost three horses. The four captured were able to escape and made it back to Fairfax Court House four days later, having "nearly perished from cold and exposure."[19]

Mosby Is Wounded Again

Two days after Sweitzer's narrow escape, Union troopers got their revenge—quite by accident—and the "Confederacy was thrown into considerable excitement," when a patrol of men from the 13th and 16th New York, led by Maj. Frazar of the 13th, surrounded the house of Mr. Ludwell Lake near Middleburg, where Mosby and some of his men were having dinner:

> The Yankees fired in the window, the ball piercing the Colonel's side. He immediately threw off his coat and the ladies [Mr. Lake's daughter and Mrs. Skinner] ripped the stars from the collar. When they entered the house they found him stretched on the floor, groaning and writhing in pain. They stripped him of his clothes, and rolled him over with their feet. They were told he was one of Mosby's lieutenants and they left him for dead, taking the other man prisoner.... His wound is very serious and is feared will prove mortal.[20]

According to the official Union report, Maj. Frazar had spied a saddled horse tied to a fence when his detachment was passing the Lake house on a routine scout. Frazar went to the front door, and a "rebel officer" came to the front door "with his boots off and fired his revolver at our men." The Union cavalrymen returned fire, and "the officer was shot in the body." At this point, according to the report, Frazar failed to take proper action:

> Major Frazar did not search the officer for papers, not inquire who he was from the people of the house; neither did he search the house; and, although two ambulances and a medical officer were with the command, the wounded rebel officer was not examined or brought in; all of which ... any good officer should have done. I am also informed that Major Frazar was too much under the influence of liquor to perform his duty at that time in a proper manner.[21]

According to Mosby's own account of the incident, during dinner he heard "the tramp of horses outside," opened the dining room door, and discovered several cavalrymen. Just as he shut the door and turned toward another, "a number of Northern officers and soldiers walked into the room." Mosby hastily covered the lieutenant colonel's insignia on his coat collar with his hands, and "a few words passed between us." A few seconds later "firing began in the back yard" and "one of the bullets passed through the window, making a round hole in the glass and striking me in the stomach."[22]

After Mosby yelled that he had been shot, "old man Lake and his daughter waltzed around the room," the gunfire outside continued, and the Union men rushed out of the room. Bleeding badly and feeling faint, Mosby was able to walk into an adjoining bedroom, where he pulled off his coat, hid it under a bureau, and lay down "determined to play the part of a dying man." When the Union soldiers returned and asked him who he was, he gave a fictitious name and unit. A Union doctor examined his wound, declared that it was "mortal," and Mosby "gasped a few words and affected to be dying."

They left the room hurriedly, after stripping me of my boots and trousers, evidently supposing that a dead man would have no use for them. The only sensible man among them was an Irishman, who said, as he took a last look at me, "He is worth several dead men yet." There was a good deal of whiskey in the crowd, but they had sense enough to take away my clothes. Fortunately they never saw my coat.[23]

After the Union cavalrymen departed, Mosby was moved to a neighboring house about two miles away. Although Col. Gamble sent Frazar back out with 300 men to scour the area, after having heard the wounded man might have been Mosby, the rebel colonel remained hidden. About a week later, he was moved to his father's house near Lynchburg, where he was attended by a doctor from Richmond and remained until he recovered. On December 27, Maj. Gen. Augur's Chief of Staff confirmed to Col. Gamble that, indeed, the wounded man had been Mosby.[24]

In his own report on December 31, Maj. Frazar—apparently now well sobered up—offered a mild mea culpa contending that "nearly every officer of my command, if not all, saw this wounded man, and no one had the slightest idea that it was Mosby." Once he returned to camp in Middleburg on that fateful night, however, an orderly had brought him the rebel officer's hat "dressed with gold cord and star." Frazar had immediately deduced that it must be a field officer, took the hat and showed it to eight prisoners who had been taken at the Lake house, and demanded to know whether it had been Mosby. They all denied it, some saying that the wounded man was "Major Johnston, Sixth Virginia Cavalry, home on leave."

Returning from his follow-up scout to Middleburg, however, Frazar was able to state, "the man shot in Lake's house was Colonel Mosby." Col. Gamble forwarded Frazar's report to Maj. Gen. Augur: "I exceedingly regret that such a blunder was made. I have given directions that all wounded officers and men of the enemy be hereafter brought in, although I thought any officer ought to have brains and common sense enough to do so without an order."[25]

That same day, General Sheridan telegraphed Maj. Gen. William Emory, 19th Corps, that he had no news "except the death of Mosby. He died of his wounds at Charlottesville." Sheridan's "news" was very premature.[26] By the end of February, Mosby would rejoin his rangers.

A Severe Winter

The final two days of 1864 "brought us violent snow-storms, gloomy and freezing-cold rains, hail and sleet," previewing what Ranger

Williamson characterized as a "very severe" winter with "snow and sleet for the greater part of the season."[27] That did not mean that the men of the 16th New York remained in their winter quarters. On the contrary, New Years Day 1865 found 100 men of the Sixteenth scouring the area "for ten to fifteen miles in front" of their lines. Earlier in the day, two men of the 13th New York on their way to Vienna had been attacked by rebels concealed in the woods near Freedom Hill, east of Vienna near Peach Grove, today's Tysons Corner. One was captured; the other was slightly wounded and managed to escape. The patrol of the Sixteenth returned at dark having found nothing. Two days later, Maj. Gen. Augur ordered Col. Gamble to take one company of heavy artillery from Prospect Hill and establish a permanent post at Freedom Hill. The company would be "assigned to the command of the senior officer at Vienna."[28]

On January 4, Lt. Wilbur wrote that the weather was "cold, but pleasant" with a dry snow on the ground. Chaplain Loyd—"a true friend, a kind associate, a noble-hearted, refined, and Christian gentleman"—had returned from Washington and would be going home in a week, discharged due to poor health.[29]

Meanwhile, routine patrolling continued, winter weather or not. On January 12 and 13, Col. Gamble sent three regimental scouting parties out to "effectually scour the country and pick up the men furloughed by the enemy to steal horses, that are now reported to me as scattered through the country." Gamble also was responding to reports several days earlier that pickets outside Lewinsville and Vienna had been fired on.

On the 13th, 200 men from the 16th New York moved out of Vienna through Hunter's Mill, Frying Pan, and Farmwell, where they met another 200 from the 13th New York. The combined force then marched to Leesburg, Mount Gilead, and Mountville, returning to their camps by way of Aldie on January 15 with three prisoners.[30]

A week later, starting early on Saturday, January 21, Vienna was hit with a major ice storm. It started with sleet and ice all day and was so severe that Sunday services were cancelled. The storm continued until Monday evening, according to Lt. Wilbur, when "the temperature became much colder. The trees are laden with ice and large branches are broken off by its weight."[31]

On February 2, Maj. Augustus P. Green, 13th New York Cavalry, was ordered out to Leesburg with 200 men to investigate reports that Mosby and 400 of his men were camped there and intended to engage in raids into Maryland or Pennsylvania. Leaving from Prospect Hill, conditions were terrible along Leesburg Pike: "It was sleeting and snowing; it was the coldest night I ever remember being out in."³² The road was so badly covered with ice that several horses had fallen and their riders were injured before they got very far.

Reaching Dranesville at day break, they met 200 men of the 16th New York under Maj. George Bosworth: "They had come by way of the Middle Pike [which extended from Alexandria to Difficult Run] and they also had suffered terribly from the cold." After a short break, the combined command started out again for Goose Creek, about 18 miles away. Arriving there around 10:00 a.m., they found the bridge had been destroyed and the river too high and ice too thin to cross. Further on, they found the same conditions at the next ford. At this point, Maj. Green halted the command:

> So I then had "Officers Call" sounded.... I told [the first officer to approach] that we would have to swim the river. He replied, "Major Green, I am now suffering from a very severe cold and if I have to swim that river a day like this it will surely kill the men." At this time it was sleeting and the thermometer below zero, and the river was about one hundred feet wide and very high, so it was a very cheerful prospect to be ordered to swim it.³³

Fortunately, a local farmer approached the cavalrymen and offered to take them to a point on the river where the ice would be thick enough to cross safely. There, the river was some 400 feet wide. The crossing was uneventful, and the command continued to march in a column of fours. About two miles outside Leesburg, Green divided his command into three platoons: "one under command of Major Bosworth to come in on the right of the town, another under command of Captain Charles H. Hatch [13th New York] to advance into town on the left side, and I advanced in the center with my command." Unfortunately, when they converged in the center of Leesburg, "the bird had flown."³⁴

Maj. Green and Maj. Bosworth searched the town and "secured a few prisoners and horses," and then started back, crossing Goose Creek safely. Rather than risk freezing if they made camp, the officers decided to continue back to Prospect Hill and Vienna. The return trip, with ten prisoners and 15 horses, was uneventful.

Two More Officer Dismissals

On February 8, Lt. Albert Wilbur noted in his diary that 1Lt. Henry G. Dow, Co. B, 16th New York Cavalry, had been discharged from the service, "his Comdg. Officers deeming him no longer of any use to it." Officially, Dow was discharged under War Department orders dated January 31, 1865.³⁵

Four days later, Capt. Charles L. J. Robin, Co. H, was tried by court-martial—Col. Sweitzer presiding as President, and 1Lt. Doherty serving as Judge Advocate—on two charges: "conduct unbecoming an officer and gentleman" and "conduct prejudicial to good order and military discipline." Specifically, he was accused of collecting the pay of a deceased soldier and converting it "to his own use," and of having, on several occasions, "obtained from Pvt. Philip Wambolt, Co. H, 16th NYC, and Paymaster Walker on account of Pvt. Wambolt, the sum of $225.00 which he has converted to his own use."[36]

Robin was found not guilty of converting the pay of the dead soldier to his own use but guilty of absconding with Pvt. Wambolt's pay. He was sentenced to be dismissed from the service. Before he could be dismissed, however, he was brought up on charges again on February 9, this time for refusing to go out on a three-day scout "on or about December 20, 1864," claiming at the time: "I am so very sick, I can not go." Again he was found guilty, but the members of the court attached "no criminality thereto" and acquitted him. Reviewing the court records, Col. Gamble found that the good captain's health "unfits him for service and he should resign on Surgeon's certificate of disability and leave the service." He was dismissed, effective February 3, 1865.[37]

Meanwhile, the 16th New York had been operating without a lieutenant colonel since Lt. Col. Hollister was dismissed back in October 1864. Col. Sweitzer took his time in selecting a replacement, apparently comfortable with having time to evaluate the regiment's majors. Albert Wilber was personally rooting for Maj. Horton, but on February 9, the Governor of New York selected Maj. Nicholson, Sweitzer's choice. Albert was devastated, writing in his diary that Maj. Horton "by every consideration of right, seniority, service, and merit" deserved the position. He speculated that Horton probably would resign.[38]

Maj. Horton did not resign. On February 28 he was ordered to Muddy Branch on the upper Potomac and placed in charge of 13 companies, including a battalion from the 13th New York Cavalry. In noting Maj. Horton's new assignment, Wilbur wrote in his diary that "rumors of a movement from here are rife. Guess we will remain here 'til this mud dries up."[39] They stayed.

More Scouts

In late February, General Grant ordered General Sheridan to "destroy the Virginia Central Railroad and the James River and Kanawha Canal," which supplied Confederate troops in Petersburg and Richmond, capture Lynchburg and continue south to join up with General Sherman in North Carolina. Sheridan left Winchester with 10,000 cavalry troops. By March 4, he was in Charlottesville. There he split his force into two commands, one targeted on the mills, factories, and locks on the James River Canal, and the other on the rail lines. These tasks completed, the two forces reunited, and by March 27, Sheridan had joined Grant at Petersburg.[40]

While General Sheridan was leaving the Shenandoah Valley, the Sixteenth was actively engaged in northern Virginia, even though the mud hadn't yet dried up. On March 2, Maj. Gen. Augur ordered Col. Gamble to send as quickly as possible a force of "not less than 500 men (cavalry) toward the Rappahannock bridge"—probably Rappahannock Station southwest of Manassas—to gather information on recent enemy movements, if any, and determine whether there were any enemy forces "on the Rappahannock." Augur had received reports that the 15th Virginia Cavalry was picketing the river.[41]

Gamble sent a combined force of 200 men from the Sixteenth, commanded by Capt. Joseph Schneider, and 400 from the 8th Illinois Cavalry, under command of Capt. Edward Russell, to Rappahannock Station by way of Warrenton, and then up the river to Sulphur Springs, returning by way of New Baltimore. The combined force met along the road to Centreville and then moved out along the Warrenton pike, camping about a mile from Warrenton. Entering the town on March 4, a number of men from the 8th Illinois "left the column in scores, spreading themselves all over the place, dismounting, and entering the houses," probably to loot. Schneider had a great deal of difficulty rounding them up to "rejoin the column."[42]

After leaving Warrenton, Schneider, now in the rear, found the corporal and four men at the far end "vigilant" with "pistols drawn." He ordered them to let no stragglers fall behind, then rode up to the front of his command. About 20 minutes later, Schneider learned from the rear guard that "about a dozen guerrillas had captured one corporal and three men of Co. I, 16th New York, and that another straggler had escaped.... The guerrillas were dressed in our uniform, and the men mistook them for members of the Eighth Illinois Cavalry. There was not a shot fired; they had got into the mountains when I arrived near the rear guard, therefore pursuit would have been useless."[43]

The joint force continued on through Bealeton Station and toward the Rappahannock, camping for the night three miles beyond Sulphur Springs. Completing their reconnaissance, they found "no rebel cavalry

Six—A New Colonel and Brigade Reorganization 123

picketing on the Rappahannock," and none on the Rapidan, "except a few straggling scouts." They also noted that the Rapidan railroad bridge had been washed out by heavy rains, that local streams were impassable, and that the roads were "exceedingly bad."

On Sunday, March 5, the command returned to camp through Warrenton, along the pike toward Salem, crossing the Bull Run mountains, picking up the Warrenton pike near New Baltimore, and following it to Centreville, and then into camp. During the ride back, Capt. Schneider's main concern was the behavior of the men of the 8th Illinois, who were "continually leaving their column, riding as far as one mile from it." Schneider's official report was damning:

> The Eighth Illinois being apparently permitted by their officers to enter farms, it acted as a bad example to our [the 16th New York] men, and to stop their following it, I threatened my platoon commanders with arrest, telling them I should put sergeants in command if they could not keep the men in the ranks. Crossing Bull Run Mountains from the Salem pike, the guerrillas again (dressed in our uniform) attacked the rear guard; succeeded in taking one corporal and two men of Company K. Two other men escaped. This time our rear guard exchanged shots with the rebels, and when I arrived at the rear, I saw the rebels on the mountains about 300 yards off. I had given Lieutenant Hoover [Co. B, 16th New York] (commanding our rear guard) orders to be from 150 to 200 yards in our rear, [and] to be more than 50 yards from his column. I thought Lieutenant Hoover rather slow in his movements, and instructed him to attack the guerrillas with his rear-guard whenever they appeared, which he had neglected before, as it seemed to me he kept marching on while the extreme rear was fighting.[44] About noon a squadron of the Eighth Illinois Cavalry took the rear, after I had been remonstrating with Captain Russell [who had overall command of the combined force], who then told me our [the 16th New York] men were continually falling out. But I convinced him that in nearly every instance his men were the perpetrators, not ours.
>
> To force those men to re-enter their ranks it would have been necessary to engage in a fight with them. One of them passed Captain Baker, Sixteenth New York Cavalry, at the head of our detachment, shouting to one of his comrades, "that son of a b___ wanted to arrest me," pointing toward the rear, where I was engaged, driving up stragglers. One party of the Eighth Illinois Cavalry left the column, went up to a house, dismounted, and entered it. A party of guerrillas attacked them. This was about a half mile from and in full view of the whole command. Captain Baker and the commanders of my rear guard greatly exerted themselves to prevent our men from straggling.[45]

Initially, Col. Gamble focused on the loss of the four men from the 16th New York, expressing his opinion that "their horses, arms and equipments [sic] should be charged to them on the payrolls."[46] On March 9, however, he zeroed in on the 8th Illinois, writing to Maj. Gen. Augur that after "numerous complaints by the people in and about Warrenton in regard to the beating of women and pillaging and robbing of houses" during the scout under Capt. Russell, he planned to "march the same officers and men back there [Warrenton] for identification and have them tried by court-martial on the spot." He hoped this swift action would bring a stop to "this beating and plundering of defenseless women by our scouting parties." Augur approved the plan, but Capt. Russell escaped disciplinary action.[47]

Two days after Capt. Schneider and his men returned from Warrenton, the Sixteenth suffered yet another indignity, once again at the hands of Mosby's men. On March 7, Lt. Olney K. Gault, carrying dispatches between Vienna and Fairfax Court House and accompanied by a sergeant and 20 men, was attacked by some 30 guerrillas. Gault, a tailor born in Smithfield, New York, had previously served as a sergeant in the 86th New York Infantry. He had been discharged for disability in November 1862 and mustered in with the 16th New York as 1st Sgt. of Co. A in 1863. In recognition of his "steady habits (being of mature age), and his being captured and suffering in a rebel prison," he was promoted to lieutenant in December 1864.[48]

Although only slightly outnumbered, Gault's patrol "disgracefully ran away without firing a shot, and let the guerrillas charge into them, killing 1, wounding 3 others, capturing several horses, arms and equipments [sic]."[49] According to Albert Wilbur, one private was killed instantly from a shot to the head, and one of the three wounded men, "with entrails protruding," died soon after he was brought back to camp.

> Both were buried at two o'clock [March 8]. The whole regiment turned out to attend the funeral, and now they who were in good health yesterday morn are sleeping a long and quiet sleep on yonder hill-side. Musketry, cannon roar and clash of hostile steel will disturb them no more. The martial array, the slow and measured tread, the dirge, the few words of the Chaplain, the farewell volley thrice repeated over the graves of the dead brave boys—in fact the whole scene was solemn and impressive—and none of it more so than the return march when the band played "Who will care for my mother now." Ah! Those mothers—who shall comfort them?[50]

In his official account of the incident, Lt. Gault reported that after passing Flint Hill on the way to Fairfax Court House, they were approached from the woods by a body of mounted men, almost all of them dressed in blue. As soon as he discovered "they were making for us," Gault ordered his men into line. "Seeing that they were too strong," however, his men "broke, and I ordered them to about face and run." Unfortunately, they ran into deep mud in which the horses had a difficult time continuing. "The enemy soon overtook us and commenced firing and killing one, wounding two, and three supposed captured." Gault and the rest of his men retreated back to the Flint Hill stockade.[51]

A report filed by Sgt. Otto Richter, Co. I, was somewhat more

Six—A New Colonel and Brigade Reorganization 125

damning as to Lt. Gault's actions. According to Richter, the patrol was marching in a column of twos but "without an advance guard or flankers." As soon as they spied the enemy cavalrymen, Richter recommended forming into line, which the lieutenant ordered. Richter then moved to his position on the right of the line and "looking around I was surprised to see the lieutenant galloping from the field to the rear, followed by the men, first from the rear and center. I heard the lieutenant give no other order than that stated above [to form into line]. The men followed the retreating officer."[52]

Col. Sweitzer, upon reviewing all accounts of the incident, placed the blame squarely on the lieutenant's shoulders:

> I [am led to] believe that the lieutenant commanding was confounded by the sudden and unexpected appearance of a body of enemy preparing to attack, and did not, by manner or example, endeavor to inspire the men to meet the attack, to which effort I believe the men would have responded with gallantry and determination. I am of the opinion this conduct of the lieutenant arose from the misfortune of his having no advantage of experience during the war, and not during his previous life having been accustomed to associations tending to prepare him from such circumstances.[53]

Col. Gamble was outraged, finding it "very disgraceful" that an officer, sergeant and 20 men would run away from 30 guerrillas "without firing a shot, the lieutenant leading the running away." He recommended to Maj. Gen. Augur that "Lieutenant Gault be sent home, out of the service. I want fighting officers to lead men in action, same as I do myself."[54]

Gault was discharged on April 21, 1865, "on tender of resignation," per Special Orders No. 94, Paragraph 9, Headquarters, Department of Washington. In an odd twist, however, the Department of Washington issued General Order No. 71 on May 19, 1865, dismissing Gault "with loss of all pay and allowances now due or to become due to him, pursuant to sentence of General Court Martial." This ex post facto dishonorable discharge was overturned by order of the Army Adjutant General in June 1868.[55]

While Capt. Schneider and Lt. Gault were engaged in northern Virginia, Maj. Horton was ordered on March 5 to move his headquarters and at least a company of men from Muddy Branch, across the Potomac above Great Falls in Maryland, about five miles north to Darnestown. Horton arrived there that night. Four days later, he reported to Maj. Gen. Augur that "a refugee" had stated that Mosby, "with 1,600 men, is at Waterford, Va., eight miles from Leesburg, conscripting." Although Augur questioned the veracity of the report, Horton sent the informant under guard to Augur's headquarters on March 10.[56]

The so-called "refugee" was Thomas McNealy, who had "crossed the river on the morning of the 9th instant [this month], and stated that he wished to take the oath of allegiance; that he had once been in the rebel army, and had been discharged." "Not wishing to be again put into the rebel army," McNealy had fled from the Leesburg area because Mosby was conscripting there.[57]

March 12 was another bad day for the cavalry brigade. A patrol of the 13th New York, with an officer, sergeant and 20 men, was attacked by guerrillas about two miles from Vienna, near Freedom Hill and the Peach Grove signal tower stockade (adjacent to the intersection of routes 123 and 7 at today's Tysons Corner). Two men were killed, eight wounded, and seven taken prisoner. The rest made it to Vienna. Col. Gamble planned to order the "whole cavalry force" out that night to sweep the countryside and examine every house "from here to Bull Run mountain."[58]

That night, however, guerrillas infiltrated the Falls Church area and "carried off a citizen and seven horses" near Upton's Hill. Another group—possibly Mosby's men who had attacked at the Peach Grove—"captured the horses of Mr. Munson, of Munson's Hill, and also those of Mr. Bailey, of Bailey's Cross-Roads." According to a local newspaper, the rebels also succeeded in "taking possession of such edibles as were available, and carrying off one colored man" at Munson's place. Munson was not home at the time. Albert Wilbur confirmed that there was a good deal of guerrilla activity in the area, noting on March 13 that "rebels have been seen during the day in various direction, in small parties."[59]

At noon on March 13, Col. Gamble reported that he had 1,200 cavalrymen out: 800 with Capt. Russell to Sperryville and some 400 with Col. Sweitzer to Waterford. Given the rebel activity close to his lines, Gamble worried that "the balance of the cavalry is barely sufficient to patrol between the posts of the line, to keep up communications, and protect public property."[60]

The morning of the Peach Grove ambush, Col. Sweitzer had left Vienna with 12 officers and 357 men from the 16th New York, heading toward Waterford in Loudoun County "to look after Mosby's conscripting parties." Two days earlier, Maj. Gen. Augur had informed Gamble of Thomas McNealy's information that Mosby was in Waterford "conscripting"—apparently horses and provisions, not men. Despite his belief that McNealy greatly exaggerated the size of Mosby's force, Augur wanted Gamble to "endeavor to ascertain [the] correctness of the report."[61]

Sweitzer and his men reached Leesburg, marching by way of Dranesville and Farmwell (today known as Ashburn) the morning of March

13, having received information all along the way that "quite a force of White's and Mosby's men were in and about" the town. He found the town empty. White had left for the Shenandoah Valley and Mosby for the area around Vienna. His troops only saw "small parties" of men around Leesburg, and these would "scatter in the woods when pursued."[62]

Thinking that he might intercept some of the rebels toward Hamilton and Waterford, Sweitzer pushed on "with an extended line of skirmishers and patrols," but they only encountered small parties of four to fifteen, all of which stayed out of range. At this point, he came to the conclusion that the reports of large guerrilla forces were a ruse to draw Union cavalry away from close-in defenses in Fairfax County. He redirected his command back to the area around Ball's Mills and Goose Creek west of Leesburg Pike, "hoping to come upon some of the parties at the fords [across Goose Creek]." He was not successful:

> From the opportunities of perfect information it is difficult to capture these guerrillas except by detachments operating in concert and rapidly, with information as to the locality of the rebels. The force [sic] of Mosby and White have been scattered about the county of Loudoun, conscripting and impressing horses and provisions, and between which two parties there is great hostility, from their stealing each other's horses, etc. This conscripting, etc., is growing very unpopular, and I anticipate good results to the Union cause, as it leads to the public moving in self-defense and anxious to assist the Union forces, in which they now do but little. In coming back I endeavored by halting and stationing parties to catch any small parties following my rear, to pick up stragglers, but the enemy was unusually wary.[63]

Sweitzer originally had planned to continue on to Harpers Ferry, obtain supplies and rations, and then return "over a route near the base of the [Blue Ridge] mountains. Upon learning that guerrillas were "taking advantage of the absence of cavalry" in Fairfax County, however, he opted to return by the more direct and faster route.

The Mission that Wasn't

On March 17, Maj. Gen. Augur queried Col. Gamble whether he could spare about 800 cavalry "in good condition" to "make an expedition" to the Northern Neck. Gamble responded that he could have that many ready to leave the morning of March 20, and that the 8th Illinois Cavalry was in the process of drawing horses and arms. Two days later, Augur again telegraphed Gamble informing him that he wanted either Gamble or Sweitzer to be in command of the expedition "in case it is sent." Gamble responded that Sweitzer would take command.

There it stood until March 22, when Augur again telegraphed Gamble that troops under General Winfield Scott Hancock—who now was commanding Union forces of the Middle Department in the Shenandoah Valley—had taken on a group of rebels some 500 strong. Augur ordered Gamble to send out about 500 to the area around Upperville to reinforce Hancock's men. The deployment to the Northern Neck was "abandoned for the present."[64]

Instead, Gamble, who had been breveted to brigadier general, conducted a formal review and inspection of all the troops of the brigade—"with the exception of some 2,000 men that we had to leave in the different camps and on the line for the purpose of doing our picket duty"—at Flint Hill. Albert Wilber was assigned to Gamble's staff which was "numerous and accompanied by several ladies. The soldiers looked well and marched well."[65]

In all, the brigade formed up with 1,000 infantrymen, a battery of light artillery, 2,500 cavalrymen, and 1,500 heavy artillerymen with muskets. For Lt. Charles Moore, "it was a most magnificent sight, the line extending some ¾ of a mile. We have quite a few ladies, officers wives & daughters. That day we had 10 of them mounted and each of the General's staff had 1 in charge." Albert Wilbur remembered that the soldiers "looked well marched well." As the review ended, guns were aimed at some woods nearby, sending "several Johnnies (rebs) who had stealthily assembled there to take notes skedaddling. After they left the woods three shells were sent screaming after them."[66]

Seven

Victory and Tragedy

April 1865 opened upon a Washington filled with hope. On April 2, Albert Wilbur wrote in his diary the news "by telegraph and signal" that General Sheridan had captured 12,000 prisoners at Five Forks southwest of Petersburg: "everybody is excited, everybody jubilant, though none forget that many a noble heart lies pulseless tonight on the red field." The following afternoon, Wilbur wrote again of victory, this time at Petersburg and Richmond:

> 1 o'clock. Petersburgh [sic] and Richmond are ours. The signal says 3 o'clock. A national salute is being fired, bands are playing, and everyone seems wild with excitement and more than one is execrating the luck that keeps us here. Am not particularly desirous of getting shot, but would be willing to run a large risk for the sake of being there. This is the greatest event of modern times.[1]

In a letter to his mother on April 5, Lt. Charles Moore also sent the "glorious news," telling her that in his view:

> Genl. Grant is the greatest General that ever lived and his officers and men all without exception worship him, fully as much as one man could another. People who when I was north, could not see what Grant had done, but was [sic] full of Sheridan, Thomas [Sherman's logistician during the "march to the sea"] & Sherman can without a doubt now see that he [Grant] was the director, they merely servants. (Good ones they were too) to carry out the plans he had established, and that the army of the Potomac that has done the hardest fighting of this war, with the least success, has at least been given the greatest boon they wished for, the taking of Richmond.[2]

Amidst the celebrations of Union victories at Petersburg and Richmond, there still was work to be done in northern Virginia. On April 7, Maj. Gen. Augur ordered (now Bvt. Brig. Gen.) Gamble "to ascertain if Mosby and his command are still in Loudoun and Fauquier Counties yet." The following day, Gamble ordered two scouting parties out after dark, one to "examine the country north of Snickersville pike" and the other the area south of the pike "as far as Sperryville, between the Blue Ridge and

Bull Run Mountains, and on their return examine the country this side of Bull Run Mountains." Gamble stressed that, in order to be successful, the reconnaissance had to be undertaken at night. The 16th New York, with 400 men, was responsible for conducting the sweep of the Loudoun Valley.[3]

Col. Sweitzer and his men left Vienna the night of April 8 along roads "to the right of the Little River turnpike." Reaching Aldie, he sent a squadron into the town, where they learned that Mosby reportedly had been staying in Harmony—now Hamilton. Based on this intelligence, Sweitzer's men crossed the Bull Run Mountains about three miles north of Aldie and moved toward Snickersville (now Bluemont), "turning toward Harmony." Near Aldie, "several shots were exchanged" with guerrillas, and between Aldie and Harmony, several guerrillas "charged by" Sweitzer's flankers. One rebel was shot.[4]

Reaching Harmony, Sweitzer discovered that Mosby had left two days earlier and rendezvoused with his command at Upperville, "for a raid, supposed to be on the Baltimore and Ohio Railroad." This information was only partially accurate. On April 8, Mosby indeed had gathered half his command in Upperville. The other half was down in the Northern Neck. From Upperville, he sent two companies off "to operate in Fairfax," and he took the other two through Ashby's Gap, crossing the Shenandoah River at "Burrell's Island," and moving toward Berryville. Learning that Federal Cavalry were camped in and around Berryville and that he was outnumbered, Mosby and his two companies returned to Fauquier the next day, after a brief skirmish with Federal pickets near the town.[5]

In talking with local citizens, however, Sweitzer did pick up some valuable information, reporting back to Brig. Gen. Gamble that Mosby's men were "becoming very obnoxious" and that recent Union victories were "creating an active and outspoken Union sentiment. The desire is to have peace—with coffee, sugar, etc." On his trip back through Leesburg, Sweitzer also found the locals "quite sociable—the formerly cold and distant secession element quite anxious that we would accept some token of their hospitality, and the Union men, formerly whispering, now quite independent." In Sweitzer's eyes the "political health" of the area was "rapidly improving."[6]

Upon his return to Vienna, Col. Sweitzer and the rest of his command got word of General Lee's surrender at Appomattox on April 9. Albert Wilber wrote in his journal: "8:30 am. Official information from the War Department has just been received to the effect that Lee has surrendered himself and his Army to Gen. Grant. Cheer after cheer is ringing through the camp."[7]

While the good news was making its way to the camp of the 16th New York Cavalry, Col. John Mosby's mother was quietly weeping as she wrote in her diary:

> I went out and heard the deep toned cannon, carrying hundreds and perhaps thousands to that long sleep that knows no waking. Oh, how my heart went up for our great, noble Lee, that God would give him strength in weakness to bring us out of battle a victorious people.... Our Lee will stand out a *man* in all the nations of the earth, nobler and greater in adversity than any other man with a crown on his head.... I hear of fearful desertions. Poor craven spirits,—I hope the Yankee bullets will yet pierce their hateful hides. General Lee surrendered to superior numbers to-day at Appomattox Court House.[8]

Despite the victory at Appomattox, there were still rebels to deal with in northern Virginia. On April 10, reports came in that 175 of Mosby's men had come down that morning to "capture the train at Burke's Station." Another report had Mosby and a battalion crossing the Blue Ridge to the Shenandoah to "capture and plunder Hancock's trains south of Winchester," while a company had been sent to Maryland "to plunder some of the banks there," and another to steal horses from Brig. Gen. Gamble's troops. Gamble sent troops from the 8th Illinois out in response.[9]

Upon learning that Mosby's other battalion had moved up from the Northern Neck to "steal the quartermaster's animals at Burke's Station," Gamble sent out another detachment from the 8th Illinois. Mosby's men were "badly whipped," with five killed: "the rebels outnumbered us three to one, but the Eighth Illinois Cavalry will fight anything." Gamble was fairly well convinced that Mosby was back in northern Virginia at full strength:

> From the conflicting accounts that have reached me I am led to believe that Mosby's entire command consists of two battalions of four companies each, and two additional companies newly organized, ten companies in all, numbering between 800 and 1,000 men. That four companies under Mosby himself crossed the Blue Ridge on Saturday [April 8] to plunder weak-guarded trains south of Winchester. One company sent to Maryland to plunder banks; one company sent to steal horses from my lines, beside the battalion from the Northern Neck.[10]

The Hunt for an Assassin

On April 14, Maj. Gen. Hancock, commanding the Middle Department and resolved to rid northern Virginia of rebel guerrillas once and for all, made the decision to "send a force of cavalry and infantry through Loudoun and Fauquier Counties with the intention of breaking up Mosby's band." Hancock requested that Maj. Gen. Augur support the operation with his cavalry. The intent was to "arrest every able-bodied man not provided with a parole, and to seize all serviceable animals found in possession of people whose loyalty is not undoubted."[11]

Augur elected to send the 16th New York and 8th Illinois, under command of Brig. Gen. Gamble. He ordered Gamble to move out early on the morning of April 15 by way of Leesburg in order to link up with Hancock's forces at Aldie on Sunday, the 16th. As the New York and Illinois troops were preparing to depart, President Lincoln was shot at Ford's Theater on Good Friday evening, April 14. All plans were cancelled:

- April 14: J.H. Taylor [Augur's chief of staff] to Colonel Thompson, Commanding at Darnestown—Colonel: An attempt has been made to assassinate President Lincoln and Secretary Seward. The assassins are supposed to have escaped toward Maryland. Send all your available people at once to scout north of Washington and arrest all suspicious persons.
- April 14: J.H. Taylor to Commander Larker, U.S. Navy, Saint Inigoes, Md.—An attempt has been made this p.m. to assassinate the President and the Secretary of State. The parties may escape or attempt to escape across the Potomac.
- April 15: Maj. Gen. H. W. Halleck to Maj. Gen. Augur: Should either of the murderers or assassins of last night be caught put them in double irons and convey them, under a strong escort, to the commander of the navy-yard, who has orders to receive them and to confine them on a monitor to be anchored in the stream.
- April 15, 1 a.m.: Maj. Gen. Augur to General Gamble—The President, Mr. Lincoln, was shot at Ford's Theater last night, and is now dying. Mr. Seward was stabbed in bed and is not expected to recover. The expedition for tomorrow will have to be abandoned, as I wish you at daylight to take your cavalry and scatter it along the river toward Leesburg to arrest and send all suspicious persons; also along your whole line between it and Washington.[12]

The brigade was in a state of shock. QM-Sgt. Cyrus Shepard recollected years later that the men of the 16th New York were in camp, "waiting and hoping for the expected orders to send in their muster-out rolls, and to be allowed to depart for home," when they were awoken Saturday morning by the "unexpected call of 'Boots and saddles!" Quickly formed up, they were told of President Lincoln's assassination and ordered to "march at

Seven—Victory and Tragedy 133

once to Washington," where they were "assigned barracks near the White House, on F Street"—probably Rush and Reynolds Barracks on the White House grounds, south of the mansion[13]—and "sent out in various directions in search of the assassins."[14] Additional men from the Sixteenth would soon be relocated to Camp Barry, formerly an artillery camp of instruction, on H Street, NE, between Maryland Avenue and Benning Road.

Meanwhile, Lt. Col. Nicholson organized a skirmish line, "extending from the Potomac River, via Vienna, Va., and Fairfax Court-House, to Fairfax Station," with 430 men and 17 officers, divided into two commands. Capt. Leahy commanded the left wing extending from Vienna to the Potomac. The right wing, commanded by Nicholson, covered a line from Vienna to the Orange and Alexandria Railroad at Fairfax Station. Starting at 11:30 a.m., the lines "moved simultaneously in direction toward the fortifications." One person "of a suspicious character" was arrested. Houses were examined, but nothing of significance, except for large quantities of Government property, was found. The two lines came together at Bailey's Crossroads and returned to Vienna around midnight.[15]

On Sunday, April 16, Lt. Moore wrote his mother from brigade headquarters in Fairfax Court House that there was "but one thought on our minds, one feeling in our hearts, and one theme of conversation among us all of which are referable to the tragedy." He continued:

> The appalling calamity of Friday night. The death of President Lincoln, if it had occurred in the course of nature, it would have been a heavy national loss, but his murder by the hand of a traitor is a calamity which the bleeding and prostrate South has far more reason to deplore than the loyal North. He was the South's best friend; no man was less disposed to enforce the extreme rigor against the Rebels, his kindness of heart had become proverbial.... The Nation well must mourn the loss of its greatest, wisest, statesman and servant. And the enemy that of a generous conqueror.[16]

On April 16, Maj. Gen. Augur ordered two battalions of the 8th Illinois Cavalry and "a squadron [several companies] and a full battalion" of the 16th New York Cavalry, along with the band, to report to his headquarters in Washington where they would serve "as part of the escort of the remains of the late President, and should march April 17 a.m."[17] In the end, the 16th New York Cavalry was the only cavalry unit that marched in the procession on April 19, following funeral services at the White House, from the Executive Mansion to the Capitol. As described by Lt. Moore:

> Genl. Gamble and Staff were ordered to town Monday [April 17] but were not used until Wednesday, then by invitation by Maj. Gen. Augur we took part on the escort that bore the remains of our late President from the White House to the Capital [sic]. It is useless for me to attempt to describe that day's proceedings, the most magnificent display of everything I ever witnessed. The Military escort proper that was limited to

President Lincoln's funeral procession in Washington, D.C., on April 19, 1865 (Library of Congress).

a certain number was marched in reverse order, the Marines with their bands, 2 Regiments of the [veterans] reserve Corps, 2 Batteries of Light Artillery, 1 Regt. of Cavalry (16th NY). By the way, the 16th had the escort duty to perform at the inauguration. The other Regt. of Cavalry about here feel very much hurt that they are always selected for such duty. After which Maj. Genl. Augur & Staff, Brig. Genl. Hardin [Hardin's Division, 22nd Corps] & Staff, and Brig. Genl. Slough [District of Alexandria] & Staff, Brig. Gen. & Staff [sic], Officers of the Navy, Officers of the Army, followed by the remains of the President which were in a magnificent hearse drawn by 6 white horses followed by the President's horse and equipment carriage, members of the Cabinet, Genl. Grant, Admiral Farragut, Senators, Congressmen & Innumerable Associations of different kinds. So long was the procession that the men marched from one curb stone to the other, making a front of 70 carriages in columns of fives. The streets were one complete mass of people, windows, roof walks, everything covered. Such a sight no city, nor even the world ever saw before. Such deep sorrow expressed on every countenance, the grief and mourning was unabated. One and all thought they had lost a friend, a father.

I felt very much honored to be in the President's escort, but imagine my feeling when I was informed I was detailed as one of the Officer's as Guard of Honor over his remains—and went on duty at 6 p.m. the same evening. Two of us, one of the Navy & the other of the Army, two hours at a time during the night.... I feel proud of my position, and how many, many times during my tours of duty watching over the head of that beloved man did the tears come to my eyes and run down my cheeks at the different expressions of sorrow, affection, and grief of the people.[18]

Where Is Booth?

On the day of the President's funeral, by order of General Grant, flags at all military facilities and on all naval vessels were flown at half mast, all labor was suspended, and 21-gun salutes were fired at noon. The next day, Albert Wilber wrote in his journal that "very large rewards are offered for the apprehension of Booth or any of his accomplices. It does not seem as if the escape of so monstrous a criminal would be permitted by the Great Ruler of us all—and I don't believe it will."[19]

Two days later, on April 22, Maj. Gen. Augur forwarded reports to the Provost Martial in Alexandria that when Booth was last heard from, he was near the Wicomico River in Maryland, and that it was feared he had crossed over into Virginia. Augur also reported that Booth had broken his leg, was on crutches, and had shaved off his mustache.

That same day, he ordered Col. Sweitzer to send a battalion (probably four companies) of the 16th New York by steamer down the Potomac, "debarking on the Virginia shore as nearly opposite the mouth of Wicomico River, probably at or near Nomini Bay, as practicable." Sweitzer was to use his men "as you may judge best" in order to find Booth and his accomplices. The Navy informed Augur that the Coan River offered a better landing site, and Augur adjusted his orders.[20]

On April 25, Sweitzer reported to Augur that he had scouted the country from Coan River "by Heathsville to the Potomac, and toward the Rappahannock," but had found "no traces" of the assassins. His plan was to start back up the coast and re-embark on a Navy vessel at Potomac Creek. Meanwhile, he had "persons on the lookout in the lower part of the Neck who will, I think, arrest any of the party escaping in this part of the country." He would also "search all the landings and their approaches and vicinity on the Northern Neck between Coan River and Potomac Creek," and arrest any suspicious person who had crossed the Potomac from Maryland.[21]

That same day, the Assistant Adjutant General, 22nd Corps, ordered Lt. Col. Nicholson to take his battalion's worth of men from the 16th New York to Coan River, leaving from Washington's 6th Street Wharf at 10:00 a.m. on April 26. He was to "scout the adjacent country thoroughly" and remain there until Col. Sweitzer joined him. On April 27, Sweitzer was told that, once he met up with Nicholson at Coan River, he must find "suitable horses" and "impress" them, since many of Nicholson's men were dismounted, which would make it more difficult to scour the area for the assassin and his accomplices.[22]

Meanwhile, back in northern Virginia, Lt. Farnesworth, Co. G, left camp in Vienna on April 25 with the last of the 16th New York's troops. Commissary Lt. Wilber was now "the last one left—A.L.R.S. (Acting Last Rose of Summer), as well as Actg. Commissary of Subsistence [for the brigade]."[23] Those men of the Sixteenth not out helping in the search for Booth remained in barracks in Washington.

On April 26, while still out searching, Col. Sweitzer was temporarily placed in command of a new "District of Northern Neck" under the Department of Washington, encompassing the area between the Potomac and Rappahannock rivers, south of the Fredericksburg and Aquia Creek Railroad line, "and all troops serving therein." He was to establish his headquarters "at any such point as he may select."[24]

Lincoln's Avengers

While Col. Sweitzer and Lt. Col. Nicholson and the main body of the 16th New York were focused on searching in the Northern Neck, reports began to trickle in suggesting that Booth and his accomplice David Herold indeed had managed to cross the Potomac. Col. Lafayette Baker, who Secretary of War Stanton had called in from New York City to help with the investigation, decided to act. On April 24, orders went out to the "Commanding Officer Detachment Sixteenth New York Cavalry," to detail 25 men, "well mounted" and commanded by a "reliable and discreet commissioned officer," and report to "Col. L. C. Baker, "Special Agent, War Department," at 217 Pennsylvania Avenue, opposite Willard's Hotel.[25]

That afternoon, Lt. Edward P. Doherty, who had just been appointed Captain of Co. B, was "seated, with another officer of the 16th New York Cavalry, on a bench in the park opposite the White House." There he received an order signed by Capt. Joseph Schneider, who was commanding the 16th New York Detachment in the city: "You are hereby detailed for the duty specified in the preceding order, and will report immediately to Col. L. C. Baker for instruction."[26]

Doherty proceeded to the 16th New York barracks and had "boots and saddles" sounded. He "took the first twenty-five men in the saddle,

Sgt. Boston Corbett being the only member of my own company." In less than half an hour, Doherty and his men, accompanied by Capt. Schneider, reported to Col. Baker's office:

> [Colonel Baker] informed me that he had reliable information that the assassin Booth and his accomplice were somewhere between the Potomac and Rappahannock Rivers. He gave me several photographs of Booth and introduced me to Mr. Conger and Mr. Baker [detectives Everton J. Conger and Luther B. Baker], and said they would accompany me. He directed me to scour the section of the country indicated thoroughly, to make my own disposition of the men in my command, to forage upon the country, giving receipts for what was taken from loyal parties, and to land at or near Belle Plain at all hazards, to swim my horses ashore if I could not land otherwise, and return when I thought proper.[27]

Capt. Edward Doherty (U.S. National Archives).

Doherty's detachment boarded the steamer John S. Ide at the 6th Street wharf and proceeded to Belle Plain, where they disembarked. Ordering the boat to stand by at anchor, Doherty marched with his men and the two detectives toward Fredericksburg. After three miles, they turned to the southwest and reached the Rappahannock, about 12 miles above Port Conway, at 6:00 a.m. on April 25.

There, two fishermen told them that a number of surgeons lived in the area. Knowing that Booth "was crippled," Doherty searched the surgeons' houses but found no traces of Booth. Conger subsequently took four men and a corporal down the Rappahannock along its banks, while Doherty marched the rest of his men some 15 miles by way of King George Court House, meeting up again with Conger at Conway's Ferry around 2:00 p.m.[28]

At the ferry, Doherty learned that men fitting the fugitives' descriptions had crossed the day before and had tried to convince the ferryman to take them to Orange Court House, which he refused. According to the ferryman, Herold maintained that he and Booth were brothers and that Booth had been wounded at Petersburg. While they were negotiating, three Confederate soldiers arrived at the ferry and agreed to take Herold and Booth with them. According to the ferryman's wife, one of the three soldiers was Capt. Willie Jett who "was courting a young lady by the name of Goldman, whose father kept a hotel at Bowling Green."

By 6:00 p.m. Doherty's command had crossed the river, and based on this information, they moved off toward Bowling Green. According to Doherty's later recollections, "at dark we passed the Garrett farm, not then dreaming that the assassins were concealed there."[29] About a half-mile from Bowling Green, Doherty sent ten men with detective Baker into the town, while Doherty, Detective Conger and the rest of the detachment rode ahead and surrounded the Goldman house, where they found Capt. Jett. Under duress, Jett admitted that he had helped Booth and Herold and agreed to take Doherty's detachment to the location where he had left the two men—at the house of Mr. Richard Garrett, about 12 miles away.

According to Doherty's account, upon reaching the Garrett farm, he ordered his men to surround the house. As a precautionary measure, he

… sent six men in rear of the barn and outbuildings. While I was placing my men around the buildings the detectives knocked at the door, which was opened by the elder Mr. Garrett, who was much excited; he said the men who had been there went to the woods the previous evening. While engaged in conversation the son of Mr. Garrett came in, advising his father to tell where they were. I

Sgt. Boston Corbett (Library of Congress).

seized this man by the collar, and pulled him out of the door and down the steps, put my revolver to his head and told him to tell me at once where the two assassins were; he replied, "in the barn."

Doherty raced to the barn and had his men surround it. Returning to the front of the barn, Doherty found Mr. Garrett coming out of it, apparently having been told by one of the detectives to go in and tell Booth to surrender. Booth, however, refused, and, according to Doherty, the detectives urged him to set it on fire. He demurred, instead suggesting they wait until daylight when he could have his men charge into the barn through all four doors and "overpower the assassin." At this point, Doherty and Baker tried negotiating with Booth, but he was "very defiant and refused to surrender." They threatened to burn the barn down and, at one point, gave him ten minutes to make up his mind.

According to Doherty, Booth finally said:

"Oh captain, there is a man here who wants to surrender awful bad." I answered, and I think Mr. Baker did at the same time, "Hand out your arms." Herold replied, "I have none." Baker said, "We know exactly what you have got." Booth replied, "I own all the arms, and intend to use them on you gentlemen." After some little parley I said, "Let him out." Someone objected. I ordered Garrett, the younger son, who had the key, to unlock the barn, which he did. I partially opened the door, and told Herold to put out his hand, which he did. I then told him to put [out] his other hand. I took hold of both his wrists and pulled him out of the barn. Almost simultaneous with my taking Herold out of the barn, the hay in the rear of the barn was ignited by Mr. Conger, and the barn fired. Sergt. Boston Corbett, Company L, Sixteenth New York Cavalry, shot the assassin Booth, wounding him in the neck. I entered the barn as soon as the shot was fired, dragging Herold with me, and found that Booth had fallen on his back. Messrs. Conger and Baker, with some of my men, entered the barn and took hold of Booth. I proceeded with Herold to find a rope to secure him, there being no irons for that purpose. The assassin Booth lived about two hours.

Wrapping Booth's body in a blanket and placing it in a wagon, Doherty and his men proceeded to Port Royal, arriving there at 9:00 a.m. on April 26. While Doherty's men were crossing the Rappahannock, detective Baker took off with Booth's body, along with Capt. Jett and two guards from the 16th New York. Doherty reached Belle Plain at 6:00 p.m., but Baker was nowhere in sight. Baker eventually arrived, absent Capt. Jett, who had managed to escape. After a short delay, Booth's body was placed on board the John S. Ide, and the command proceeded to Washington, "where I delivered over the body of Booth, Herold, and the two Garretts to Col. L. C. Baker, at 3 a.m. the 27th day of April 1865."

According to Pvt. John Millington of Co. H, Garrett's two sons, who had returned home just before the Union troopers arrived, had been with Mosby's command. Millington wrote years later that "one of them had a

"The Killing of Booth, the Assassin" (Library of Congress).

young wife and there was a tearful scene when our officer told the boys they would have to go to Washington with us."[30]

In concluding his report, Doherty gave "great credit" to his men for their "fortitude and eagerness," noting that for nearly 60 hours, "hardly an eye was closed or a horse dismounted until the errand was finished." He singled out Sgt. Boston Corbett, "who was untiring in his efforts to bring the murderers to justice. His soldierly qualifications have been tested before this occasion, and, in my judgment, are second to none in the service." He also praised Mr. Rollins, at Port Conway, for "his willingness to impart all the information he possessed."

The following day, writing in his diary, Commissary Lt. Albert Wilber offered another, less generous, assessment of Sgt. Corbett, remarking that he was "a man of great determination—is absolutely inflexible when doing what he believes to be right. 'Tho he is entirely deficient in judgment, and, hence, is apt to be in the wrong when thinking himself right. He is said to have disobeyed orders in shooting Booth, but will hardly receive much censure. The country and the world will be only too glad to be rid of the monster, to find fault with the manner of his taking off." Indeed, Boston Corbett would remain a man of controversy and would end his life a man of mystery.[31]

According to QM-Sgt. Cyrus Shepard, another detachment of the 16th New York, in which he served, was responsible for arresting assassination "conspirator" Dr. Samuel Mudd on April 21. Official records indicate that the force that arrested Dr. Mudd was under Maj. James O'Beirne, Provost Martial in Washington. It could well be that this "force" was from the 16th New York. In any case, as told by Shepard many years later, he and other men from the 16th New York, were ordered to report to Col. Lafayette Baker "with all possible dispatch" and "were directed by him to march to Bryantown, about thirty miles out in Maryland, and arrest and bring to Washington Dr. Mudd, who was known to be in the conspiracy with the other assassins."

As related by Shepard, the detachment crossed the eastern branch of the Potomac and began to string out as it raced through Maryland, so much so that by the time they reached Bryantown, "there were only eight or ten of the company, which originally numbered twenty-five, remaining. We found Dr. Mudd, arrested him, and took him to Washington. We also found in his house a boot belonging to Booth, which had been stripped from his wounded leg."[32]

Mosby's Rangers Disband

On April 17, while preparations for President Lincoln's funeral were being made, Maj. Gen. Hancock, commanding in the Shenandoah Valley, telegraphed from Winchester that General Chapman (2nd Division, Cavalry Corps, Army of the Shenandoah) was to meet with Colonel John Mosby on the day of the funeral at Millwood in Clarke County, southwest of Berryville. Hancock believed Mosby intended to surrender. He was wrong. There was no surrender.[33]

On April 21, having agreed to a ceasefire with representatives of Gen. Hancock, Mosby brought his men together at Salem (now Marshall) to bid them farewell. Telling them that he was disbanding the organization "in preference to surrendering it to our enemies," he stated that he was no longer their commander:

> After an association of more than two eventful years, I part from you with a just pride in the fame of your achievements and a grateful recollection of your generous kindness

to myself. And at this moment of bidding you a final adieu, accept the assurance of my unchanging confidence and regard. Farewell![34]

On April 23, Hancock's chief of staff informed Maj. Gen. Augur that Mosby's deputy, Col. Chapman, had surrendered some 380 of Mosby's men, but that Mosby had fled.[35] After disbanding the command at Salem, Mosby and a few of his men had traveled south, hoping to join up with General Joe Johnson's army. Learning that Johnson also had surrendered, however, Mosby disbanded this last group of followers near Frederick Hall between Fredericksburg and Richmond. Mosby continued on to Lynchburg. There he would apply for and receive a parole in June.[36]

Eight

At War's End

With the end of hostilities in the east—negotiations for the surrender of Confederate armies in the "western" theater would stretch out into late May—and the surrender of Mosby's men, the spring and summer months found the men of the 16th New York Cavalry largely back to the regularity and boredom of garrison duty. Commissary Lt. Albert Wilber remained in camp at Vienna through the middle of the month, when he turned his brigade responsibilities over to another lieutenant from the 5th Pennsylvania Artillery and reported back to Col. Sweitzer and the Sixteenth in Washington.[1] Sweitzer had just been recommended for promotion to Brevet Brigadier General "for meritorious and distinguished" service in the Department of Washington in addition to his combat service before taking command of the Sixteenth.[2]

On May 18, Sweitzer's temporary command of the District of the Northern Neck came to a close when it and the District of the Patuxent were abolished and folded into the Districts of Washington and Alexandria.[3] That same day, General Grant ordered preparations for a two-day grand review on May 23 and 24, "with marching salute" of the Armies of the Potomac, Tennessee, and Georgia, and General Sheridan's cavalry. Maj. Gen. Augur, commanding the Department of Washington, was ordered to provide the "necessary guards posted in the street along the route, keeping the street clear of all horsemen and carriages."[4] While the men of the Sixteenth did not march in this parade, they certainly were present along the parade route, providing security.

Two Testimonials

On the evening of June 27, a group of officers of the Sixteenth gathered in Capt. Baker's (Co. E) quarters to discuss "presenting a suitable testimonial of respect" to Bvt. Brig. Gen. Sweitzer, their commanding officer. Maj. Horton was elected chairman and regimental Surgeon Joseph Homiston treasurer. Lt. Wilbur was appointed secretary. A committee, including Wilbur, Dr. Homiston, Lt. Col. Nicholson, Maj. Bosworth, Capt. William J. Keays, and Quarter-Master Ladue, went into the city the following day and selected "a beautiful sabre with solid silver scabbard—cost $260—a belt $50—a silk sash $35—and a knot $10." Meeting again that evening, the group instructed Wilbur to draft an inscription for the scabbard and agreed that Dr. Homiston should make the presentation speech. The presentation would take place on July 3.[5]

The presentation was a huge success. According to Lt. Wilbur, "a number of ladies and several military guests were present." Sweitzer's speech was "quite felicitous," wine was passed around, "toasts given, speeches made, and songs sung." The ladies present left early but the party broke up "only 'when 'twas morning.' The whole thing passed off pleasantly to everyone and none seemed to enjoy it more than the Gen."[6]

A week later "a subscription" was started to purchase a brace of revolvers, costing $150, as a testimonial to Edward Doherty, promoted to captain in April, in recognition of his role in the capture of Booth and Herold. On July 11, Lt. Wilbur and Dr. Homiston purchased the pair of revolvers, "richly mounted in gold and silver and pearl," and on display in a jeweler's store window.[7] A few days later, Capt. Keays, who had overseen one of the regiment's early operational disasters, gave the presentation address:

> Your brother officers of the 16th New York Cavalry are pleased to present you with this brace of pistols, as a testimonial for your distinguished services in the pursuit and capture of Booth and Herold, the assassins of President Lincoln. It is a matter of pride and satisfaction to the officers of the regiment that, after two years service in the field in the same organization, it has fallen to the lot of one of their members to capture and bring to justice the assassins of our late beloved and good President—prominent members of a band of conspirators and murderers, which had for its chief Jefferson Davis, late President of the late bogus Southern Confederacy, and embracing in its folds a set of men who, for fiendish malignity and hellish designs, have never been surpassed in any age or any clime. In future years this testimonial will serve to remind you of your old comrades-in-arms of the 16th New York Cavalry, and of the many incidents that occurred during your two years' association with them, in the camp and in the field, on lonely scout and daring raid, and in the secret night-watches from the Potomac to the Rapidan, and from the Rapidan back again to the Potomac—a two years' service which has made the by-paths, thickets, and wilds of Virginia its mountain passes and guerrilla-haunts, as familiar to our minds as the places that were once our homes.
>
> It will also serve to remind you of the memorable morning of the 15th of April 1865, when our skirmish line, under the eye of our veteran commander, Brevet

Brigadier General Sweitzer, stretched from the Orange and Alexandria railroad to the Potomac, when officers and men with solemn mien and determined will scoured the country in search of the assassins; and during the subsequent twelve days, before your successful capture of the assassins, our regiment was in Maryland; it was on the north side of the Potomac, on the side of the Potomac, and away to the Rappahannock. Receive this testimonial, then, and should ever a righteous cause again beckon thee to its aid, use these weapons in its defense.[8]

In response, Doherty expressed his gratitude "beyond expression" to receive the pistols from such "gallant defenders of the nation." Recognizing the "honor this confers on me," he assured his follow officers he would keep the gift "with jealous care," and that, once they had gone their separate ways, the gift would "bring to my mind many happy recollections of hours so pleasantly passed in the society of the officers of the 16th New York Cavalry."[9]

"Lincoln Avengers" Medals and Certificates

At some point prior to the consolidation of the two New York regiments, most likely in July 1865, now Bvt. Brig. Gen. Sweitzer awarded special "Lincoln Avenger" medals to "meritorious officers" of the 16th New York. A certificate embossed with the medal's ten-pointed star accompanied each medal:

> Pro Ejus Merito
> Sixteenth N. Y. Cavalry
> By approval of the General Commanding
> (name, rank, company)
> 16th N. Y. Cavalry, is entitled, as a meritorious officer, to
> wear the Cross of the L.A.
> N.B. Sweitzer
> Brevt Brig Genl

At least eleven officers had the medal, certificate or both after the war. With the exception of Capt. James McPherson who resigned in March 1865, all were serving with the regiment when it was consolidated with the 13th New York in August. Those known to have had the award are:

- Capt. Francis Baker, Co. E: a certificate still in family possession.
- Capt. Edward Doherty, Co. B: a medal and certificate in private archive, Steven G. Miller, Lake Villa, IL.
- Capt. Charles Farnsworth, Co. K: medal mentioned in his obituary, *Brooklyn Daily Eagle*, December 29, 1926.
- 1st Lt. William Farrell, Co. F: medal described in the *Poughkeepsie Evening Enterprise*, October 20, 1909.

- Dr. Joseph Homiston, regimental surgeon: photograph after the war shows him wearing the medal.
- 2nd Lt. John F. Hoover, Co. B: certificate in family possession.
- Capt. William Keays, Co. G, and Capt. James A. McPherson, Co. G: medals mentioned in the *Livonia (NY) Gazette*, July 2, 1885.
- Capt. Joseph Schneider, Co. C: medal in family possession.
- 1st Lt. Matthew Tuck, Co. K: medal mentioned in obituary, *New York Sun*, February 5, 1892.
- Assistant Surgeon Samuel P. Vandersmith: medal and "diploma" mentioned in obituary, *Journal of the American Medical Association*, 1895.[10]

Consolidation with the 13th New York Cavalry

Meanwhile, on June 29, the battalions of the 13th New York Cavalry stationed at Fairfax Court House and Fairfax Station had been ordered to Prospect Hill, Virginia, "preparatory to consolidation with the 16th N.Y. Cavalry."[11] Shortly after President Lincoln's assassination, according to Maj. Augustus Green, the officers of the Thirteenth, worried about rumors they would be merged with the Sixteenth, had drawn up and "signed a petition" to General Grant asking him to intercede and permit them to "return home the way they went out, as the 13th N.Y.C." Green took 40 men with him "well mounted as I knew Grant would see them" down the Leesburg Pike from Prospect Hill, across Chain Bridge and into Washington.

> We marched into Georgetown and found the General living in a large mansion, guarded by dismounted cavalry, but having the countersign I was admitted upon the lawn.... My men were marching in column of fours. I formed them on the lawn and dismounted them. General Grant was standing on the stoop watching us. He did not know who we were or where we came from until I saluted him ... and handed him the petition. He read it and told me to inform the officers of the 13th when I had returned to camp that the regiment would not be consolidated with the 16th New York Cavalry and would be mustered out as the 13th.[12]

General Grant's assurances to the officers of the Thirteenth were for naught. War Department orders dated June 23, 1865, made the consolidation official. On July 9, Col. Sweitzer told his fellow 16th New York officers that the Thirteenth and Sixteenth would be consolidated "within three or four days under the name of the 3rd Provisional Cavy."[13] On August 17, 1865, the two regiments were officially consolidated, at Camp Barry in Washington, as the Third Provisional Regiment of New York Volunteer Cavalry.[14]

Camp Barry in Washington (Library of Congress).

"Shooting Affair at Washington"

That same day, the shocking news of the accidental shooting death of a young lady visiting Washington from Baltimore by Pvt. Henry Raymond of Co. C, 16th New York Cavalry, was splashed across the pages of national newspapers. According to these accounts, 23-year-old Miss Mary Ann Goode, her cousin Miss Eliza Ward, and a "young man named Chatham," were walking from Miss Goode's aunt's house at the corner of 2nd and L Streets, NE, around 7:00 p.m. on August 17, past Camp Barry, to another relative's house on G Street, near the Eastern Branch. About 70 or 80 yards after passing a sentry on G Street, "a shot was fired, and Miss Goode fell, the ball having entered her back about two inches to the right of her back bone, passing through the right lung, and coming out the breast, and then inflicting a flesh wound of Miss Ward's right shoulder."[15]

The sentry, Pvt. Raymond, had fired the shot on order of 1st Lt. Charles Farnsworth, Co. K, who was commanding a patrol, "from which a soldier named Murphy, brought in by them, was endeavoring to escape." Apparently, Pvt. Raymond initially refused to fire at Murphy for fear of hitting an innocent civilian. After a third order to fire, however, he did so, the bullet striking Miss Goode. Regimental Surgeon Homiston was called out from Camp Barry immediately and did what he could for the victims. An ambulance carried both wounded ladies back Miss Goode's aunt's house, where she died the following afternoon.[16]

On August 18, the local coroner and 12 "jurors" heard testimony about the incident. Pvt. Raymond testified that while he was at his sentry post, a corporal told him to take two drunken prisoners to the guardhouse. When one refused to go and apparently began to run away, Lt. Farnsworth told Raymond to load his carbine; when the prisoner refused a third time to halt, Farnsworth told him to fire. He fired above the man's head. Capt. Julius Windsbecker of Co. F testified to Farnsworth's character, as did Dr. Homiston, who stated that the lieutenant was "one of the most temperate men in the regiment" who "would not have ordered the gun to be fired if he knew the ladies were about."[17]

The jury quickly concluded that the killing was "accidental," but it condemned "in the severest terms" the "reckless shooting" on a public road, after dark, since "it too frequently happens that innocent persons are injured, and often, as in this instance, lives are taken."[18]

Except for Capt. Gaylord of Co. K being thrown from his horse and severely injured on August 26—he was drunk—this would be the last incident involving troops from the 16th New York Cavalry. On September 9, Albert Wilbur wrote in his diary that the morning papers were saying the men of the 3rd Provisional Regiment of Cavalry were to be mustered out. There was "general rejoicing" in camp.[19]

A Job Well Done?

The 16th New York Cavalry was officially mustered out of the Federal service on September 21, 1865. However, a number of its men had already been discharged and sent home. Some, including a few members of the detachment that had captured Booth, left Washington as early as May and June. In all, the regiment lost 140 men: one officer—Capt. James Fleming—and 139 enlisted men. Capt. Fleming and twelve enlisted men were "killed in action" and eight more enlisted men died of "wounds received in action." Another 119 enlisted men died of "disease and other causes." Of the 139 enlisted deaths, 44 occurred "in the hands of the enemy," including 28 at Andersonville.[20]

In terms of the total number of men killed in action or by disease and other causes, the Sixteenth—at 140—stood about in the middle of all New York cavalry regiments. In general, the regiments that served outside of

Washington in the field saw far more intense combat and suffered many more casualties. The two highest in total deaths from combat and disease were the 2nd New York Cavalry, assigned the Army of the Potomac Cavalry Corps (357 dead) and the 11th New York Cavalry, assigned to the 18th Corps (344 dead).[21]

Despite General Halleck's contention in October 1864 that the men of the 16th New York Cavalry were "cowed and useless" because they had been "so often cut up by Mosby's band," it can be argued, to the contrary, that the regiment did the best that it could have, against considerable odds. Indeed, the Sixteenth had "cut up" Mosby several times, wounding him twice and coming very close to capturing him.

In his memoirs, General Sherman likened the Army regiment to the soldier's "family," contending that the commander, "as the father, "should have a personal acquaintance with every officer and man." He also wrote that "a good captain makes a good company," and "should be appointed by the colonel or some superior authority."[22]

From the very start, Col. John Singleton Mosby's 43rd Battalion, Virginia Cavalry, was such a "family," with officers, sergeants, and enlisted men who were hand-picked by Mosby, came from the same regions of Virginia, knew each other well, and had a tremendously high degree of esprit and dedication to their cause. Mosby's Rangers would have satisfied General Sherman's criteria for an effective combat command.

The 16th New York Cavalry, on the other hand, was the organizational antithesis of Mosby and his rangers. As a consolidation of three partially-formed regiments, with recruits from widely dispersed cities, towns and villages across the state, it was far from a "family" with a shared identity other than as New Yorkers. Col. Lazelle had not been afforded the opportunity to select his staff or company officers, nor had he overseen the limited training the regiment's companies received before arriving in Vienna. When he was able to get rid of ineffective junior officers, he had little say in the selection of their replacements, except when he promoted men from within the unit.

Finally, the cavalry regiments assigned to 22nd Corps and the defenses of Washington were forced, by their very mission, to operate in a largely static defensive and reactive mode. With only two under-manned regiments after the 2nd Massachusetts left for the Shenandoah Valley in August 1864, the cavalry brigade had to maintain three stockades and an extensive defensive line of pickets and patrols, while also routinely undertaking scouting missions out as far as the Bull Run and Blue Ridge mountains.

At the same time, officers and men who, to the degree they had been trained at all, were most comfortable and familiar with standard Army formations and tactics, were forced time and again to deal with an enemy who had become exceptionally adept at unconventional guerrilla warfare tactics. According to one analysis, Mosby created what Prussian military theorist Carl von Clausewitz "described as a 'feeling of uneasiness and dread' in the enemy" and "achieved [Swiss military theorist Antoine-Henri] Jomini's aim of making everything outside the invaders' camp hostile and multiplying 'a thousandfold the difficulties he meets at every step.'"[23]

By his own accounting, Mosby's main objective in making his pin prick attacks against Washington's outer defenses was to keep Washington's cavalry regiments tied down and unable to reinforce Union armies in the Shenandoah Valley and southern Virginia. He was partially successful, in that the two New York regiments remained in Fairfax. However, his tactics did not prevent the 2nd Massachusetts from being tagged to join the valley campaign. Moreover, Mosby's daring operational tactics were not cost-free. By one estimate, his total casualties throughout the war ranged between 35 and 40 percent, with at least 477 of his men captured, some of these at the hands of the 16th New York Cavalry.[24] Since these were virtually all battle casualties, Mosby's losses were very high compared to regular units.

It also can be argued that, despite less than adequate manpower and its weaknesses in organization, command, and training, the 16th New York did accomplish its defensive mission, particularly after Col. Lazelle altered his tactical scheme to one he had learned as a lieutenant out in Texas territory and created his "line of stockades."[25] While small detachments of Mosby's men were able to sneak through the lines—for example infiltrating into Falls Church under cover of darkness and murdering the Reverend Read—in the greater scheme of things, they did little damage. And a much larger force, supported by artillery, was unable to mount a successful attack against the Annandale stockade, ably commanded by Capt. Schneider. In short, Mosby never truly threatened Washington or northern Virginia. And, indeed, his Rangers faced some close calls including his injury and near-capture.

The larger, multi-company scouting and "reconnaissance in force" operations of the New York cavalrymen generally met with "success," in that they achieved their objectives: obtaining intelligence on enemy locations, activity, and objectives. With the exception of the debacle at Anker's Shop in Dranesville, few of these "scouts" were challenged seriously by Mosby and his men, most garnered the tactical intelligence they were after, and many returned with Confederate prisoners. The Rapidan Station raid, under Col. Lazelle, which destroyed a major Confederate logistical hub, was marred only by the unexpected encounter with a larger force of General Kershaw's infantry at Culpeper Court House.

So, on balance, while there certainly were some tactical failures and embarrassing moments, most often at the hands of John Singleton Mosby, the men of the 16th New York Cavalry could return home with heads held high. At least in a small way, they had helped win the war. Moreover, 26 of them had captured and killed the assassin!

NINE

Postwar Fortunes and Failures

Across the Potomac, the guns had fallen silent. The guards were gone from the Washington bridges. Virginians were no longer enemies, but farmers who trundled their crops to the city markets. Rich with the wastage of armies, the perennial fields were green. On the Capitol dome, Armed Freedom rested her sheathed sword.[1]

When the 3rd Provisional Regiment of Cavalry was mustered out at Camp Barry in Washington, most of the men of the 16th New York Cavalry returned home to very ordinary lives, as farmers, laborers, and tradesmen. A few took up the professions and a handful went on to Army careers. A small number gained some notoriety in their postwar lives.

Brig. Gen. Nelson B. Sweitzer

Bvt. Brig. Gen. Sweitzer returned to the regular Army and was on "recruiting service" at Carlisle, Pennsylvania, and Cincinnati, Ohio, from November 1865 until July 1866, when he was promoted to major in the 5th U.S. Cavalry Regiment. He joined the regiment on November 2, 1866, at Washington, D.C., and commanded Sedgwick Barracks and a detachment of the regiment until the end of February 1867. After another short recruiting tour, he was transferred to the 2nd U.S. Cavalry Regiment, reporting for duty at Fort Laramie, Wyoming, in June 1867. He remained with the 2nd Cavalry on frontier duty and as Acting Assistant Inspector General for the Department of the Platte until he was promoted to lieutenant colonel.[2]

During his tour of duty with the 2nd Cavalry, Sweitzer was involved in numerous scouting operations and expeditions in support of efforts to establish safe wagon routes and the Union Pacific Railroad line across the plains. He selected the location for Fort Fetterman, Wyoming, and laid out the road route from Fort Fetterman south to the projected route of the Union Pacific near Fort Laramie. Following his stint as Inspector General, he commanded Fort Ellis, Montana, guarding the Gallatin Valley and scouting along the Yellowstone, Musselshell and Missouri Rivers. In September 1875 he was appointed to an Army board on wagon transports in Washington, D.C. In February 1877 he returned west, now commanding the regiment at Fort Sanders, near Laramie.[3]

On June 25, 1877, Sweitzer was promoted to lieutenant colonel of the 8th U.S. Cavalry, and took command of the regiment at Fort Brown, Texas, near the current city of Brownsville. He remained on frontier duty at Fort Brown and Ringgold Barracks near Rio Grande City until October 1880 when the regimental headquarters was relocated to Fort Clark, Texas. In 1886 he was promoted to Colonel of the 2nd Cavalry, taking command of the regiment and post at Walla Walla, Washington, on May 1. He retired from active service on October 29, 1888.[4]

Sweitzer is credited, at a date uncertain at the end of the Civil War, with having a special medal, known by some as the "Cross of Lincoln Avenged," struck and presented to some, if not all, members of the 16th New York Cavalry. Accompanied by a presentation certificate signed by Sweitzer, it has been referred to as the "Lincoln Avengers" medal. A top bar with crossed swords carries the inscription "16 N.Y. Cav." Hanging from the bar by one or two short chains, a multi-pointed star backed by a wreath, carries the inscription "Pro Ejus Merito L.A." None of the three known recipients—Capt. Francis M. Baker, Co. E; 2nd Lt. John Frank Hoover, Co. B; and Sgt. Ernest Diezelsky, Co. K—were members of the detachment that captured and killed John Wilkes Booth.[5]

Col. Sweitzer married Helen M. McGregor of Terre Haute, Indiana, in December 1867. They had two sons and a daughter. After he retired, Sweitzer and his wife lived for a while in Cincinnati, Ohio, but they returned to Washington, D.C., where he died on March 7, 1898. He and his wife, who lived until August 1914, are buried at Arlington National Cemetery.[6]

Colonel Henry M. Lazelle

Following his resignation from the 16th New York Cavalry in October 1864, Henry Lazelle rejoined the 8th U.S. Infantry Regiment, once again a captain. Requiring a warm climate due to a severe case of rheumatism, however, he was sent to the headquarters of the Military Division of West Mississippi in New Orleans, first as Acting Assistant Inspector General and then as Assistant Provost Martial General. He rejoined his 8th Infantry company when it moved to North Carolina to administer law and order, governance, and public services in Charlotte. Capt. Lazelle and his company remained in the Carolinas until late 1870, when the regiment was sent west into the tribal hunting grounds of the Sioux and Cheyenne, supporting the Yellowstone Expeditions for the Northern Pacific Railroad and the opening of the Black Hills to settlers and prospectors.

In December 1874, after a ten-year wait, Lazelle was promoted to major with the 1st Infantry Regiment at Fort Sully, South Dakota. There, in the spring and summer of 1877, he and a battalion's worth of infantry and cavalry troops operated against the remnants of Sioux Chief Sitting Bull's warriors along the Tongue, Powder and Little Missouri Rivers and into the Black Hills. The following year, he was ordered away from Fort Sully to establish Fort Meade, in the eastern Black Hills. His family joined him there the winter of 1878/79, in a four-room log cabin. That June, the family prepared to move again, this time to West Point, when Lazelle was appointed Commandant of Cadets.

As Commandant, Maj. Lazelle was a principal actor in one of the most damning incidents in the early history of African American cadets at West Point, when Cadet Johnson Chestnut Whittaker, a former slave from South Carolina, was attacked in his room, allegedly by masked strangers. Lazelle and West Point Superintendent Maj. Gen. John Schofield quickly concluded, and a Court Martial agreed, that Whittaker had contrived the incident. President Chester A. Arthur eventually overturned the verdict, but the die had been cast. Cadet Whittaker was dismissed after failing one of his examinations.

The Whittaker affair cost Schofield his job, tarnished Lazelle's image, and brought Maj. Gen. Oliver Otis Howard to the academy as Superintendent. Almost immediately, he and Lazelle clashed over policy and command issues, as Howard was intent on reforming the West Point disciplinary system. Lazelle won a few battles, but in the end he lost the war and was dismissed from the Commandant's position a year short of tour.

During the Whittaker controversy and prior to his battles with Howard, Lazelle had been promoted to lieutenant colonel. However, he began his next assignment with the 23rd Infantry Regiment at Fort Craig, New Mexico, one of the most desolate Army posts in the country. Rescued in 1884, in part by ill health at Fort Craig's high altitude, and reassigned to the Military Division of the Pacific as Assistant Inspector General, Lazelle moved his family from its rough adobe cabin to more opulent quarters, first at the Presidio of San Francisco and then at Vancouver Barracks in Washington State. In the fall of 1885, he was selected to attend British military maneuvers in India as the American representative.

Returning from India in early 1887, Lazelle received new orders, this time back to Washington, D.C., to oversee publication of the Official Records of the War of Rebellion. He was almost immediately caught up in intense partisan political maneuvering by Republicans intent on unseating Grover Cleveland, the first Democrat elected to the Presidency since before the Civil War. Seizing on allegations in the press that Lazelle had purposely allowed non-official information to be inserted in the Official Records, the Republicans launched Congressional investigations and hearings. After nearly a year, Lazelle was fully exonerated, but the damage had been done. Once again he was dismissed short of tour.

In October 1889, Lazelle and his family returned to Texas for his assignment as Colonel of the 18th U.S. Infantry and post commander at Fort Clark and then, shortly before his retirement in 1894, as post commander at Fort Bliss, where his Army career had begun 38 years earlier.

As his career progressed, Lazelle authored articles on military strategy and tactics, challenging Maj. Gen. Emory Upton, the "father" of post–Civil War U.S. Army tactics, and winning the Military Service Institution's coveted Gold Medal for an 1882 essay on improvements in the art of war. He also took up spiritualism and scientific inquiry, publishing books on force theory and the relationship between science and theology. In 1904, he was promoted, in retirement, to Brigadier General.

In the later years of his career, Lazelle proved to be a very complex and, at times, highly conflicted man. He lost his wife Rebecca to gall bladder disease in 1893. Coming from a prominent Maryland banking family, she had shared years of hardship and sacrifice with him in the far West and the Dakotas, along with brief periods of "high living." Five years later, his eldest son, Jacob, who had followed in his father's footsteps at West Point, was taken by encephalitis as a young first lieutenant on his way to the Philippines. After Rebecca's and Jacob's deaths, Lazelle became somewhat a lost soul, roaming from place to place, never quite able to settle down. After marrying his second wife, 40 years his junior, he became distant from his surviving younger son. He died in 1917 and was buried at his summer cabin on Lake Memphremagog in Quebec, Canada.[7]

Lieutenant Colonel George S. Hollister

Following Lt. Col. Hollister's dismissal from the volunteer service in October 1864 for licentious sexual behavior, his supporters and detractors continued to press their cases. "Fourteen officers of Hollister's cavalry regiment petitioned for his reinstatement, while seven others, including the regimental chaplain, signed a petition asking for just the opposite result."[8]

Finally, retired Maj. Gen. John Dix came to his rescue. Writing to Secretary of War Edwin Stanton in November 1865, Dix stated that he had examined the papers related to the case and had received affidavits of Capt. Charles Robin, Surgeon Joseph Homiston, and Assistant Surgeon Samuel Vandersmith. Noting that the court-martial had never completed its deliberations and that Hollister's dismissal was based solely on accusations not fully proven, Dix urged that Hollister be reinstated "as of the date of the muster out of his regiment." He based his recommendation on several factors:

- Hollister had "no opportunity of producing testimony in his defence [sic], except in the single case of Capt. Washburn, whose character he was allowed to impeach."
- The "infamous" accusations against Hollister were based on the testimony of Washburn, "a man of disreputable character who was dishonorably discharged from the service, of Private (Lieut.) Farrell who was confined in the Old Capitol Prison for desertion and was reduced to the ranks for infidelity to his oath and his flag, and of Lieut. Grosvenor who was also dishonorably dismissed." Moreover, Washburn had later denied the charges and later still claimed they were true.
- Seventeen fellow officers signed a petition stating that Hollister was "sacrificed to personal malice."
- No man accused of "acts which degrade him to the level of the brutes" should be judged guilty "unless the proof is clear and unquestionable."[9]

Maj. Gen. Dix's letter apparently had an impact. On January 25, 1866, War Department Special Orders No. 32 revoked Hollister's original dismissal and "honorably mustered" him out of the Volunteer service, effective October 7, 1864. On February 7, 1866, the Adjutant General's Office, on behalf of the Secretary of War, directed that "as the vacancy in the Regular service caused by this dismissal has been filled and he cannot be restored to it," Hollister should fill the first vacancy available in his rank of Captain.[10]

The reaction within the "Regular service" was swift. On March 1, 1866, Col. John T. Sprague, former Adjutant General of the State of New York and namesake of the Sprague Light Cavalry, now commanding the 7th U.S. Infantry and Eastern District of Florida, wrote a scathing letter to the Adjutant General asking that, when Hollister's name came before the Military Committee for onward assignment, the words of the Secretary of War to Hollister's mother about the nature of his offenses be kept in mind: "Madam, he replied, they are of such a degrading, and of so debasing a character [that] delicacy, and respect for your sex, forbids my repeating them to you."[11]

Sprague went on to assert that from his military duties in Albany he received much information relating to Hollister's conduct and character and that if Hollister were ever to return to the 7th Infantry, his reception would be "anything but an agreeable one." His entreaties went unheeded, however, and Hollister returned to the Seventh.

His reception, indeed, was less than hospitable. On January 24, 1867, he complained to the Assistant Adjutant General in Washington that his fellow officers believed that his restoration to duty was "the result of political influence, rather than that of a thorough investigation and disproval of the calumnious charges preferred against me." Moreover, they were limiting all contact with him to official business only.[12]

Hollister, or perhaps his mother, again orchestrated a writing campaign on his behalf. On October 23, 1867, two Florida attorneys and a "planter" co-signed a letter to Maj. Gen. John Pope, Commanding the Third District (Georgia, Alabama, and Florida), expressing their concern over alleged efforts to remove Hollister from command of the Post of Tallahassee on the grounds that he had "taken a part in politics." The three petitioners vowed that to their knowledge he had never "interfered in political matters," and pled that Hollister remain in his position. The same day, they forwarded a petition with many signatures favoring Hollister's retention to Florida Governor David Walker. Walker expeditiously forwarded the letter and petition to Maj. Gen. Pope. Walker also professed to have never known Hollister to interfere with politics "in the slightest degree," and assured Pope that he would be pleased to see Hollister in a colonel's position someday.[13]

Hollister's brother, W. H. Hollister of New York City, joined the letter-writing campaign in November, appealing to Commanding General Ulysses S. Grant for a thorough investigation of allegations against Capt. Hollister. He asserted that Col. Sprague was prejudiced against his brother "through false and malicious statements made to him" and maintained that he could "prove that he is an Excellent officer & performs his duties faithfully."[14]

The allegations of Hollister's politicking had been made by Republican Party officials Thomas W. Osborn and Sherman Conant. In a letter written to General Grant on September 19, 1867, the two officials had asked that Hollister be "ordered to duty out of the State of Florida or retired from active service," claiming that he had "thrown himself actively into the present political campaign and is exerting himself in every way to disparage the cause of liberty and the policy of the Government." They went on to charge that he was associating with "the lowest and most degraded people of the Country," that he was "dissipated in his habits," and "continually drunk and conducting himself without respect or shame." They concluded that he was a "disgrace to the Government as well as to the Service" and asked that he be removed from the state."[15]

A month later, having reviewed the case, General Grant's terse instructions to the Adjutant General were very clear:

> Return to Gn. Pope with suggestion that Capt. Hollister be brought before Court Martial on charge of "Utter worthlessness" and such other charge as Dist. Commander may prefer. If not thought advisable to bring him before Ct. Mar. enquire if his case will warrant his being ordered before the Retiring Board. Law prohibits striking an officer's name from the Army without trial.[16]

Meanwhile, Hollister had married 18-year-old Philoclea Fisher, the daughter of a farmer, in the Florida Governor's living room, so there was some substance to the rumors of his political connections. Marriage neither reformed the man nor eliminated controversy.[17]

On January 28, 1868, he once again faced a court-martial, charged with absence without leave, drunkenness on duty, and conduct to the prejudice of good order and military discipline. The specifics of his offenses, while not nearly as debasing as those with the 16th New York Cavalry, were serious nonetheless:

- He was drunk on April 26, 1867, while on duty as Officer of the Day. He was drunk again and "unable properly to perform the duties which were required of him as Commanding Officer of the Post of Tallahassee, Florida, on May 10, 1867, on June 5, 1867, and again on September 18, 1867.
- From October 6–19, 1867, he left his company and command of the Post of Tallahassee, Florida, failed to report his absence to Col. Sprague, and was out of communication with Col. Sprague.
- He asked Lt. William H. Nelson, 7th U.S. Infantry, Post Adjutant

at Tallahassee, to date the Post Order granting him a leave of absence for seven days on October 10, 1867, instead of his actual day of departure on October 6.[18]

On February 18, 1868, Hollister was found guilty of all charges and specifications and recommended for dismissal. On March 8, Maj. Gen. George S. Meade, Commanding the 3rd Military District, forwarded the proceedings to Washington "for the action of the President of the United States." On March 21, the Judge Advocate General recommended to the President that it would be in the best interest of the service if Hollister were dismissed.[19]

This was not the end of the Hollister's career, however. Prominent Floridians wrote many letters on his behalf, and on May 21 his mother dispatched her own plea to President Andrew Johnson. Expressing her confidence that "my son has not been guilty of the charges preferred against him. I know his innocence," she prayed for clemency and begged for a "full pardon" so that he could return to duty.[20]

Apparently taking pity on the captain, the President commuted Hollister's sentence on May 25, 1868, and ordered that he be "reprimanded in General Orders by the Commanding General of the Department." Meade ordered the captain's return to duty on June 1.[21]

Hollister remained with his regiment in Florida through April 1869 when it was ordered to Salt Lake City, Utah. Traveling by way of Omaha Barracks, Nebraska, he arrived at Camp Douglas on June 8 after several weeks of leave.[22]

Hollister and his company remained on garrison duty at Camp Douglas until April 1870 when, along with two other companies and the regimental staff, they departed for the Department of the Platte and Camp Baker (later known as Fort Logan) on the Smith River in Montana. He remained there until he was "honorably" mustered out of the service—for reasons not stated—on January 1, 1871.[23]

Following his discharge, Hollister made one last attempt to clear his name and be restored to duty, again using his political contacts. On January 30, 1871, Secretary of War William W. Belknap passed final judgment in a letter to the Honorable Roscoe Conkling, Senator from New York:

> I have the honor to acknowledge your reference to the Dept. of a telegram from Georg. Hollister, late a captain in the 7th Infantry, asserting that his recent discharge from the Army is an act of great injustice and that he and his family are left utterly destitute in consequence, and to inform you, in reply, that the military record of this officer is such as fully to justify the action taken in his case and to preclude any thought of his restoration, even were such a restoration not ... a legal impossibility.

With regard to his alleged destitution, it is only necessary to remark that under the generous provisions of the law for reducing and reforming the Army, he has been discharged with one year's full pay.[24]

George S. Hollister died "of uremic convulsions" while a patient at the "Jackson Sanitorium" in Dansville, New York, on June 9, 1881. On May 27, 1891, his widow, Philoclea A. Hollister, then living in Michigan, filed for his pension.[25]

Lieutenant Colonel John Nicholson

Nicholson, a native of Elbridge in Onondaga County New York, had lived a life of much adventure before the war, having "sailed in all the known seas all over the world and visited many foreign countries," as well as serving in the Mexican war.[26] In 1849, he had settled down and married the former Mary C. Holway. By 1861, when he first enlisted in the 21st New York Volunteer Infantry, the couple already had three sons.[27]

Following the Civil War, having been promoted to lieutenant colonel after George Hollister was dismissed, Nicholson and his family first settled in Buffalo where he served for several years as Captain of Police. According to his obituary, however, the injuries that he suffered "while in his country's service," were debilitating enough that he was "invalid all the rest of his life."[28]

By 1870, he and the family had moved to Monroe, Wisconsin, where his oldest son, Frederick, was already engaged as a photographer. "Deeply religious" and a member of the Methodist Church in Monroe, Nicholson apparently held down menial jobs as a "laborer" and "night watchman."[29]

Nicholson died of a stroke on September 14, 1901, while visiting his youngest son in Janesville a few miles from Monroe. Nicholson was a member of the W. H. Sargent Post No. 20 of the Grand Army of the Republic, whose members served as his pall bearers. He and his wife, who died in 1907, are buried at Oak Hill Cemetery in Janesville.

Bvt. Lieutenant Colonel (Surgeon) Joseph M. Homiston

Following his discharge, Dr. Homiston returned home to Brooklyn where he was "welcomed by his fellow townsmen at an open-air meeting ... in front of the Pierrepont House" and given a medal for his service. In

Brooklyn, he opened "one of the largest medical and surgical practices in the city" on Sands Street, near Jay, where his offices remained until his death. Homiston had married the former Caroline J. Madden of New York City in May 1858, and their first son Ezra had been born in 1860; their second son Harry was born in 1867.[30]

Homiston was active in both fraternal and military organizations after his return to Brooklyn. He was a Freemason, belonging to the Clinton Commandery No. 14, Knights Templar, and a member of the 14th Regiment Veteran's Association. He continued his military service as Colonel and surgeon of the 2nd Division, New York National Guard in 1869, a position he held until April 1875. He also was a member of Grand Army of the Republic and an original member of the Military Order of the Loyal Legion of the United States.[31]

Dr. Homiston died on April 8, 1879, at the age of 50. According to his death notice, the cause of death was "nervous prostration,"[32] a condition in those days described as "extreme exhaustion from inability to control physical and mental activities." His biography published by the Green-Wood (Brooklyn) Cemetery Civil War Project, however, identifies the cause of death as "general paresis," a form of severe mental impairment caused by damage to the brain from untreated syphilis, which usually doesn't emerge until 15 to 20 years after infection.[33]

Homiston died intestate. On May 9, 1879, his wife petitioned the Kings County Surrogate's Court to administer his estate, which was estimated to be worth no more than $300. The Homiston house on Sands Street had been offered for rent in mid–March. She applied for his Civil War pension in February 1880. He was buried at Brooklyn's Green-Wood Cemetery.[34]

Captain Nathan H. Mooney

Paroled in Charlotte, North Carolina, after his third escape attempt, Capt. Mooney first made his way to Wilmington, North Carolina, and then on to Annapolis, Maryland. He was discharged from volunteer service in August 1865 and returned "to the peaceful seclusion of his country home" in Beekmantown, New York, where he engaged in farming. In October 1868 he married the former Elizabeth E. Dunn, of nearby Chazy, New York. Their first child, W. Grant Mooney, was born a year later.[35]

In November 1880, running on the Republican Party ticket, Mooney was elected Sheriff of Clinton County, receiving nearly 60 percent of the votes cast.³⁶ His three-year term as Sheriff was largely routine but marked by occasional events that drew headlines in the local papers. One such episode, a year after his election, involved the nearly-botched execution of a convicted murderer. With headlines screaming "From Time to Eternity! The Hanging of Henry King, the Convict Murderer! His Last Hours! Full Particulars of the Execution!," the *Plattsburgh Sentinel* provided lurid details of the preparations and execution of a "life convict" who had killed a fellow convict at Clinton Prison. After listening to Sheriff Mooney read his death warrant and remarking "That don't amount to much, does it?" the doomed man was led to the gallows by Mooney and the undersheriff. Mooney and three other officers

> ... stepped into the enclosure, and at 11:43 the weight dropped and the prisoner was suspended in mid air. For half a moment he was motionless, and then commenced breathing heavily, and it was evident that his neck was not broken. There were muscular convulsions which continued for about four minutes. At 11:48 Drs. Dunham, of Plattsburgh, and Honsinger, of Chazy, commenced the examination, the pulse then being 96.³⁷

It would take nearly fourteen minutes for the condemned man's heart to stop beating. Nonetheless, Essex County Sheriff Talbott and other official witnesses declared the execution "very successful."³⁸

In late August 1883, Mooney was in the news again, having been struck by one of three "crazy drunk" and disorderly brothers whom he and other officers were attempting to apprehend on an otherwise orderly Saturday afternoon.³⁹ However, the sheriff is probably best known locally as the first man to "confirm" the existence of Lake Champlain's sea serpent, known by aficionados as "Champ" or "Champy," and rumored to exist dating as far back as early Indian legends.

On July 27, 1883, after camping on South Hero Island, due east of Plattsburgh in the middle of Lake Champlain, Sheriff Mooney and friends were returning to Plattsburgh on the steam yacht *Nellie*, Mooney at the helm. Having reached Plattsburgh's Cumberland Bay:

> ... he saw a black object ahead, nearly on a line with the tack of the steamer. He at first thought it was a man overboard from the [steamer] *Maquam* [which was ahead of him] but finally concluded it was not, as it was lying perfectly still, about five feet in length being out of the water.⁴⁰

Mooney, described by the newspaper as "a gentleman of unquestioned truthfulness, not easily disturbed, and in no way given to sensations of any kind," gave the *Sentinel* a detailed accounting of what he had seen:

> ... I then discovered that it was an enormous snake or water serpent. It stood out about five feet from the water, with a long jaw, a snake-shaped head, at least eight

inches across at the top or flat part, and ten inches from the top of the head to the lower end of the jaw. I saw him distinctly.... Its body, which must have been from twenty-five to thirty-five feet in length, was pointed to the north.[41]

While the existence of Lake Champlain's reputed serpent remained highly disputed, Mooney finished out his three-year term as sheriff and, with his wife and son, returned to farming. Elizabeth Dunn Mooney died during the winter of 1899 at the age of 53 and was buried at the Point Au Roche Cemetery outside Beekmantown. Mooney remained on the farm with his son's family, but at some point after 1900 father and son apparently were estranged. In 1905, Nathan Mooney was boarding with William and Margaret Oliver in Beekmantown, although his son and family still lived in the area. In 1910, now 70, he was still a border with another local family.[42]

Capt. Nathan H. Mooney died January 10, 1914, in Beekmantown and was buried, with his wife, at the Point Au Roche Cemetery.

Captain Joseph Schneider

The stalwart defender of "Fort Schneider" in Annandale was mustered out on August 17, 1865, and returned to New York City where he gained American citizenship on August 26. His naturalization certificate described him as 5' 4.75" tall with blue eyes, dark brown hair, a fair complexion, a high forehead, oval chin and face, straight nose and medium mouth.

Joseph's father had died in Germany during the war, so he had been unable to return home at the time. Thus, after being discharged, he traveled to Cologne, returning to the United States in March 1866. On March 19, 1866, Joseph married Gertrude Pauline Wirz in Manhattan. Most likely they met in Cologne, where she was born and lived before their marriage.[43]

The couple remained in New York and had nine children. In 1870, Joseph was working as a lithographer when he was hired by the Internal Revenue Service as a "deputy collector." In 1880 Joseph was working as a "weigher" at the U.S. Custom House. When he retired, around 1906, at the age of 72, he was again a deputy collector for the Internal Revenue Service.

Joseph was a member of the New York Grand Army of the Republic (GAR) Post 192 in New York City. An active supporter of the Republican Party, he served as Deputy Marshal in the Southern District of New York for the 1870 congressional election and as a "doorkeeper" at the Chicago national Republican Convention in June 1888.

Joseph remained very close to his family, living next door to his eldest son in the Bronx until the end of his life. He died of pneumonia and cardiac arrest on April 17, 1908, and was buried in St. Michael's Cemetery in Queens.[44]

The "Garrett's Farm Patrol"

On April 20, 1865, five days after President Lincoln's death, the War Department offered a $100,000 reward for the "apprehension" of Booth and his fellow conspirators: $50,000, "in addition to any reward offered by municipal authorities or State executives," for Booth's capture, and $25,000, each, for the capture of John Surratt and David Herold. The announcement also offered "liberal awards" for any information leading to their arrests.[45]

On November 24, 1865, the War Department issued a second order that anyone who believed they were "entitled to a share of the rewards," must file a claim by the end of the year. The Army Judge Advocate General Joseph Holt and his assistant, E.D. Townsend, chaired a commission that decided how rewards would be distributed.[46]

The commission issued its report in April 1866, and Capt. Edward Doherty, who had filed a claim, was among those deemed worthy of reward. A few weeks later, however, a Pennsylvania congressman introduced a resolution directing the House Committee on Claims to review the "fairness and propriety" of the award distribution plan. The committee's July 1866 report was debated on the house floor, amended, and eventually a bill was sent to the Senate and passed unanimously.[47]

In the end, Capt. Doherty was awarded $5,250. Sgt. Boston Corbett and the other 25 members of Doherty's detachment received $1,653.85 each. The members of the detachment came from across the state of New York, and among them, eleven were foreign-born:

- Sgt. Andrew Wendell: Co. E, a shoemaker born in Germany, enlisted at Buffalo.
- Cpl. Michael Hornsby (Hormsby): Co. H, born in Green, Georgia, enlisted at New York City.
- Cpl. Oliver Lonkey (Lonpay): Co. E, a farmer, enlisted at Massena.
- Cpl. Herman (Herron) Newgarten (Neugarten): Co. H, a "soldier" born in Prussia, enlisted at New York City and had previously served with the 8th New York Infantry.

Nine—Postwar Fortunes and Failures 165

- Cpl. Michael Uniac (Uniace): Co. C, enlisted at Buffalo.
- Cpl. John Walz (Wallz): Co. H, a "clerk" born in Germany, enlisted in New York City and was mustered in initially as a wagoner.
- Cpl. Charles Zimmer: Co. C, a laborer born in Germany, enlisted at Buffalo.
- Pvt. David Baker: Co. H, a farmer, enlisted at Plattsburgh.
- Pvt. William Byrne: Co. C, a farmer born in Ireland, enlisted at Plattsburgh.
- Pvt. Frederick Dietz (Deitz): Co. E, a farmer born in Germany, enlisted at Concord, south of Buffalo.
- Pvt. Godfrey Phillip Hoyt: Co. C, a joiner born in New Hampshire, enlisted at Plattsburgh.
- Pvt. Martin Kelley: Co. C, a farmer, enlisted at Saranac.
- Pvt. Frank (Franklin) McDaniel(s): Co. C, a farmer, enlisted at Plattsburgh.
- Pvt. William McQuade: Co. H, a carpenter, enlisted at Tarrytown on the Hudson River, north of Yonkers.
- Pvt. John Meyers (Myers, Mayers): Co. C, a laborer born in Germany, enlisted at Buffalo.
- Pvt. John W. Millington: Co. H, a laborer, enlisted at Plattsburgh and had previously served in the 93rd New York Infantry.
- Pvt. Emery Paraday: Co. H, a farmer, enlisted at Plattsburgh.
- Pvt. Henry Putnam, Co. C, enlisted at Alexandria, VA.
- Pvt. John Ryan (Rina): Co. C, a "sailor" born in Ireland, enlisted at Buffalo and was a blacksmith when transferred to the 3rd Provisional New York Cavalry in August 1865.
- Pvt. Lewis Savage: Co. A, a farmer, enlisted at Plattsburgh.
- Pvt. John Adolph Singer: Co. M, a "soldier" born in Prussia, enlisted in New York City and had previously served in the 20th New York Infantry.
- Pvt. Abraham (Abram) Snay (Genay): Co. A, a farmer from Saranac, enlisted at Plattsburgh.
- Pvt. Carl Steinbrigge (Steinbrugge): Co. M, enlisted at Greenburgh, near Tarrytown.
- Pvt. John Winter: Co. I, a "sailor" born in Germany, enlisted at Buffalo.
- Pvt. Joseph Zisgen: Co. M, a "laborer" born in Prussia, enlisted at New York City and had previously served in the 1st and 42nd U.S. Infantry.[48]

Captain Edward Doherty

Following the capture and killing of John Wilkes Booth, Doherty remained with Co. B until the two New York regiments were consolidated into the Third Provisional New York Cavalry. He was mustered out of the volunteer service on September 21, 1865.

Reportedly in recognition of his role in capturing the Lincoln assassins, Doherty was offered an appointment as a second lieutenant in the 5th U.S. Cavalry, effective April 19, 1866. He had begun lobbying for a regular army commission well before he was mustered out of the volunteer service, and had managed to secure a meeting with President Johnson on April 11. In a follow-up letter that same day, accompanied with a list of numerous high-level supporters—including Lt. Col. Nicholson—who had sent letters to the Secretary of State, he formally requested a cavalry commission.[49]

Doherty joined Co. H of the 5th Cavalry in July 1866 on reconstruction duty in South Carolina and was sent to Sumter about 40 miles east of Columbia, commanding a detachment of two non-commissioned officers and 45 privates. In September, his company was reassigned to Aiken, South Carolina, where Doherty served as Acting Post Adjutant.[50]

On June 1, 1867, having been promoted to first lieutenant of Co. C, Doherty reported for duty at Atlanta, Georgia. There he served as Acting Assistant Adjutant General at Headquarters, Department of Georgia, but was back with his company in March 1868. Meanwhile, in January, again with an endorsement from Lt. Col. Nicholson, he had applied to President Johnson for a promotion to brevet major. It was not forthcoming.[51]

In August 1868, Doherty and his company were transferred to the Headquarters, Department of the South, in Atlanta where they served as the commanding general's "cavalry escort." Lt. Doherty also served as Acting Post Adjutant, a position normally held by a junior lieutenant.[52]

All was not well, however. On September 29, his company commander, Capt. Thomas E. Maley, wrote from Camp Emory near Atlanta to the Adjutant of the 5th U.S. Cavalry requesting that Doherty be transferred to another company. Maley did not cite a reason for his request but stated that it would be in the "best interest of the regiment, certainly for the best interest of this company." Maley's request was routed through Washington. Although Commanding General George Meade "strongly recommended" the transfer, the Army Adjutant General declined, noting that if Doherty was not fit to serve in Mahley's company, the issue of his fitness for duty should be handled through normal procedures.[53]

In February 1869, Doherty was transferred to Fort McPherson in

Nebraska with the bulk of the 5th Cavalry, where he participated in the Republican River expedition. According to the regimental history he was "engaged in the affair at Rock Creek, the brilliant action at Summit Springs [against Cheyenne Dog Soldiers led by Tall Bull], the affair in the sandhills south of Julesburg, and in the Niobrara pursuit." He also served at Plum Creek, Nebraska, in September and October 1869, when, along with five other companies, Doherty and Co. C were ordered to Fort D.A. Russell, Wyoming, where they went into winter quarters.[54]

Initially, things went well for Lt. Doherty at Fort D.A. Russell, but eventually his fortunes would decline precipitously. In December 1869 and again in March 1870 he was temporarily in command of Co. C. In April and May, his company scouted the country near Hillsdale Station outside of Laramie, and for three weeks in June and July, now assigned to Co. K, he was stationed at the Chug Water Mail Station. Once back at D.A. Russell, he was placed in charge of a detail away from the fort to purchase supplies.[55]

After the procurement mission, the Army began to suspect there were irregularities in 1st Lt. Edward P. Doherty's official actions. On May 5, 1870, Lt. Col. Thomas Duncan, commanding the 5th Cavalry Detachment at Fort D. A. Russell, visited Hillsdale Station to investigate charges of inferior rations and improper punishments meted out to enlisted men for being several hours late from leave. Duncan found no basis for complaints about the quality of rations or evidence that "any rations had been misapplied or disposed of." While the punishments inflected by Doherty—requiring them carry heavy logs for a prolonged period and tying up two who refused—were harsh, Duncan accepted the lieutenant's reasoning that "having no officers to compose a Court Martial, he found it necessary to resort to arbitrary means to enforce his orders and maintain discipline." Doherty also maintained, and Duncan apparently agreed, that he "had no idea of treating the men cruelly" and was unaware that one of the men had fainted until it was reported to him. Although no charges were brought against Doherty, his men clearly were not happy with his leadership.[56]

Several months later, however, a more serious issue arose. On September 7, 1870, Lt. Col. Duncan wrote to the regimental headquarters Adjutant at Fort McPherson that Doherty had received several letters from the Headquarters of the U.S. Army in Washington stating that "he has a wife and child whom he has utterly neglected to provide for and refused to recognize."

Indeed, General Sherman had received and forwarded to Doherty several letters from Mrs. Nellie Doherty, the last one, apparently, dated

July 30, 1869, asking him to "assist me through your influence in compelling Capt. E. P. Doherty of the 5th U.S. Cavalry to contribute to the support of his child." Mrs. Doherty—only a portion of the letter is in the official files—went on to describe her precarious circumstances:

> For nearly four years I cheerfully have labored to care for my child, while the father with ample means has never showed one interest in it. I have at last been compelled to part with everything I possessed on earth to enable to support my child. I have a mother residing in Cincinnati and have begged him (Capt. D.) to send me money to enable me to reach her with a little assistance for the child out of his ample means. I asked him to send me a certain trifling sum so I never would trouble him again. I love my child and as a mother should have done everything in my power to honestly maintain it but everything at last has failed and I am dependent on charity. I am compelled to once more beg of you to compel Capt. Doherty to listen to me.[57]

In his September 1870 memorandum, Lt. Col. Duncan went on to describe more serious charges:

- In December 1869, Doherty had taken an ambulance from Fort D.A. Russell in broad daylight and had himself driven to the house of Ida Hamilton, "a common, public prostitute" in Cheyenne, opposite the Rectory of the Episcopal church. He was seen by the wife of one of the regiment's captains, as well as the church rector and others, entering and leaving the residence in uniform.
- Later that month, Doherty was on the organizing committee for an officers' "hop" on post. The captain's wife and other ladies refused to attend, maintaining that "if the 5th Cavalry placed such officers on their Committee, they would not associate with the regiment."
- Duncan attempted to gather testimony to bring formal charges against Doherty, but "all the witnesses had such a repugnance to being brought up in a case of this kind that it was impossible for me to ascertain the facts in the case until recently."
- It was also alleged that Doherty lacked "integrity in his pecuniary transactions." Specifically, the post trader held a debt against him which he "neglected to pay although frequently called upon," until the trader was compelled to sue him. He also refused to settle a bill with the post laundress until she complained to Doherty's commanding officer.

In concluding, Duncan reported that Doherty had a general reputation in the regiment of being "a man of rather low tastes and instincts," and he

Nine—Postwar Fortunes and Failures 169

recommended that the lieutenant be brought before a War Department Board considering officers for possible dismissal.[58]

As it turned out, these were but the first charges against Doherty. Apparently while he commanded his company at Plum Creek, Nebraska, from late August to mid–November 1869, some questions arose as to his financial transactions related to the procurement of supplies. In early October 1870, Lt. Col. Duncan, having "heard whispering in regard to these and many other similar transactions several months ago," took it upon himself to investigate and ordered a lieutenant to obtain affidavits from soldiers stationed at Pine Bluffs. The question at hand was whether Doherty had refused to fully pay bills, presumably pocketing the difference.

This investigation, however, paled in comparison to three formal charges for "conduct unbecoming an officer and a gentleman" brought against Doherty on November 1, 1870:

> First: that he publicly appeared in uniform in the town of Cheyenne on or about November 1, "in a state of intoxication thereby bringing scandal and discredit on the service."
>
> Second: that, while in uniform, publicly entered and remained in a "Chinese house of prostitution" in Cheyenne on or about November 1.
>
> Third: that he "falsely and visibly represented himself to the inmates of a Chinese house of prostitution as Judge Jones, meaning thereby, William Jones, Associate Justice, Supreme Court of Wyoming," in Cheyenne on or about November 1.[59]

Although he escaped a formal court-martial, action against Doherty was swift. Under an act passed by Congress July 15, 1870, Army commanders were required to identify officers deemed "unfit for the proper discharge of their duties" for whatever reason—except injury or illness in the line of duty—to be reviewed for dismissal by a board of officers in Washington. Doherty's file was sent to Washington on November 3, 1870, and the board took up his case on November 28. On December 24, the board rendered its opinion that Doherty was "unfit for the service by reason of lack of good moral character" and recommended he be mustered out of the service. He was mustered out on December 27.[60]

Following his dismissal, Doherty married the former Catherine Josephine Gautier. "Kate" was the daughter of the prominent Washington restaurateur and caterer Charles Gautier. By 1880 he and his wife were established in New Orleans with a six-year-old son.[61] He already had established himself as a government contractor, and they had a small house on Dauphine Street in the French Quarter.

In March 1876, Doherty attempted to have his dismissal case reopened, complaining to President Ulysses S. Grant that Maj. Vincent, an Assistant

Adjutant General, had been sharing with "persons not connected with the government the allegations which I thought I had disproved, without giving me the benefit of the evidence on file, explaining or disproving these malicious false charges." His case was not reopened.[62]

Doherty had a mixed record as a contractor. In March 1871 he successfully bid on a contract to provide mail service on route 7505 "White River to Vicksburg, 229 miles and back, twice a week by steamboat," but failed to begin service when required. He lost the contract.[63] In 1879, he had a contract with the City of New Orleans, "filling up the batture holes for the city, employing a force of from 150 to 175 men daily."[64]

In 1882 he again was low bidder and won a Federal contract for the "removal of rock from the bed of the Red River, at the falls in the vicinity of Alexandria, La." Work was delayed due to "continuous high water," but eventually began in August 1883. Progress was slow, however, due to the "lack of proper plant on the part of the contractor and the high stage of the water." Doherty was given several contract extensions, and the work was finally completed in October 1884.[65]

Doherty and his family returned to New York City in 1886, and he was appointed "Inspector of Street Pavings [sic]." In March of that year he made one final attempt to clear his name and be restored to Army service. His request was referred to the Senate Committee on Military Affairs and Secretary of War. It went nowhere. The closest he got to "military service" was as Commander of Veteran Post No. 436, Grand Army of the Republic and of the Press Veterans. Twice he served as Grand Marshal in New York City Memorial Day celebrations. Doherty died of heart disease on April 3, 1897, and was buried at Arlington National Cemetery.[66]

Sergeant Boston Corbett

By the time the man who survived Andersonville Prison joined the 16th New York Cavalry, he already was a deeply troubled man, yet a preacher with an uncommonly high degree of religious fervor. Among other things prior to the war, Corbett was so wracked with puritanical guilt over his sexual desires that he had castrated himself with a pair of scissors to fend off the temptations of local ladies of the night. Some have speculated that his strange behavior may have been caused by exposure to mercury (II) nitrate used in making felt in his trade as a hatter.

His life following the war, while productive in some ways, was just as conflicted. In the end, he remained a man of great mystery, vanishing forever from a Kansas insane asylum in the spring of 1888.[67]

Nine—Postwar Fortunes and Failures

Still basking in the glory of killing Booth, Corbett mustered out with Co. L in Washington, D.C., on August 17, 1865, and returned to working as a hatter, initially in Boston, then Danbury, Connecticut, and finally in Camden, New Jersey. He retained his religious fervor and was appointed the second pastor of the Memorial Methodist Protestant Church on Broadway in Camden, when it moved from temporary quarters in 1866, but was replaced in 1867.[68]

In 1869 Corbett was appointed pastor of Camden Mission "for the Conference Year" of 1869 by the President of the New Jersey District of the Methodist Church. In the 1870 Federal census he was living with Isaac Boggs, a teamster, and his wife Sarah, with the occupation of "preach gospel." His church duties probably did not cover fully his living expenses, as he was still listed as a hatter in the local directory in 1874.[69]

Corbett left Camden for Cleveland, Ohio, in 1874, where he lived in a local boarding house and worked as a hatter for the Barrett hat factory.[70] He also preached at a local Methodist church. A newspaper account of one of his sermons noted that he attracted a large crowd due to his "notoriety as an historic character, and his reputation as a zealous and devoted Christian of the Methodist persuasion," and that he conducted the evening service "in a simple, earnest, and unostentatious manner, greatly interesting his audience."[71]

By 1876, Corbett was back in Camden. According to a Portsmouth, New Hampshire, paper he was living alone in a "little forlorn-looking house" where he did his own cooking and housekeeping and saw no one "but the members of his little flock of Methodists which meet nightly at his house."[72]

In January 1878—now serving as pastor of the Independent Methodist Church where he also resided—he wrote to President Rutherford B. Hayes, appealing for a government position for "one who has risked his life ... and lost his health ... by four months imprisonment at Andersonville." In closing his letter, he urged the President to "read the Words of Solomon."[73]

Corbett failed in his bid for a government job and left Camden for the farming country near Concordia in Cloud County, Kansas.[74] According to a local history, he found 80 acres a few miles southeast of Concordia, "overlooked by the homestead settlers" and lying among some hills, where he built a "hermit-like quarter" to "live the life of a recluse." His homestead was extremely basic, described as a partial dugout built into a hillside:

> The floor and roof were of dirt after the fashion of the Kansas dugout; in dimensions it is about twelve by fifteen feet. In one corner of the room, from an excavation under the rock wall, a spring of water bubbled up and flowed through an aperture to the outside. The furniture of this queer domicile, long since removed, was very meager; it

consisted of a home-made bedstead, a chair or two, an old musket and a Bible, the yellow leaves of the latter being well worn with time and frequent turning.[75]

Described as "small in stature" with "swarthy skin, a "scant beard" and "long dark hair floating over his shoulders," Corbett joined the local Methodist Episcopal Church, was "very enthusiastic in revival work," but thought by some to be "mentally disordered."[76] In 1887, some "sympathizing friends" managed to secure an appointment for him as an assistant doorkeeper for the House of Representatives at the Capital in Topeka. His new position was reported in the Christian press.[77]

Not long after arriving on the job, however, he went berserk over an assumed slight by one of his fellow doorkeepers, brandished a knife and in the ensuing uproar pulled a gun on the Sergeant-at-Arms. He was eventually subdued by three policemen. On February 16, 1887, following the altercation, Corbett appeared before Probate Judge Quinton of Topeka. He was "adjudged insane and placed in the [Topeka] asylum."[78]

The following year, allowed outside for exercise, Corbett managed to escape, and wanted posters soon were up throughout the region:

INSANE MAN ESCAPED

Topeka, Kansas, May 26, 1888

BOSTON CORBETT, an insane man, escaped from the Insane Asylum at Topeka this morning, and is supposed to be heading for Cloud County. He is about 55 years of age; about 5 feet, 4 inches high; has plucked all his beard out down to the lower part of his ears; has gray chin whiskers and moustache; gray hair, cut square at bottom, and parts his hair in the middle; he wore a dark jeans suit, and black soft hat; and was riding a bay or sorrel pony with a boy's saddle.

He is regarded as a dangerous man, but was unarmed when he escaped. If he comes your way arrest him and return him to the Asylum at once, or telegraph Dr. B.D. Eastman, Superintendent Insane Asylum, Topeka, for orders.

G.A. Huron,
Guardian Boston Corbett[79]

Following his escape, Corbett made his way to the farm of Irvin DeFord, brother of Capt. Harvey DeFord who had befriended Corbett while both were incarcerated at Andersonville Prison. Corbett and Harvey DeFord had kept in touch after the war. According to Harvey's niece, it was Harvey who arranged for Boston's appointment at the Capital building.[80]

Corbett remained in Irvin DeFord's barn for several days, departing on June 1, 1888. DeFord gave him a horse along with "food, a blanket and some money, with the promise he would keep going and not come back." Corbett told them he was going to Mexico and would not return. And with that, he vanished.[81]

Corporal Michael Hornsby

Just four days before his company was consolidated into the 3rd Provisional Cavalry Regiment, Hornsby deserted, "place not stated," but most likely from Camp Barry. Nonetheless, he still collected his Booth capture award and apparently soon drifted westward, living in Denver, Cheyenne and Deadwood, South Dakota, among other locations, working as a "freighter and teamster." According to family lore, he was one of the teamsters for the 1874 scientific expedition surveying the Black Hills, along with Colonel George Custer and the 7th Cavalry.[82]

Hornsby's first wife had died in 1860, and he remarried in 1872. He and his new wife apparently continued working together as freight haulers, but eventually settled down in Cocolalla, Idaho, northeast of Spokane, Washington. He died of stomach cancer in nearby Sagle on February 18, 1914, and was buried in the Westmond Cemetery.[83]

Private John W. Millington

Millington returned to his family's farm in Chestertown, near Lake George. He used $800 of his reward money to buy a farm and married Miss Phoebe St. Francis in nearby Johnsburg. They would have five children between 1866 and 1880. There, while still farming, he started working as a carpenter. In 1870, the family was still in Chestertown, but by 1880 they had moved to Summit Lake in Nobles County, Minnesota, northeast of Sioux Falls, where Millington was again a farmer. In 1895, they moved to Sioux City, Iowa. John, now 52, and Phoebe, 49, still had two children at home—17-year-old George and 14-year-old Benjamin. Their son James, his wife and newborn son lived nearby.

John, Phoebe and George remained in Sioux City through 1900, but Phoebe died sometime between 1900 and 1904. After her death, John moved to Portland, Oregon, and in 1910, at the age of 67, was working as a self-employed carpenter. He also had a new wife, Mary, a native of Illinois. Millington died in Portland on November 11, 1914, and was buried in Portland's Grand Army of the Republic Cemetery.[84]

Private Emery (Emory) Parady (Paraday)

John Millington's fellow member of Co. H also eventually settled in Portland, Oregon, after wandering a bit. In 1870, Emery Parady moved from his home in Beekmantown, along with his wife, Francis, son and younger brother Alfred, to Berlin, Michigan, east of Grand Rapids, where he and Alfred were farmers. His farm was valued at $1,700. In 1880, now with three children, he and Francis had moved to nearby Nashville, Michigan, where he once again had taken up business as a cobbler. He did well in Nashville, serving as postmaster from 1881 to 1886 and getting elected to a term as village president.[85]

Emery and Francis were still in Nashville in 1900, but ten years later had moved to Portland with their 30-year-old daughter, Elizabeth. There he again worked as a cobbler in his own repair shop. In 1920, at the age of 75, he was still working as a "shoemaker" in Portland. His unmarried daughter, Elizabeth, was still living with him and his wife, as were daughter Nellie Parady Brown and her two children. Elizabeth and Nellie both were working as "retouchers" in a photo studio.[86]

Sometime after they both had relocated to Portland, Emery Parady and John Millington reconnected. Both were members of Portland's Benjamin F. Butler Post 67 of the Grand Army of the Republic.[87]

Emery Parady died on March 14, 1924, and was buried at Lincoln Memorial Park in Portland. Francis filed for his Civil War pension in April. She died two years later to the day, and was buried beside her husband.[88]

Private Abraham (Abram) Snay

Born in Saranac, Abraham returned to his hometown and married the former Mary Peck, probably a local girl. Both were 19 years old. By 1870, they were living on a farm, valued at $500, in nearby Franklin. By 1880, still in Franklin, they had five children. Abraham was farming 29 acres with a value of $900 and producing an estimated $250 a year in revenue. By 1892, however, they had moved to Schuyler Falls, still near Saranac and Plattsburgh, where Abraham and his son William were farming. Mary died in in 1894.

Abraham remarried in 1897. His new wife, Margaret, a French Canadian with German heritage, came from Quebec. By 1910, his son, William had married and, along with his wife Anna and their son, was living and farming in Schuyler Falls with Abraham and Margaret. William, Anna and their children remained on the family farm.[89]

Abraham died on February 9, 1928, and was buried in the Peasleeville Cemetery a few miles west of Schuyler Falls.

Other Members of the 16th New York

Lieutenant George F. French

After Col. Lazelle's nephew was captured at Culpeper Courthouse on September 9, 1864, he was sent to Danville Prison, a collection of six large, three-story tobacco warehouses that had been "stripped of all furnishings including lamps and chairs."[90] With floors encrusted with dirt and barely heated by a single potbellied stove at one end of each floor, living conditions were brutal, especially in winter.

By the time French arrived at Danville in the fall of 1864, a smallpox epidemic the previous winter had run its course, only to be replaced by scurvy and chronic diarrhea that summer. In late 1864, Danville's facilities were "officially declared to be 'filled to utmost capacity,' which meant that over 4,500 men were quartered on the upper floors of the six buildings." French and his fellow prisoners faced an especially harsh winter:

> By this time most of the prisoners were one step removed from nakedness. Some possessed a piece of tattered blanket for a shawl, although Major Putnam calculated that among the 350 men who occupied the second floor of Prison No. 3, no more than 70 had even a scrap of a blanket. Those few men who owned pieces of shoes had to guard them literally with their lives. Men died in droves that winter from starvation and exposure.[91]

George French was among the lucky first group of officers and men released from Danville starting on February 18, 1865. Four days later, he was paroled at Aiken's Landing on the James River. Soon he was back with his regiment, promoted to 1st Lieutenant of Co. K. On August 17 he was transferred, along with the rest of the regiment, to the 3rd Provisional Cavalry and mustered out of Federal service in September.

After he was mustered out, French returned to Hagerstown, Maryland, where his father, a lawyer, was running (successfully) for State Circuit Court Judge. In May 1869 he secured a position as an Internal Revenue Service "store-keeper" for a local bonded warehouse.[92]

In May 1873, French was promoted to the position of Custom House Inspector, a political appointment. The following December, he married the former Susan Virginia Brown of Washington County. The young couple moved to Baltimore where George had taken up his Customs position.[93] He remained Customs inspector until after the 1882 Congressional elections when the Republicans lost control of the House of Representatives. In all likelihood, George, appointed by Republicans, lost his position as a result. In 1883, the local business directory listed him as a "salesman." In

1885, however, he and Samuel W. Coover, a flour merchant, entered into a joint venture, Coover and French, as "commission merchants" or brokers.[94] George's partnership with Coover lasted for three years. In 1888, Coover and French became "Coover and Smith," and French struck out on his own as a flour merchant. The *Baltimore City Directory* variously identified him as a "clerk" or "salesman" through 1894 and a "commission merchant" or "flour merchant" through 1901.

George and his wife never had children. In 1900, her sister and niece were living with the couple in Baltimore. The following year, on March 7, George died "of a sudden illness" at the age of 58 in their home on Park Avenue. He was buried at Rose Hill Cemetery in Hagerstown. His wife, Susan Virginia Brown French, lived another 25 years and was buried in the French family plot at Rose Hill.[95]

Lieutenant William J. Keays

After he was mustered out of Federal service, Keays returned to Canada and went into business in the town of Sarnia on Lake Huron in Ontario Province. In 1868–69 he was listed as a "forwarder," and in 1871 as owning a foundry. In 1869, he also was appointed "Official Assignee" for the County of Lambton, essentially responsible for handling the assets involved in bankruptcy cases, a position in which he served while running his business. He also served in the local militia.[96]

Keays married the former Emily DiRenzie Horton in 1869. Seventeen years younger than William, she was the daughter of a London, Ontario, barrister whom Keays had come to know before he and his first wife had left Canada for Buffalo in 1861. He and Emily would have four children, however the youngest, Ernest F. Keays, born in 1882, would live only a year.[97] Their other two sons both graduated in engineering from Cornell University.

According to the Keays family history, William "was greatly responsible for pushing the idea of a steamship line to the Northwest out of Sarnia." He also patented and found investors to build a device to keep winter ice in Lake Huron from blocking Sarnia's harbor. Unfortunately "it didn't work."[98]

When Keays was reappointed Lambton County Assignee in 1875, he also was serving as an agent for the Grand Trunk rail line, which ran through Sarnia. In 1878, as Official Assignee for the County of Lambton, he was a named party in a bankruptcy cased tried in the Michigan State Supreme Court, *Burrows vs. Keays*.[99] That same year, "having removed to the city of Toronto" and claiming that there was insufficient business in the County of Lambton since the duties were divided between him and the sheriff, he tried to obtain a transfer as Official Assignee for the County of York. He was unsuccessful, and a month later he accepted an appointment as Deputy Maritime Marshal for Lambton County.[100]

In 1881, living in Clifton Town (Niagara Falls), Ontario with his wife and young children, Keays was offered a position as Agent for the Grand Trunk Railroad in Buffalo, New York. The family settled in Eden, a suburb of Buffalo, where he held a number of positions including Captain of the steamer "McPherson" on Conesus Lake, one of New York's finger lakes east of Buffalo and south of Rochester. The McPherson had been built by "Colonel" James A. McPherson of Avon, New York, who had commanded Co. G of the 16th New York Cavalry.[101]

Between 1884 and 1891, Keays' health deteriorated—rheumatism, inflammation of his nasal passages, piles, and rectal fistulas—mostly the result of his Civil War service. In 1890 his doctor described him as having "yellow eyes and skin and looking emaciated." At the time, the family was living on White's Corner's Road just south of Buffalo (today's suburb of South Park). He was granted full disability in 1891.[102]

His health improved, and from 1895 through at least 1900 he was working in the real estate business. In 1905, William, now age 76, and Emily, age 57, were living in Chautauqua, but by 1910 they were back in Eden. That year, Emily D. Horton Keays died and was buried at the Forest Lawn Cemetery in Buffalo.[103]

On May 5, 1911, William J. Keays, occupation "merchant," was admitted to the Bath Branch National Home for Disabled Volunteer Soldiers, in Bath, Steuben County, New York, with cardiac hypertension. He was discharged on November 10, 1911, and returned to Buffalo. His son, Reginald, living in New Palz, New York, was listed as his nearest relative.[104]

In 1913, Keays entered Sisters' Hospital on Main Street in Buffalo. He died in Buffalo on April 24, 1914, from kidney failure brought on by "chronic interstitial nephritis." He was buried beside his wife in Forest Lawn Cemetery.

Lieutenant Charles Moore

There is limited information on the postwar life of the young staff officer who stood watch over President Lincoln's bier and wrote so eloquently of it to his mother. Apparently, however, it was not a happy one. He was dead of a self-inflicted gunshot wound at the age of 35.

After he was mustered out of the Federal service, Moore returned to New York and found a job as a clerk with the Peck and Hillman life insurance agency in Troy. He then opened an insurance office in partnership with A. G. Peck. At some point afterwards, he opened a real estate brokerage in partnership with another Troy businessman, Lansing Smith. The two partners had "a very successful business," and Moore "speculated considerably," most successfully in West Troy.[105]

In 1870 he was still single and living in a boarding house in Troy, where he was employed as a "life insurance agent" for J. McKillopp & Co. Two years later, he was working in Troy as a real estate agent and "commissioner of deeds."[106] By 1874, however, he had relocated to New York City and was working on his own as a real estate and insurance broker. Apparently his business was not doing well. In November he wrote his mother explaining he could not return home for Thanksgiving because "business is not so rushing, but so mighty slow that I cannot afford the time or lose the chance of some of the little pickings."[107]

In 1875, he became the agent for McKillopp & Co. Commercial Agency, which was associated with McKillop & Sprague of New York City and specialized in "the collection of claims."[108] Moore then "leased the State of Connecticut" from the McKillopp Agency "with the intention of establishing offices in all the large cities" and building the commercial agency business in the state "on a more elaborate scale than ever before attempted." While in Connecticut a few months before his death, he contracted "miasmatic fever," (thought to be caused by exposure to contaminated water, foul air or poor hygienic conditions) a condition "from which he has since been a great sufferer." The *New York Tribune* speculated that "fears of financial ruin" were the cause of his suicide.[109]

The local paper agreed that he probably became despondent over the likelihood that his new venture would prove "a bad investment and cause a serious loss," and "his shattered health would not bear the strain." It opined that Moore could well have endured his own misfortunes, but the "possibility of causing loss or embarrassment to friends whom he had induced to invest in the project, caused him great suffering" and in the end contributed to "mental derangement."[110]

Following his suicide, Moore's body was brought back to Plattsburgh from Troy, and his funeral was held at the family's "old homestead" at the corner of Peru and Bridge Streets, on November 30, 1877. He was buried in Plattsburgh's Riverside Cemetery.[111] In death he was described as:

> ... a young man of excellent character. He served faithfully and with honor in the Union army during the late war. He was highly esteemed for his many estimable

qualities of head and heart. He was an earnest worker, and recognized integrity as a guiding principle. He loved life and it was his aim to make it useful. In his right mind Charles F. Moore would never have taken his own life.[112]

Lieutenant (Regimental Commissary) Albert B. Wilbur

Returning to New Haven after he was mustered out, Albert married Sophie Morgan on October 18, 1865. The couple moved to Port Jervis, New York—on the Delaware River in Orange County—where he first taught at a "select school," and then opened a "Classical and Commercial Day School for Ladies and Gentlemen" in November 1866. In April 1867, he established the "Mountain Home Institute for Young Ladies and Gentlemen." He closed this school in December 1870 and became Superintendent of Public Schools in Port Jervis in January 1871.[113]

In December 1883, Albert, now 49, resigned his position in Port Jervis. He and Sophie, now 45, left the following month for France, "for her health," and returned in August. They spent the next year in Florida, New Mexico, and "elsewhere," and subsequently moved to Middletown, New York, where he became Superintendent of Schools in September 1886. He noted in his Yale biography that he found "considerable satisfaction" in education but only "a little bread and butter."[114]

Wilbur resigned as school superintendent in July 1891 and, according to his biography, "occupied himself with private interests in the west." In 1900, he and Sophie were still in Middletown—and childless—where he was working as a real estate agent.[115]

Sophie Wilbur died on May 17, 1911, at the age of 72. She was buried in the Wilbur family plot in Amenia, New York, northwest of Poughkeepsie. Albert, now 75, was still working in real estate in Middletown and continued to do so at least through 1916. His sister, Sarah, was living with him in 1920. Albert died on June 18, 1926, and was buried in the family plot, along with Sophie, in Amenia.[116]

Private George Bunn

Born in New York City around 1850 and raised in Utica, Bunn enlisted on July 6, 1863, at Rochester and was mustered in as a bugler in Co. G the following month. Official records list his age as 18, but newspaper accounts maintain he was 15 at the time. He deserted on June 20, 1864, but later (the date not specified) returned to the regiment and was transferred to the Third New York Provisional Cavalry in August 1865.[117]

Following the war, Bunn served in the Navy's Pacific Squadron for three years aboard the USS *Pensacola*, a "screw steamer" that had patrolled the Gulf of Mexico off Mississippi during the war. Returning to Utica, he established a sign painting business "now and again, in desultory fashion, painting maritime pictures, which he sold among his acquaintances."[118]

George remained in Utica as a sign painter and artist until late 1886 or early 1887, when he moved to Hartford, Connecticut, taking up residence as an artist. The following year, he left for Europe, apparently under sponsorship of a Hartford art dealer. Going first to Brussels, he eventually settled in Antwerp, "where he found, along the docks and canals, the class of subjects that suited his talent."[119]

Bunn met his ultimate downfall, "a young servant girl" named Anna Hoffman at his rooming house in Antwerp. Apparently he was smitten with the housemaid, but she spurned his advances and "eventually left the house." In June 1893, learning that Anna had become engaged to a young German man named Boutman, Bunn "forced his way into a house in the Rue Escant, where the Hoffman girl was staying, and shot her dead." In August, he was convicted of murder and sentenced to 15 years at hard labor.[120]

George apparently survived only a few years of his prison term, although his paintings continued to sell in Europe and the United States. Announcing an exhibition and sale in London in 1902, the Grave Galleries identified the artist as "the late George Bunn," and that same year the *New York Times* reported that he had died "about five years ago."[121]

Bunn's paintings continue to appear on the U.S. market occasionally, fetching between a few hundred to over a thousand dollars.

The Kenelty Brothers

Privates Edward, James and John Kenelty remained with Co. A through the end of the war and were mustered out together on May 31, 1865. All three initially returned home to Saranac, New York. James and John lived rather ordinary lives as farmers and laborers. Edward gained some prominence as a local official.

James returned to farming and married after the war. In 1870 he and his wife, Maria, were living in Saranac, where his farm was valued at $500. His brothers John and Hubert, both day laborers, were living with them. They had no children. James died on November 14, 1874, and was buried in Assumption of Mary Cemetery in nearby Redford, New York.[122]

John, whose occupation at the time he enlisted was identified as

Nine—Postwar Fortunes and Failures

"laborer," returned to manual labor after the war. By June 1875, he may have moved to Brooklyn's Ward 5 where a John "Kennelty," age 28 (the Kenelty name was sometimes spelled as "Kennelty" or "Kenalty"), was a "boarder" with a James and Bridget Kennelty, probably family relatives. John Kennelty continued to live at various addresses in Brooklyn, working as a laborer, in 1885, 1888, and 1889. John "Kenelty," of the 16th New York Cavalry, died on March 1, 1891, and was buried in Brooklyn's Cypress Hills National Cemetery.[123]

Edward Kenelty had married the former Ann Pickett on December 8, 1859, and their first two children, Richard and Jane, were born before the war. They would eventually have nine children. Ann was the daughter of a Saranac farmer and sister of Edmund J. Pickett, who also had enlisted in Co. A with the Kenelty brothers in September 1864.[124]

In 1880, still living in Saranac, now with six children, Edward "took charge of the Saranac Plank Road." A local newspaper expected to find "a good smooth road" and believed Kenelty knew "how to make it so." Six years later, Edward still had an association with the plank road, serving on the Board of Inspectors of the Saranac Plank Road Company.[125]

By 1900, Edward and Anne, with five children ages 16 to 33 still living with them, had moved to the town of Dannemora, about 16 miles from Saranac, where they ran a boarding house with eight boarders. There, Edward's wife died on November 30, 1906, at the age of 63.[126]

A year later, Edward was elected "Overseer of the Poor" for the town of Dannemora, reporting to the Clinton County Superintendent of the Poor and the State Board of Charities. He would hold this position until his death. While serving in this position, he continued to run his boarding house. In 1910, three of his children still lived with him.[127]

On February 10, 1917, Edward Kennelty, "one of the best known and most popular residents" of Dannemora, died at the age of 77. According to his obituary, Edward had been "rugged and well preserved," but his Civil War service eventually "began to tell upon him and he failed in health rapidly." He was buried on February 12, 1917, in St. Joseph's Cemetery in Dannemora.[128]

Private Edmund J. Pickett

Edward's brother-in-law, who was born in Saranac and worked on the family farm and in log-driving and lumbering until he enlisted at the age of 19, returned to Saranac and initially returned to the lumber business, riding and guiding logs downstream, until 1867 when he opened a mercantile business at Pickett's Corners in Saranac. Pickett was active in the Grand Army of the Republic (GAR), serving as post commander in Saranac for ten years, and in the Clinton County Veterans' Association. Also active in politics, he served on the county board, was appointed Postmaster at Saranac during the Cleveland administration, and was elected to the State Assembly in 1897 for the first of two terms, serving on the Excise, State Prisons and Fisheries and Games Committees.

Toward the end of his life, Pickett suffered an attack of gangrene and both legs had to be amputated. Apparently, his affliction did not slow him down: "His abounding good nature and power of will refused to succumb even to this great misfortune." In the end, however, it probably contributed to his fast decline in 1908. He died on September 10, 1908, at the age of 64 and was buried in Cadyville.[129]

Private George Westinghouse

Westinghouse, of Co. M, had enlisted in April 1863 to serve for three years and was appointed Corporal on October 19. He had previously volunteered in the 12th New York State Militia (30 days).[130] Following the death in combat of his brother, Albert, in late 1864, George obtained a transfer to the U.S. Navy and was commissioned as an engineering officer aboard the newly built USS *Muscoota*, which entered service in January 1865. That May, his ship was ordered south to Key West as part of an effort to block Jefferson Davis from escaping the country.[131]

Upon his release from the Navy, George, who had invented a rotary engine at the age of 15, enrolled at Union College near his parent's home in Schenectady. He quickly lost interest in its liberal arts curriculum and dropped out during his first term. In October 1865, at the age of 19, he obtained his first patent—for the rotary engine he had designed before the war. He went on to found the Westinghouse Air Brake Company in 1869 and Westinghouse Electric Company in 1886. In 1911, he received the Edison Medal from the American Institute of Electrical Engineers.[132]

Westinghouse was afflicted with a heart ailment in 1913 and semi-retired to an estate in Lenox, Massachusetts. He died on March 12, 1914, "in a chair beside a blueprint of yet another invention—an electric wheelchair—in a New York hotel." He was buried in Arlington National Cemetery.[133]

Appendix A
Roster of Officers and Sergeants

This roster was extracted from *New York in the War of the Rebellion, 1861 to 1865*, compiled by Frederick Phisterer, Third Edition, Volume 2 (Albany: J. B. Lyon Company, State Printers, 1912), 1010–1042, and from *A Record of the Commissioned Officers, Non-Commissioned Officers and Privates of the Regiments Which Were Organized in the State of New York and Called into the Service of the United States to Assist in Suppressing the Rebellion, Vol. I,* Adjutant General's Office, State of New York (Albany: Comstock & Cassidy, Printers, 1864), 397–423. The full roster compiled by Phisterer is available online at the New York State Military Museum website at http://dmna.ny.gov. The Adjutant General's Report is available on line at the Fold3 website at www.fold3.com/image/#312064820.

The Adjutant General's report reflects those officers and men on the rolls of the 16th New York Cavalry as of each company's official muster date. Phisterer's list, on the other hand, included all officers and men enlisted, enrolled and mustered in during the regiment's existence.

Unless noted otherwise, all officers and men were transferred from the 16th New York Cavalry Regiment to the 3rd New York Provisional Cavalry on August 17, 1865.

Company A Roster

Name & Rank	Enrolled at	Date of Rank	Remarks
CAPTAIN			
Mooney, Nathan H.	Albany	Apr 24, '63	Enlisted as Pvt., 96th New York Infantry, Jan '62. Promoted to 1st Lt. after 3 months. Disability discharge Sep '62. Mustered as Capt., Co. A, Apr 24, '63. Captured Apr 16, '64; paroled Mar '65. Discharged May 15, '65.
1ST LIEUTENANTS			
Anderson, George H.	Albany	May 20, '63	Enlisted as Pvt., 118th New York Infantry Aug 13, '62. Discharged

183

Name & Rank	Enrolled at	Date of Rank	Remarks
			May 12,'63. Mustered as 1st Lt., Co. A, May 20,'63. Resigned Jan 11,'64.
Pettit, John	Syracuse	July 22,'63	Enlisted Dec 16,'62; mustered as Sgt., Co. A, Feb 17,'63; 1st Sgt., Apr 8,'63; 1st Lt., July 22,'63. Mustered out Oct 14,'63 at Albany; not commissioned.
Keays, William J.	Albany	May 29,'63	Mustered in June 1,'63 as 1st Lt., Co. B. Dismissed Oct 10,'63 & restored to duty Dec 31,'63. Transferred to Co. A Jan 13,'64. Mustered as Capt., Co. G, Apr 10,'65.

2ND LIEUTENANTS

Name & Rank	Enrolled at	Date of Rank	Remarks
Moore, Charles F.	Plattsburgh	June 19,'63	Mustered in May 15,'61 as QM-Sergeant, 16th New York Infantry; discharged on disability Feb '62. Mustered in June 19,'63 as 2nd Lt., Co. A; 1st Lt., Co. C, Sep 1,'64.
Gault, Olney R.	Syracuse	June 16,'64	Enlisted Jan 22,'63 & mustered in as Sgt., Co. A, Apr 8,'63. 1st Sgt. June 19,'63. Mustered as 2nd Lt. Dec 23,'64.
Mueller, Gabriel A.	Buffalo	May 11,'65	Enlisted July 31,'63 & mustered in as Pvt., Co. E Aug 13,'63. Appointed QM-Sgt. Aug 14,'63; Regimental Commissary Sgt. July 26,'64. Mustered as 2nd Lt., Co. A, Apr 22,'65.

SERGEANTS

Name & Rank	Enrolled at	Date of Rank	Remarks
Gault, Olney R.			See Above.
Ferguson, William H.			See Co. E.
O'Brien, John	New York	June 19,'63	Enlisted Mar 11,'63 & mustered as Pvt., Co. A, Apr 9,'63. QM-Sgt. June 19,'63.
Carey, Henry	Plattsburgh	June 19,'63	Enlisted May 27,'63 & mustered as Commissary Sgt., Co. A, June 19,'63. Deserted Nov 26,'63 at Vienna, Va.

Roster of Officers and Sergeants 185

Name & Rank	Enrolled at	Date of Rank	Remarks
Smith, James H.	Syracuse	Feb 7, '63	Enlisted Jan 2, '63 & mustered as Pvt., Co. A, Feb 17, '63. Appointed Sgt. Apr 8, '63. Deserted June 26, '63 at South Amboy, N.J.
Bardell, Francis A.	New York	Apr 9, '63	Enlisted Mar 6, '63 & mustered as Pvt. Co. A. Appointed Sgt., no date stated; Sgt-Maj. Apr 13, '63. Mustered in as 2nd Lt. Jan 16, '64; 1st Lt. Co. I, Feb 8, '64. Dismissed Sep 20, '64.
Millard, Elvin L.	Plattsburgh	Apr 8, '63	Enlisted Mar 26, '63 & mustered as Sgt., Co. A, Apr 8, '63. Sentenced by general court-martial to forfeit $10 of his monthly pay for one year. AWOL Aug 17, '65.
Sample, Robert	Plattsburgh	Apr 8, '63	Enlisted Apr 7, '63 & mustered as Pvt, Co. A. Appointed Sgt. June 19, '63. Deserted Mar 25, '64 at Fairfax Court House, Va.
Bedlinger, William	Plattsburgh	Mar 12, '63	Enlisted Feb. 17, '63 & mustered in as Sgt., Co. A, Mar 12, '63. Deserted as Pvt. May 3, '63, no place stated.
Gadbaw, John	Massena	Sep 7, '64	Enlisted May 7, '63 & mustered in as Pvt., Co. A, May 18, '63. Appointed Cpl. Apr 30, '64; Sgt. Sep 7, '64. Also borne as Gadbow & Gadbeau.
Healy, James	New York	—	Enlisted Feb 3, '63 & mustered in as Pvt., Co. A, Apr 9, '63. Appointed Cpl. Feb 26, '64; QM-Sgt. date not stated. Also borne as Haley.
McAvoy, John	Plattsburgh	—	Enlisted Apr 15, '63 & mustered in as Pvt., Co. A, Apr 9, '63. Appointed Cpl. June 19, '63; Commissary Sgt., date not stated. Mustered out Aug 17, '65 at Washington. Prior service in Co. H, 60th New York Volunteers.
McGinnis, Joseph	Plattsburgh	May 21, '64	Enlisted Apr 21, '63 & mustered in as Pvt. Co. A, Apr 22, '63. Appointed Cpl. June 19, '63; Sgt. May 21, '64. Wounded by guerrillas while on picket, date not

Appendix A

Name & Rank	Enrolled at	Date of Rank	Remarks
Reynolds, Harmon	Plattsburgh	Sep 7, '64	shown. Died Sep 2, '64 in Brigade Hospital, Falls Church, Va. Enlisted Mar 21, '63 & mustered in as Pvt. Co. A, Apr 8, 63. Appointed Sgt. Sep 7, '64.

Company B Roster

Name & Rank	Enrolled at	Date of Rank	Remarks
CAPTAIN			
Doherty, Edward P.	Albany	Apr 3, '65	Enrolled Aug 17, '63 & mustered in as 1st Lt., Co. L, Sep 5, '63; transferred to Co. I, Dec 8, '63; to Co. H, Jan 22, '64; to Co. L, Oct 5, '64. Mustered in as Capt. Co. B, Apr 3, '65.
Mickles, Phil D.	Washington	Dec 15, '63	Enlisted as Corporal, 1st New York Cavalry, July '61; promoted to Sgt.; promoted to 2nd Lt., Oct '62. Resigned May '63. Mustered in as Capt., Co. B, 16th New York Cavalry, Jan 6, '64; resigned Mar 31, '65.
Nicholson, John			See Field & Staff
1ST LIEUTENANTS			
Dow, Henry G.	Washington	June 16, '64	Sgt., Co. H, 3rd New York Cavalry, Aug 20, '61; promoted to 1st Sgt., Jan 1, '63; discharged July 14, '63. Enrolled Nov 16, '63 & mustered in as 2nd Lt. Co. D, Nov 16, '63; 1st Lt. Sep 1, '64; transferred to Co. K, Sep 21, '64; to Co. B, Jan 11, 65. Discharged Jan 31, '65 per S.O. No. 49, War Dept.
Kavanaugh, William J.	Albany	Sep 16, '63	Enrolled Sep 16, '63; mustered in as 1st Lt., Co. M, to serve 3 years; transferred to Co. B, Apr 1, '64; to Co. H, Oct 23, '64; Co. M, Nov 21, '64.
Keays, William J.			See Company A
Nicholson, John			See Field & Staff

Roster of Officers and Sergeants

Name & Rank	Enrolled at	Date of Rank	Remarks
2ND LIEUTENANTS			
Dean, Herman B.	Buffalo	—	Mustered in as 1st Sgt., Co. A, 50th New York Engineers, Sep 18, '61; discharged Feb 10, '63. Enrolled in 16th New York Cavalry May 14, '63 & mustered in as Pvt., Co. B, June 19, '63. Reported on rolls for Aug 31, '63 as 2nd Lt. Deserted Sep 15, '63. Enrolled & mustered in Feb 26, '64 at Brooklyn in 1st New York Engineers under name of Henry B. Drew. Recognized as deserter from 16th NY Cavalry Apr 21, '64; transferred back to 1st NY Engineers by sentence of court-martial, Oct 22, '64. Mustered out June 30, '65.
Larned, Henry S.	Buffalo	Aug 20, '63	Mustered as Pvt., 49th New York Infantry, Dec 2, '61 (3 years); discharged Aug 15, '63. Enrolled Aug 20, '63 & mustered in as 2nd Lt. Co. B. Fractured leg at Fairfax Court House, date not reported. Dishonorably dismissed per War Dept. S.O. No. 327, Oct 1, '64.
Hoover, John Frank	Buffalo	Nov 15, '64	Enrolled May 25, '63 & mustered in as Commissary Sgt. June 19, '63. Reduced to ranks Aug 11, '64. Mustered as 2nd Lt., Co. B, Feb 12, '65.
SERGEANTS			
Baldwin, Thomas C.	Buffalo	Nov 1, '63	Enlisted May 23, '63 & mustered in as Pvt., Co. B, May 25, '63. Appointed QM-Sgt. Nov 1, '63; Regimental QM-Sgt., Nov 4, '63. Reduced & transferred to Co. B Nov 26, '63. Discharged Apr 21, '64 for the purpose of enlisting in the U.S. Navy.
Bell, James	Buffalo	June 19, '63	Enlisted Apr 6, '63 & mustered in as Pvt., Co. B. Appointed Sgt.

Name & Rank	Enrolled at	Date of Rank	Remarks
Clarke, James	Buffalo	June 19,'63	June 19,'63. Deserted June 28,'63 at Washington. Enlisted May 18,'63 & mustered in as Pvt., Co. B, May 20,'63. Appointed Sgt. June 19,'63. Deserted June 21,'64 at Annandale, Va.
Cooper, James	Buffalo	Apr 30,'64	Enlisted & mustered in as Pvt., Co. B, May 12,'63. Appointed Sgt. Apr 30,'64. Deserted while on pass to Washington Oct 21, '64. Returned Dec 11,'64. Deserted again Aug 12,'65.
Cunningham, Henry	Buffalo	Aug 15,'64	Enlisted May 23,'63 & mustered in as Pvt., Co. B, May 28,'63. Appointed Cpl. Apr 30,'64; Sgt. to date Aug 15,'64.
De Carroll, Henry	Buffalo	June 19,'63	Enlisted Apr 15,'63 & mustered in as Pvt., Co. B. Appointed Commissary Sgt. June 19,'63; deserted July 5,'63 & sentenced by court-martial to forfeit all pay & allowances due & confined for 12 months & dishonorably discharged. Committed to Old Capitol Prison, Feb 3,'65. Discharged Mar 27,'65 by order of the President.
Drake, Humphrey W.	Buffalo	—	Enlisted May 14,'63 & mustered in as Pvt., Co. B, May 29,'63. Appointed Cpl. June 19,'63; sergeant, date not stated. Reduced July 24,'64.
Goulding, John			See Co. C.
Greggs, John	Buffalo	Apr 30,'64	Enlisted June 5,'63 & mustered in as Pvt. Co. B, June 19,'63. Appointed Cpl. Feb 28,'64; Sgt. Apr 30,'64. Captured while on scout July 24,'64. Reduced, no date stated. Also borne as Griggs.
Hemenway, Danforth G.	Buffalo	June 19,'63	Enlisted Apr 25,'63 & mustered in as Pvt., Co. B. Appointed Sgt. June 19,'63. Killed "by guerrillas" Oct 1,'63 at Lewinsville, Va.

Roster of Officers and Sergeants

Name & Rank	Enrolled at	Date of Rank	Remarks
Hickey, Patrick	Buffalo	June 19, '63	Enlisted May 21, '63 & mustered in as Pvt., Co. B May 22. Appointed 1st Sgt. June 19, '63. Mustered out with detachment Aug 17, '65.
Kelley, John N.	Buffalo	Jan 1, '65	Enlisted & mustered in as Pvt., Co. B, May 1, '63. Appointed Cpl. Date not stated; Sgt. Jan 1, '65. Mustered out with detachment Aug 17, '65 at Washington.
Lathrop, Charles E.	Buffalo	June 19, '63	Enlisted Apr 11, '63 & mustered in as Pvt., Co. B. Appointed QM-Sgt. June 19, '63; reduced Oct 8, '63. Reported AWOL Aug 17, '65.
Lee, James	Buffalo	June 19, '63	Enlisted May 6, '63 & mustered in as Sgt., Co. B, June 19, '63. Reduced Apr 6, '64.
Mackin, Thomas A.	Buffalo	Sep 13, '64	Enlisted & mustered in as Pvt. Co. B, May 13, '63. Appointed Sgt. Sep 13, '64. Mustered out with detachment Aug 17, '65 at Washington.
Nye, Sidney	Buffalo	Apr 30, '64	Enlisted Apr 30, '63 & mustered in as Pvt., Co. B, May 1, '63. Appointed Cpl. Date not stated; Sgt. Apr 30, '64. Died of disease, July 21, '64, at hospital, Alexandria, Va.
Stark, Henry	Buffalo	Jan 1, '65	Enlisted & mustered in as Pvt. Co. B, May 9, '63. Appointed Cpl. Aug 15, '64, to date Aug 1, '64; Sgt., to date Jan 1, '65. Reduced to the ranks June 11, '65.
Stigler, Stephen	Buffalo	Apr 23, '64	Enlisted June 5, '63 & mustered in as Pvt., Co. B, June 23, '63. Appointed QM-Sgt., rank from Apr 23, '64. Reduced Jan 1, '65. Died of disease May 22, '65, in Regimental Hospital, Lincoln Barracks.
Torrence, Edwin H.	Buffalo	—	Enlisted May 19, '63 & mustered in as Pvt., Co. B, June 8, '63. Appointed Cpl. June 19, '63; Commissary Sgt., no date stated.

Appendix A

Name & Rank	Enrolled at	Date of Rank	Remarks
Wright, Frederick	Buffalo	June 19, '63	Mustered out with detachment Aug 17, '65 at Washington. Enlisted May 26, '63 & mustered in as Pvt., Co. B, June 8, '63. Appointed Sgt. June 19, '63; reduced to ranks Jan 25, '64. Wounded & captured Sep 19, '64 at Culpeper Court House, Va. Released Oct 8, '64 at Varina, Va. Appointed Sgt. to date July 15, '64.

Company C Roster

Name & Rank	Enrolled at	Date of Rank	Remarks
CAPTAIN			
Schneider, Joseph	Buffalo	May 25, '63	Mustered in as Capt., Co. C, June 2, '63. Mustered out Aug 17, '65.
1ST LIEUTENANTS			
Baker, Francis M.	Albany	May 2, '63	Enrolled June 2, '63 & mustered in as 1st Lt., Co. C, June 2, '63. Promoted to Capt., Co. E, Jan 27, '64.
Windsbecker, Julius	Albany	May 25, '63	Enrolled May 25, '63 & mustered in as 2nd Lt., Co. C, May 25, '63. Promoted to 1st Lt. Jan 21, '64; Capt. Co. F, Aug 1, '64. Captured at Flint Hill, Va., Nov 27, '64; rejoined company Apr 6, '65.
2ND LIEUTENANTS			
Goulding, John	Buffalo		Enlisted Apr 7, '63 & mustered in as Pvt., Co. B. Appointed Sgt. May 5, '63; regimental QM-Sgt., June 13, '63. Returned to company Nov 4, '63; mustered in as 2nd Lt., Co. C, Dec 27, '64. Resigned June 26, '65.
Moore, Charles F.			See Company A
SERGEANTS			
Beerworth, Phillipp A.	Buffalo	May 5, '63	Enlisted & mustered in as 1st Sgt., Co. C May 1, '63. Mustered

Roster of Officers and Sergeants

Name & Rank	Enrolled at	Date of Rank	Remarks
			out as Commissary Sgt. Aug 17, '65.
Collingwood, Harry	Buffalo	May 30, '63	Enlisted & mustered in as Pvt., Co. E, 21st New York Infantry, Mar 29, '62. Deserted Aug 6, '62 at Fredericksburg, Va. Returned in arrest Apr 10, '63 & sentenced by general court-martial to lose pay and allowances and to be confined 6 months. Enlisted May 21, '63 & mustered in as Sgt. Co. C, May 30, '63. Captured Aug 8, '64; paroled Feb 20, '65.
Currier, Thomas	Buffalo	Aug 1, '64	Enlisted Apr 11, '63 & mustered in as Pvt., Co. C, Apr 18, 63. Appointed Cpl. Apr 5, '64; Sgt. Aug 1, '64.
Elsasser, George	Buffalo	Oct 1, '64	Enlisted May 16, '63 & mustered in as Pvt., Co. C, Apr 18, '63. Appointed Cpl. Apr 6, '64; Sgt. Oct 1, '64.
Frederick, Louis	Buffalo	May 5, '63	Enlisted May 4, '63 & mustered in as commissary Sgt. May 5, '63. Deserted Apr 1, '64 at Annandale, Va.
Herwill, Daniel	Buffalo	June 19, '63	Enlisted May 12, '63 & mustered in as Pvt., Co. C, May 18, '63. Appointed Sgt. June 19, '63; 1st Sgt. Mar 1, '64. Deserted Mar 26, '65, while on furlough at Buffalo.
Lillick, Michael	Buffalo	Apr 22, '63	Enlisted & mustered in as Sgt. Co. C, Apr 22, '63. Reduced May 27, '64.
Linkelmann, Gustav	Buffalo	May 1, '63	Enlisted Ap. 29, '63 & mustered in as Sgt., Co. C, May 1, '63. Deserted Nov 10, '63 at Alexandria, Va.
Miller, Henry	Buffalo	Apr 26, '63	Enlisted May 7, '61 & mustered in as Pvt. Co. E, 21st New York Infantry May 20, '61. Wounded Sep 17, '62 & discharged for disability Jan 6, '63. Enlisted Apr 20, '63 & mustered in as Sgt. Co. C, 16th New York Cavalry, Apr

Name & Rank	Enrolled at	Date of Rank	Remarks
			26, '63. Appointed 1st Sgt. Apr 1, '65.
Place, Ovet	North Collins	June 19, '63	Enlisted May 18, '63 & mustered in as QM-Sgt., Co. C, June 19, '63. Deserted Sep 20, '63 at Buffalo.
Schamberger, Adam	Buffalo	May 1, '64	Enlisted May 25, '63 & mustered in as Cpl., Co. C, June 19, '63. Appointed Sgt. Oct 1, '64. Prior service in Co. K, 21st New York State Volunteers.
Seckler, James	Buffalo	May 13, '63	Enlisted May 3, '63 & mustered in as Sgt., Co. C, May 13, '63. Reduced on consolidation July 15, '63. Appears on list of deserters dated Jan 1, '64. Dishonorably discharged Nov 7, '65 by S.O. No. 42, District of Southern New York.
Waring, Thomas	Buffalo	Apr 5, '64	Enlisted & mustered in as Cpl., Co. C, Mar 21, '63. Appointed Sgt. Apr 5, '64.
Webber, John	New York	May 1, '64	Enlisted Jan 5, '63 & mustered in as Cpl. Co. C, June 19, '63. Appointed QM-Sgt. May 1, '64.

Company D Roster

Name & Rank	Enrolled at	Date of Rank	Remarks
CAPTAIN			
Washburn, A. Livingston	Albany	June 13, '63	Enrolled & mustered in as Capt., Co. D, June 15, '63. Dismissed dishonorably for conduct unbecoming an officer and gentleman Oct 6, '64.
Cameron, William A.	Washington	Nov 28, '64	Enrolled & mustered in as Capt. Co. D, Dec 6, '64. Mustered out Aug 17, '65.
1ST LIEUTENANTS			
Grosvenor, George H.	Albany	July 20, '63	Enrolled June 1, '63 & mustered in as 1st Lt., Co. D, June 19, '63. Transferred to Co. F, Feb 14, '64. Dismissed Sep 27, '64, "for conduct unbecoming an officer and gentleman, breach of arrest, and

Roster of Officers and Sergeants

Name & Rank	Enrolled at	Date of Rank	Remarks
Dow, Henry G.			obtaining the countersign by surreptitious means." See Co. B
Slorah, Andrew	Ogdenburgh	Dec 1, '64	Enlisted July 15, '63 & mustered in as Pvt., Co. F. Appointed QM-Sgt. Aug 13, '63; 1st Sgt. Mar 22, '64. Mustered in as 2nd Lt., Co. I, Sep 1, '64; 1st Lt. Co. D, Jan 10, '65.

2ND LIEUTENANT

Name & Rank	Enrolled at	Date of Rank	Remarks
Dow, Henry G.			See Co. B

SERGEANTS

Name & Rank	Enrolled at	Date of Rank	Remarks
Armstrong, Samuel	Buffalo	June 19, '63	Enlisted Apr 25, '63 & mustered as Sgt. Co. D, June 19, '63. Discharged for disability Jan 27, '64, at Convalescent Camp, Va.
Chateaubriand, Gustave	Buffalo	—	Enlisted Jun. 16, '63 & mustered in as Pvt., Co. D, Jun. 19, '63. Appointed QM-Sgt., date not stated.
Davis, Norman	Buffalo	—	Enlisted Apr 28, '63 & mustered in as Pvt., Co. D, May 5, '63. Appointed Cpl. June 19, '63; Sgt., date not stated. Reduced Feb 28, '64.
Hoover, John F.	Buffalo	June 19, '63	Enrolled May 25, '63 & mustered in as Commissary Sgt., Co. D, June 19, '63. Reduced to ranks Aug 11, '64. Mustered in as 2nd Lt. Co. B, Feb 12, '65.
Lott, Amos B.	Buffalo	May 29, '63	Enlisted May 29, '63 & mustered in as Pvt., Co. D, June 8, '63. Appointed Commissary Sgt., to date May 29, '63. Died of disease, as Sgt., Dec 22, '63, at Fort Ethan Allen, Va.
Marsh, Robert	Buffalo	June 19, '63	Enlisted May 27, '63 & mustered in as Pvt., Co. D, May 30, '63. Appointed 1st Sgt., June 19, '63. Deserted June 24, '63, location not stated.

Appendix A

Name & Rank	Enrolled at	Date of Rank	Remarks
McNaughton, Peter	Buffalo	June 19, '63	Enlisted Mar 30, '63 & mustered in as Pvt., Co. D, May 25, '63. Appointed Sgt. June 19, '63; 1st Sgt. July 2, '64. Mustered in as 2nd Lt., Co. H., Feb 12, '65.
Meredith, H. J.	Buffalo	June 19, '63	Enlisted Apr 22, '63 & mustered in as Pvt. Co. D, May 18, '63. Appointed Sgt. June 19, '63; reduced date not shown.
O'Mais, Charles	Buffalo	Feb 15, '65	Enlisted June 16, '63 & mustered in as Pvt., Co. D, June 19, '63. Appointed Cpl. July 25, '64; Sgt. Feb 15, '65.
Platt, John F.	Buffalo	—	Enlisted May 29, '63 & mustered in as Cpl., Co. D, June 19, '63. Appointed QM-Sgt., no date stated; 1st Sgt. Feb 15, '65. Mustered out Aug 17, '65 at Washington.
Pritchard, S. M.	Buffalo	June 19, '63	Enlisted Apr 27, '63 & mustered in as Pvt., Co. D, May 6, '63. Appointed Sgt. June 19, '63. Deserted June 30, '63 at Washington.
Rankin, James A.	Buffalo	Nov 28, '64	Enlisted Apr 28, '63 & mustered in as Pvt., Co. D, May 5, '63. Appointed Cpl., to date Apr 28, '63; Sgt. Nov 28, '64.
Reeves, Charles E.	Buffalo	June 19, '63	Enlisted May 12, '63 & mustered in as QM-Sgt. June 19, '63. Discharged as Sgt. Oct. 5, '64, for promotion to 2nd Lt., Co. M, 2nd Mounted Rifles.
Steffen, Henry	Buffalo	Nov 16, '64	Enlisted May 7, '63 & mustered in as Pvt., Co. D, May 8, '63. Appointed Sgt. Nov 16, '64; reduced to ranks, date not stated. Appointed Cpl., May 7, '65. Mustered out as Sgt., June 17, '65 at Point Lookout Hospital, Md.
Taylor, James	Buffalo	June 19, '63	Enlisted Apr 17, '63 & mustered in as Pvt. Co. D, May 18, '63. Appointed Sgt. June 19, '63; reduced July 2, '64. Deserted Sep 26, '64 at Ft. Buffalo, Va.

Roster of Officers and Sergeants

Name & Rank	Enrolled at	Date of Rank	Remarks
Tracy, Alfred	Buffalo	Jan 1, '64	Enlisted May 18, '63 & mustered in as Pvt., Co. D, May 25, '63. Appointed Cpl. June 19, '63; Sgt. Jan 1, '64. Mustered out as Commissary Sgt., Aug 17, '65. Also borne as Tracy, Alfred S.
Young, George	Buffalo	July 25, '64	Enlisted June 6, '63 & mustered in as Pvt., Co. D, June 19, '63. Appointed Cpl., to date June 6, '64; Sgt. July 25, '64.

Company E Roster

Name & Rank	Enrolled at	Date of Rank	Remarks
CAPTAINS			
Morse, Charles E.	Buffalo	Aug 1, '63	Enrolled Sep 23, '61 & mustered in as Capt. Co. I, 100th New York Infantry, Jan 7, '62. Discharged Nov 15, '62. Enlisted & mustered in as Pvt. Co. B, 16th New York Cavalry, May 6, '63. Mustered in as Capt., Co. E, Aug 1, '63. Resigned Feb 8, '64.
Baker, Francis M.			See Co. C
1ST LIEUTENANTS			
Wells, William H.	—	July 31, '63	Enrolled at Albany & mustered in as 2nd Lt., Co. B, 100th New York Infantry, Sep 13, '62. Dismissed No. 15, '62; dismissal revoked June 17, '63. Enlisted as Pvt. Co. D, 74th Rgt. (Buffalo) N.G.N.Y. Mustered in as 1st Lt, Co. E, 16th Cavalry, Aug 5, '63. Discharged Jan 21, '64.
Hildebrand, Henry A.	—	Oct 1, '63	Enlisted & mustered in as 1st Sgt., Co. B, 41st New York Infantry, June 6, '61. Promoted Sgt.-Maj. Sep 1, '61. Discharged for disability Mar 7, '62, near Hunter's Chapel, Va. Mustered in as 2nd Lt., Co. I, 16th Cavalry, Sep 22, '63. Mustered as 1st Lt., Co. E, Feb 4, '64. Resigned Aug 25, '64.

Appendix A

Name & Rank	Enrolled at	Date of Rank	Remarks
French, George F.	—	Jan. 16, '65	Mustered as Pvt., 1st Maryland Cavalry, Sep. 3, '61. Discharged Apr. 18, '64 & mustered in as 2nd Lt., Co. E, 16th Cavalry, May 30, '64. Transferred to Co. K, Aug. 11, '64. Captured at Culpeper Court House, Va., Sep. 19, '64 & sent to Danville Prison, Va. Paroled Feb. 22, '65 at James River & mustered in as 1st Lt., Co. E, Apr. 13, '65.

2ND LIEUTENANTS

Name & Rank	Enrolled at	Date of Rank	Remarks
Ferguson, William H.	Mooers	Jan 16, '65	Enlisted May 17, '63 & mustered in as Cpl., Co. A, June 19, '63. Appointed Sgt., date not stated. Mustered in as 2nd Lt., Co. E, Apr 14, '65. Resigned May 31, '65.
French, George F.			See above.
Moore, Norman T.	Buffalo	Aug 1, '63	Enlisted Aug 13, '62 & mustered in Aug 18, '62 as Pvt. Co. F, 11th New York Cavalry. Appointed Cpl. Nov 11, '62. Discharged Aug 28, '63 to accept commission in 16th New York Cavalry. Mustered in as 2nd Lt., Co. E, 16th Cavalry Aug 29, '63. Resigned Jan 19, '64.

SERGEANTS

Name & Rank	Enrolled at	Date of Rank	Remarks
Bridges, Lucius L.	Plattsburgh	Aug 12, '63	Enlisted & mustered as Pvt., Co. A, Apr 8, '63. Transferred to Co. E & appointed Commissary Sgt. Aug 12, '63; Regimental Commissary Sgt. Aug 13, '63. Reduced to ranks and assigned to Co. C June 12, '64. Discharged for promotion Aug 1, '64.
Briggs, W. A.	Buffalo	Aug 13, '63	Enlisted June 10, '63 & mustered in as Pvt., Co. E, July 25, '63. Appointed Sgt. Aug 13, '63. Mustered out Aug 17, '65 at Washington.

Roster of Officers and Sergeants

Name & Rank	Enrolled at	Date of Rank	Remarks
Craozia, Benjamin	Buffalo	Aug 13, '63	Enlisted June 24, '63 & mustered in as Pvt., Co. E, July 25, '63. Appointed QM-Sgt. Aug 13, '63. Deserted as Pvt. Nov 28, '63, at Vienna, Va.
Hasenger, Phillip	Plattsburgh	Aug 13, '63	Enlisted Aug 3, '63 & mustered as Sgt., Co. E, Aug 13, '63. Reduced Apr 23, '64. Also borne as Hassenger, Philip.
Lauber, Mathias	Buffalo	Aug 13, '63	Enlisted June 29, '63 & mustered in as Pvt., Co. E, July 25, '63. Appointed Sgt. Aug 13, '63. Reduced July 25, '64. Mustered out June 6, '65 at Washington.
Linsinger, Earnest	Buffalo	Sep '63	Enlisted July 17, '63 & mustered in as Pvt., Co. E, July 30, '63. Appointed Sgt. Sep, '63. Deserted Apr 17, '64 at New York City. Also known as Von Linenger.
Lonkey, Oliver	Massena	May 20, '65	Enlisted June 21, '63 & mustered in as Pvt., Co. E, Aug 13, '63. Appointed Cpl. Apr 23, '64; Sgt. May 20, '65.
Meaden, James C.	Buffalo	Mar 15, '65	Enlisted July 1, '63 & mustered in as Pvt., Co. E, July 25, '63. Appointed QM-Sgt. Mar 15, '65.
Mitchell, Samuel	Buffalo	May 8, '64	Enlisted Dec. 12, 63 & mustered in as Pvt., Co. E, Dec. 18, '63. Appointed Cpl. Apr. 27, 64; Sgt. May 8, '64; 1st Sgt. Dec. 25, '64.
Palmer, David A.	Buffalo	Aug 1, '64	Enlisted July 23, '63 & mustered in as Pvt., Co. E, July 30, '63. Appointed Cpl. Sep 11, '63. Reduced at his own request Feb 29, '64, to join regimental band. Appointed QM-Sgt. Aug 1, '64. Mustered out with detachment, as Sgt., Aug 17, '65 at Washington.
Pratt, Edwin	Buffalo	Oct 6, '64	Enlisted July 1, '63 & mustered in as Pvt., Co. E, July 25, '63. Appointed Cpl. May 8, '64; Sgt. Oct 6, '64. Mustered out with detachment Aug 17, '65, at Washington.

Appendix A

Name & Rank	Enrolled at	Date of Rank	Remarks
Roberts, John	Buffalo	Oct. 6, '64	Enlisted July 16, '63 & mustered in as Pvt., Co. E, July 25, '63. Appointed Cpl. Aug 1, '64; Sgt. Oct 6, '64. Transferred Aug 17, '65, as Commissary Sgt., to Co. D, 3rd New York Provisional Cavalry.
Smith, J.F.	Buffalo	July 25, '63	Enlisted June 25, '63 & mustered in as Sgt., Co. E July 25, '63. Sentenced by general court-martial, for two desertions, fined $60 & $8 per month for balance of enlistment. Confined in General Hospital, Washington. Dishonorably discharged Sep 13, '65. Also borne as Jackson P. Smith.
Sullivan, Felix	Buffalo	Aug 1, '64	Enlisted July 8, '63 & mustered in as Pvt., Co. E, July 25, '63. Appointed Cpl. Apr 27, '64; Sgt. Aug 1, '64. Reduced Oct 5, '64. Again appointed Sgt. Dec 10, '64; QM-Sgt., date not stated. Reduced Mar 15, '65. Deserted June 1, '65 at Washington.
Taylor, B. P.	Buffalo	Aug 13, '63	Enlisted June 27, '63 & mustered in as Pvt., Co. E, July 25, '63. Appointed Sgt. Aug 13, '63; 1st Sgt. Feb 29, '64; reduced Apr 27, '64; appointed 1st Sgt. May 8, '64; reduced to ranks July 27, '64.
Wendell, Andrew	Buffalo	Feb 18, '65	Enlisted June 23, '63 & mustered in as Pvt., Co. E, June 25, '63. Appointed Cpl. Sep 14, '63; Sgt. Feb 18, '65.
Whipple, E. L.	Buffalo	Aug 13, '63	Enlisted July 9, '63 & mustered in as Pvt., Co. E, July 25, '63. Appointed 1st Sgt. Aug 13, '63. Discharged for disability at Boston, Mass. Apr 1, '64.

Company F Roster

Name & Rank	Enrolled at	Date of Rank	Remarks
CAPTAINS			
Schlaefer, John J.	Albany	Aug 7, '63	Enlisted Apr 26, '61 at Troy & mustered in as Cpl., Co. K, 2nd

Roster of Officers and Sergeants

Name & Rank	Enrolled at	Date of Rank	Remarks
Windsbecker, Julius			New York Infantry, May 14, '61. Mustered as 2nd Lt. Sep 4, '61. Resigned July 29, '62. Enrolled & mustered in as Capt. Co. F, 16th New York Cavalry, Aug 7, '63. Dismissed June 1, '64. Recommissioned Capt. Nov 22, '64. See Co. C.

1st Lieutenants

Name & Rank	Enrolled at	Date of Rank	Remarks
Moffat, James	Albany	July 16, '63	Enrolled & mustered in as 1st Lt., Co. F July 16, '63. Resigned Feb 1, '64.
Grosvenor, George H.			See Co. D.
Farrell, William	Troy	Jan 24, '64	Enlisted at Troy & mustered in as Pvt. Co. D, 27th New York Infantry, Oc. 15, '61. Deserted Jan 24, '62 at camp near Falmouth, Va. Enlisted June 5, '63 at Troy & mustered in as Pvt. Co. F, 16th New York Cavalry, Aug 3, '63. Mustered as 2nd Lt. Aug 13, '63. Arrested for desertion in '64 & sentenced by general court-martial to make good time lost & serve one year & three months extra time. Sentence remitted July 2, '64 & returned to former rank of 2nd Lt., 16th Cavalry, upon condition that he serve out the term of his enlistment and six months for unauthorized absence. Mustered in as 1st Lt., July 8, '64.

2nd Lieutenants

Name & Rank	Enrolled at	Date of Rank	Remarks
Farrell, William			See above.
Hall, John T.	Rochester	Feb 1, '65	Enlisted May 7, '61 at Rochester & mustered in as Pvt. Co. E, 27th New York Infantry, May 21, '61. Mustered out with company May 31, '63 at Elmira. Enlisted July 8, '63 at Rochester & mus-

Appendix A

Name & Rank	Enrolled at	Date of Rank	Remarks
			tered in as Pvt. Co. G, 16th New York Cavalry, Aug 8, '63. Appointed Sgt. Aug 13, '63; regimental QM-Sgt., Dec 18, '63. Mustered in as 2nd Lt., Co. F, May 19, '65.
SERGEANTS			
Barron, Richard W.	Troy	July 6, '64	Enlisted June 20, '63 & mustered in as Pvt., Co. F, Aug 13, '63. Appointed Cpl., no date stated; Sgt. July 6, '64. Reduced to the ranks Nov 26, '64.
Bradley, Francis	Troy	Aug 13, '63	Enlisted June 6, '63 & mustered in as Pvt. Co. F, Aug 5, '63. Appointed Sgt. Aug 13, '63. Transferred to the Navy June 4, '64.
Corker, Marshall	Fort Covington	Aug 13, '63	Enlisted May 6, '63 & mustered in as Sgt., Co. F, Aug 13, '63. Reduced Sep 20., '63. Appointed Cpl. Jan 1, '65.
Eagle, Richard	Troy	Aug 13, '63	Enlisted June 5, '63 & mustered in as Pvt., Co. F, July 1, '63. Appointed Sgt. Aug 13, '63. Reduced by sentence of court-martial, Jan 18, '64. Confined at Dry Tortugas Mar 13, '65. Transferred Aug 17, '65 to Co. B, 3rd New York Provisional Cavalry.
Field, Henry P.			See Co. H.
Hendrix, Simeon	Plattsburgh	May 20, '64	Enlisted June 27, '63 & mustered in as Pvt. Co. F, July 1, '63. Appointed Cpl. Aug 13, '63; Sgt. May 20, '64. Reduced July 27, '64. Captured at Fairfax Nov 27, '64. Released at Aiken's Landing Feb 17, '65. Appointed Cpl., date not stated. Mustered out June 8, '65, at York, Pa.
Keefe, John	Troy	Jan 1, '65	Enlisted June 8, '63 & mustered in as Pvt. Co. F, Aug 5, '63. Appointed farrier Aug 13, '63; Cpl. Nov 1, '64; Sgt. Jan 1, '65. Reduced to ranks Jan 27, '65.

Roster of Officers and Sergeants

Name & Rank	Enrolled at	Date of Rank	Remarks
Marriner, Edwin	Oswego	Jan 1, '65	Enlisted Apr 8, '63 & mustered in as Pvt., Co. F, May 7, '63. Appointed Commissary Sgt. Jan. 1, '65. Reduced June 11, '65.
McCracken, William	Troy	July 27, '64	Enlisted June 18, '63 & mustered in as Pvt. Co. F, July 1, '63. Appointed Cpl. May 20, '64; Sgt. July 27, '64. Reduced Sep 28, '64.
McDonnell, John	Troy	Jan 20, '64	Enlisted June 5, '63 & mustered in as Pvt., Co. F, July 1, '63. Appointed Cpl. Aug 13, '63; Commissary Sgt. Jan 20, '64. Wounded at Centerville, Va., no date stated. Died July 4, 1864 at Falls Church.
McFarland, Terence	Malone	Apr 22, '64	Enlisted June 24, '63 & mustered in as Cpl., Co. F, Aug 13, '63. Appointed Sgt. Apr 22, '64. Mustered out Aug 17, '64, place not stated.
Moore, James M.	Ogdensburgh	Jan '64	Enlisted June 23, '63 & mustered in as Pvt., Co. F, Aug 5, '63. Appointed Cpl. Nov 1, '63; Sgt. Jan., '64. Reduced Apr 22, '64. Reappointed Sgt. May 20, '64. Reduced Oct 26, '64. Appointed Sgt. Nov 1, '64; Orderly Sgt. Jan 1, '65. Reduced, date not stated. Deserted May 8, '65, place not stated.
Moore, William J.	Ogdensburgh	—	Enlisted July 2, '63 & mustered in as Pvt., Co. F, Aug 5, '63. Appointed Sgt. Date not stated. Deserted Apr 28, '64.
Morrison, Andrew	Troy	Sep 20, '63	Enlisted June 14, '63 & mustered in as Pvt. Co. F, Aug 5, '63. Appointed Cpl. Aug 13, '63; Sgt. Sep 20, '63. Reduced to ranks Nov. 2, '63. Reappointed Sgt. Apr 10, '64. Transferred June 4, '64 to the Navy. Prior service in Co. C, 2nd New York Volunteers.
Nineman, Anthony	Troy	Aug 13, '63	Enlisted July 20, '63 & mustered in as Sgt., Co. F, Aug 13, '63.

Appendix A

Name & Rank	Enrolled at	Date of Rank	Remarks
Payne, Cyrius	Champlain	June 1, '63	Captured June 26, '64 at Annandale, Va. Returned Apr 1, '65. Enlisted May 28, '63 & mustered in as Sgt., Co. F, June 1, '63. Reduced to ranks, date not stated. Mustered out Oct 22, '63, at New York, by reason of promotion to 1st Lt., 18th New York Cavalry.
Porter, William	New York	Jan 1, '65	Enlisted & mustered in Dec 2, '64 as Pvt. Co. F. Appointed Sgt. Jan 1, '65; 1st Sgt. Mar 21, '65. Mustered out with detachment Aug 17, '65 at Washington.
Sheperd, Cyrus G.	Malone	—	Enlisted June 19, '63 & mustered in as Pvt., Co. F, Aug 13, '63. Appointed QM-Sgt., date not stated.
Sholtus, Edward H.	Buffalo	Aug 13, '63	Enlisted July 18, '63 & mustered in as Pvt. Co. F, Aug 5, '63. Appointed Commissary Sgt. Aug 13, '63; reduced Jan 20, '64. Appointed Cpl. July 15, '64; Sgt. Nov 1, '64. Reduced Jan 1, '65. Died of disease Apr 5, '65 at Alexandria, Va.
St. Dennis, Peter	Masena	May 12, '65	Enlisted June 24, '63 & mustered in as Pvt., Co. F, Aug 13, '63. Appointed Cpl. Apr 22, '64; Sgt. May 12, '65. Missing in action at Annandale, Va., June 26, '64. Returned Jan '65.
Waller, Charles H.	Troy	May 20, '64	Enlisted July 15, '63 & mustered in as Pvt., Co. F, Aug 5, '63. Appointed Sgt. May 20, '64. Reduced Dec 26, '64. Deserted June 20, '65 at Lincoln Barracks, Washington.

Company G Roster

Name & Rank	Enrolled at	Date of Rank	Remarks
CAPTAINS			
McPherson, James A.	—	Aug 13, '63	Enlisted Sep 18, 62 as Pvt. in Barnes' Rifle Btty (26th Ind. Lt. Artillery Btty.) & commissioned

Roster of Officers and Sergeants 203

Name & Rank	Enrolled at	Date of Rank	Remarks
Keays, William J.			but "not mustered" 1st Lt., Nov 29, '62. Mustered out spring '63. Mustered in as Capt., Co. G, 16th New York Cavalry, Aug 13, '63. Resigned Mar 28, '65. See Co. A.
1st Lieutenants			
Jones, Seldon L.	Rochester	Aug 13, '63	Enlisted June 13, '61 at Rochester & mustered in as Pvt. Co. A, 3rd New York Cavalry, July 17, '61. Discharged for promotion June 29, '63. Mustered in as 1st Lt., Co. G. 16th New York Cavalry, Aug 13, '63. Resigned Jan 4, '65.
O'Keefe, Arthur A.	New York	Jan 31, '65	Enlisted Sep 19, '63 & mustered in as Pvt., Co. L, Oct 18, '63. Appointed Sgt. Oct 20, '63; 1st Sgt. Dec 16, '63. Mustered in as 2nd Lt. Co. G, Jan 10, '65; 1st Lt. Apr 5, '65.
2nd Lieutenants			
Farnsworth, Charles H.	—	Aug 13, '63	Enlisted at Plattsburgh & mustered in, date unknown, as Pvt., Co. K, 96th New York Infantry. Promoted to Commissary Sgt., Mar 10, '62. Discharged Nov 15, '62. Mustered in as 2nd Lt., Co. G, 16th New York Cavalry, Aug 13, '63; 1st Lt., Co. K, Jan 10, '65.
O'Keefe, Arthur A.			See above.
Sutter, Charles	New York	Jan 31, '65	Enlisted Jan 3, '63 & mustered in as Pvt. Co. H, Apr 8, '63. Appointed QM-Sgt. Aug 13, '63. Reduced to Cpl. Sep 2, '63. Appointed Sgt. Mar 3, 64; 1st Sgt. June 16, '64; Sgt, Maj. Feb 28, 65. Mustered in as 2nd Lt. Co. G, Jan 31, '65.
Sergeants			
Biddlecomb, George W.	Buffalo	Aug 13, '63	Enlisted July 22, '63 & mustered in as Sgt. Co. G Aug 13, '63.

Appendix A

Name & Rank	Enrolled at	Date of Rank	Remarks
Black, James	Rochester	—	Mustered out as 1st Sgt. June 10, '65. Prior service in Co. I, 2nd U.S. Infantry. Enlisted June 16, '63 & mustered in as Pvt., Co. G, Aug 8, '63. Died of gunshot wound, accidentally received, July 12, '64, as Sgt., in Brigade Hospital, Annandale, Va. Prior service in Co. G, 28th New York State Volunteers.
Carolan, Thomas	Rochester	Aug 13, '63	Enlisted May 7, '61 at Rochester & mustered in as Pvt., Co. E, 27th New York Infantry, May 21, '61. Promoted to Cpl. Sep 1, '62. Mustered out with company May 31, '63 at Elmira, N.Y. Enlisted July 9, '63 & mustered in as Sgt., Co. G, 16th New York Cavalry, Aug 13, '63. Prisoner of war July 30, '64. Appointed Sgt., date not indicated; to Sgt.-Maj. May 20, '65.
Gardener, William	Rochester	Aug 1, '64	Enlisted Aug 4, '63 & mustered in as Pvt., Co. G, Aug 8, '63. Appointed Cpl. Aug 13, '63; Sgt. Aug 1, '64. Reduced May 14, '65.
Gunn, William	Rochester	Aug 8, '63	Enlisted Apr 27, '61 at Seneca Falls & mustered in as Pvt. Co. C, 19th Infantry, May 22, '61. Designation of regt. Changed to 3rd Artillery, Dec 11, '61. Appointed Sgt., date not stated. Mustered out with battery June 2, '63. Enlisted July 8, '63 & mustered in as Sgt. Co. G, 16th New York Cavalry, Aug 13, '63. Reduced Feb 27, '64.
Hall, John T.			See Co. F.
Hickman, Joseph H.	Rochester	July 20, '64	Enlisted July 7, '63 & mustered in as Cpl., Co. G, Aug 8, '63. Appointed Sgt., July 10, '64. Reduced Feb 21, '65. Prior service in Co. E, 27th New York State Volunteers.

Roster of Officers and Sergeants

Name & Rank	Enrolled at	Date of Rank	Remarks
Lee, Richard H.	Rochester	Aug 8, '63	Enlisted July 21, '63 & mustered in as Sgt., Co. G Aug 8, '63. Appointed Regimental Commissary Sgt. June 21, '64. Reduced to ranks & returned to Co. G July 30, '64. Discharged for disability July 22, '65. Prior service in, but no record of, 27th New York Infantry.
McComb, John	Rochester	—	Enlisted July 29, '63 & mustered in as Pvt., Co. G, Aug 8, '63. Appointed Commissary Sgt., date not stated. Mustered out Aug 17, '65 at Washington.
Neeley, Albert	Rochester	Feb 26, '64	Enlisted June 10, '63 & mustered in as Cpl., Co. G, Aug 8, '63. Appointed Sgt. Feb 26, '64. Reduced, date not stated. Mustered out while in hospital Aug 9, '65 at Rochester, N.Y.
Sumner, Henry L.	Plattsburgh	Aug 13, '63	Enlisted Nov 17, '61 at Chazy & mustered in as Cpl., Co. F, 96th New York Infantry, Nov 25, '61. Discharged for disability Feb 1, '63 at New Berne, N.C. Enlisted July 15, '63 & mustered in as Commissary Sgt., Co. G, 16th New York Cavalry, Aug 13, '63. Reduced Jan 15, '64.
Talladay, John	Oswego	Aug 13, '63	Enlisted Apr 30, '63 & mustered as Pvt. Co. G May 30, '63. Appointed Sgt. Aug 13, '63. Reduced, date not stated. Transferred Sep 5, '63 to Co. H. Deserted Aug 7, '65, place not stated. Also carried as Talliday and Toloday.
Thorpe, Manser J.	Buffalo	—	Enlisted July 25, '63 & mustered in as Pvt., Co. G, July 30, '63. Appointed QM-Sgt., date not stated. Discharged for disability June 23, '65 at Washington.
Tuck, Matthew	Rochester	Aug 13, '63	Enlisted May 27, '63 & mustered in as 1st Sgt., Co. G, Aug 13, '63. Promoted to 1st Lt., Co. K, Feb

206 Appendix A

Name & Rank	Enrolled at	Date of Rank	Remarks
			3, '64, and Capt., Co. I, Aug 4, '64.

Company H Roster

Name & Rank	Enrolled at	Date of Rank	Remarks
CAPTAIN			
Robin, Charles	Albany	June 19, '63	Enrolled & mustered in June 19, '63 as Capt., Co. H. Dismissed Feb 3, '65.
1ST LIEUTENANTS			
Lazarus, Louis Henry	Albany	June 13, '63	Enrolled May 27, '63 & mustered in June 9, '63 as 1st Sgt. Mustered as 1st Lt, Co. H, July 15, '63. Resigned Jan 19, '64.
Doherty, Edward P.			See Co. B
Kavanaugh, William J.			See Co. B
Lee, Phillip Ludwell	New York	Mar 25, '65	Enlisted & mustered in as Pvt., Co. F, 2nd New York Cavalry, Aug 28, '62 at New York. Transferred to Co. L Aug 29, '64; to Co. M Dec 15, '64. Discharged for promotion Apr 7, '65. Mustered in as 1st Lt., Co. H, 16th New York Cavalry, Apr 7, '65.
2ND LIEUTENANTS			
Moody, Horace D.	Canton	June 13, '63	Enlisted & mustered in as Pvt., Co. D, 11th New York Cavalry, Aug 7, '62. Appointed Sgt., date not stated. Discharged for promotion July 25, '63. Mustered in as 2nd Lt., Co. H, 16th New York Cavalry, Aug 7, '63. Resigned Nov 2, '63.
Bardell, Francis A.	New York	Nov 2, '63	Enlisted Mar 6, '63 & mustered in as Pvt., Co. A, Apr 9, '63. Appointed Sgt., date not stated; Sgt.-Maj. Apr 13, '63. Mustered in as 2nd Lt. Jan 16, '64 & 1st Lt, Co. I, Feb 8, '64. Dismissed Sep 20, '64.
Field(s), Henry P.	Troy	Mar 1, '64	Enrolled Aug 16, '62 at Ogdensburg & mustered in as 2nd Lt.,

Roster of Officers and Sergeants

Name & Rank	Enrolled at	Date of Rank	Remarks
			Co. I, 106th New York Infantry. Discharged dishonorably Mar 9, '63, "while under charges." Enlisted June 5, '63 at Troy & mustered in as 1st Sgt., Co. F, 16th New York Cavalry, Aug 13, '63. Promoted to 2nd Lt., Co. H, Mar 23, '64. Discharged Oct 1, '64.
Keller, Wallace	Buffalo	Aug 1, '64	Enlisted July 11, '63 & mustered in as Pvt. Co. E, July 30, '63. Appointed Commissary Sgt. Aug 11, '63; 1st Sgt. Aug 1, '64. Mustered in as 2nd Lt., Co. H, Nov 5, '64. Promoted to 1st Lt. Dec 30, '64. Not mustered. Dismissed Jan 23, '65.
McNaughton, Peter	Buffalo	Dec 1, '64	Enlisted Mar 30, '63 & mustered in as Pvt., Co. D, May 25, '63. Appointed Sgt. July 19, '63; 1st Sgt. July 2, '64. Mustered in as 2nd Lt., Co. H, Feb 12, '65.

SERGEANTS

Name & Rank	Enrolled at	Date of Rank	Remarks
Benway, Washington	Plattsburgh	Aug 13, '63	Enlisted May 20, '63 & mustered in as Pvt., Co. H, May 30, '63. Appointed Sgt. Aug 13, '63. Reduced June 16, '64. Discharged July 25, '65 at Washington.
Burk, William O.	New York	Aug 13, '63	Enlisted May 31, '63 & mustered in as Sgt., Co. H, Aug 13, '63. Discharged for disability June 10, '64, location not stated. Also borne as Burke, William C.
Gessner, Edward	New York	Aug 6, '64	Enlisted May 13, '63 & mustered in as Pvt., Co. H, Aug 13, '63. Appointed Cpl. Aug 14, '63; QM-Sgt. Aug 6, '64.
Haefeli, Jacob	New York	June 16, '64	Enlisted June 12, '63 & mustered in as Cpl., Co. H, Aug 13, '63. Appointed Sgt. June 16, '64.
Herard, Arsene	Plattsburgh	Feb 1, '65	Enlisted May 11, '63 & mustered in as Pvt., Co. H, Aug 13, '63. Appointed Commissary Sgt. Feb 1, '65.

Name & Rank	Enrolled at	Date of Rank	Remarks
Herrmann, Lewis	New York	Aug 13, '63	Enlisted Mar 1, '63 & mustered in as Pvt. Co. H, Apr 9, '63. Appointed Commissary Sgt. Aug 13, '63. Deserted Sep 1, '63 at Baltimore. Also borne as Herman, Lewis.
Hornsby, Michael	New York	Nov 18, '64	Enlisted June 4, '63 & mustered in as Pvt., Co. H, Aug 13, '63. Appointed Cpl. June 16, 64; Sgt. Nov 18, '64. Reduced Feb 1, '65. Appointed Cpl. Apr 14, '65. Deserted Aug 13, '65, place not stated.
Johnes, Charles J.	New York	—	Enlisted June 6, '63 & mustered in as Pvt., Co. H, Aug 13, '63. Appointed Cpl. Feb 7, '64; Sgt., date not stated. Deserted Aug 13, '65, place not stated. Also borne as Charles C. and J. Jones.
Klassen, Adam	New York	Mar 2, '65	Enlisted Apr 28, '63 & mustered in as Pvt., Co. H, May 18, '63. Appointed Cpl. June 16, '64; Sgt. Mar 2, '65. Also borne as Kleeson.
McCormeck, James	New York	Aug 13, '63	Enlisted Jan 27, '63 & mustered in as Pvt., Co. H., Apr 9, '63. Appointed Sgt. Aug 13, '63; reduced Feb 27, '64; again appointed Sgt. Mar 27, '64 & 1st Sgt. Mar 4, '65. Reduced July 16, '65. Also listed as McCormick, James.
Meyer, John	New York	Aug 13, '63	Enlisted May 8, '63 & mustered in as Pvt., Co. H, May 18, '63. Appointed Sgt. Aug 13, '63. Also borne as Mayer.
Nelling, James S.	New York	Aug 13, '63	Enlisted June 3, '63 & mustered in as Sgt., Co. H, Aug 13, '63.
Smith, Charles	New York	June 16, '64	Enlisted June 16, '63 & mustered in as Pvt., Co. H, Aug 13, '63. Appointed Sgt. June 16, '64. Captured at Piedmont Oct 12, '64. Reported at Camp Parole, Md. Feb 19, '65. Mustered out Aug 17, '65.

Name & Rank	Enrolled at	Date of Rank	Remarks
Sutter, Charles			See Co. G
Thompson, James			See Field & Staff–Adjutants

Company I Roster

Name & Rank	Enrolled at	Date of Rank	Remarks
CAPTAINS			
Kleinschmidt, Otto	—	Sep 1, '63	Enrolled and mustered in at New York as Adjutant, 41st New York Infantry, June 6, '61. Transferred to Co. I as 1st Lt. Sep 1, '61. Reappointed Adjutant May 1, '62. Discharged for disability Oct 31, '62. Mustered in as Capt., Co. I, 16th New York Cavalry, Sep 2, '63. Cashiered June 14, '64, reason not stated.
Tuck, Matthew			See Co. G.
1ST LIEUTENANTS			
Schultz, Joseph N.	Albany	June 19, '63	Enrolled & mustered in as 1st Lt., Co. I June 19, '63. Transferred to Co. L Jan 22, '64. Dismissed Oct 3, '64.
Tuck, Matthew			See Co. G.
Bardell, Francis A.			See Co. H.
Cannon, Patrick	New York	Dec 1, '64	Enlisted May 3, '61 & mustered in May 4, '61 at New York as Pvt., Co. G, 9th New York Infantry. Wounded in action Apr 19, '62 at Camden, N.C. Promoted to 1st Sgt. Nov 26, '62. Mustered out with company May 20, '63 at New York. Enrolled Aug 5, '63 at Albany & mustered in Sep 5, '63 as 2nd Lt., Co. L, 16th New York Cavalry. Captured Feb 22, '64, location not stated; paroled, date not stated. Mustered in as 1st Lt., Co. I May 8, '65. Mustered out Aug 17, '65.

Appendix A

Name & Rank	Enrolled at	Date of Rank	Remarks
2ND LIEUTENANTS			
Barnes, Thomas	Albany	June 19, '63	Enrolled June 19, '63 & mustered in as 2nd Lt., Co. I, Sep 2, '63. Transferred to Co. K Feb 15, '64. Tried by court-martial and dismissed May 11, '64 "for conduct unbecoming an officer and gentleman."
Hildebrand, Henry A.			See Co. E.
Smith, Annseley B.	Washington	Apr 23, '64	Enlisted & mustered in as Pvt., Co. E, 90th New York Infantry, Jan 3, '62. Promoted to Sgt. Mar 1, '62. Discharged Oct 30, '62. Enrolled & mustered in May 31, '64 as 2nd Lt., Co. I, 16th New York Cavalry. Dismissed July 29, '64 for "drunkenness on duty, breach of arrest, and attempting to purloin from a government stable a saddle and bridle belonging to an officer."
Slorah, Andrew			See Co. D.
Lowery, John	New York	Dec 1, '64	Enlisted & mustered in July 30, '63 as Pvt., Co. I. Appointed Sgt.-Maj. Apr 25, '64. Mustered in as 2nd Lt., Co. I, Jan 10, '65. Discharged June 9, '65.
SERGEANTS			
Brodie, William John	New York	Feb 8, '65	Enlisted June 17, '63 & mustered in as Pvt., Co. I, Sep 2, '63. Appointed Regimental Saddler Sgt. Feb 8, '65.
Candee, William E.	New York	May 22, '65	Enlisted July 10, '63 & mustered in as Pvt., Co. I Sep 2, '63. Appointed Cpl. Nov 21, '64; Regimental QM-Sgt. May 22, '65. Also borne as Cander.
Crosby, Charles S.	New York	Dec 26, '63	Enlisted Apr 23, '63 & mustered in as Pvt., Co. I, Sep 2, '63. Appointed Commissary Sgt. Dec 26, '63; Regimental Commissary

Roster of Officers and Sergeants

Name & Rank	Enrolled at	Date of Rank	Remarks
Delany, Andrew	New York	Not Reported	Sgt. May 31, '65. Mustered out Aug 17, '65. Enlisted May 16, '63 & mustered as Pvt. Co. I, Sep 2, '63. Appointed Sgt. Deserted Sep 9, '63, location not stated.
Hoefield, Hermann	New York	Sep 2, '63	Enlisted June 29, '63 & mustered in as Pvt. Co. I, Sep 2, '63. Appointed Sgt. Sep 2, '63; 1st Sgt. May 15, '64.
Johnson, Charles	Buffalo	Oct 20, '64	Enlisted Aug. 10, '63 & mustered in as Pvt., Co. I, Sep. 2, '63. Appointed Cpl. May 28, '64; Sgt. Oct 20, '64.
Laury, Thomas	New York	Not Reported	Enlisted June 23, '63 & mustered as Pvt., Co. I, Sep 2, '63. Appointed Sgt., date not stated. Died Jan 7, '64 at Fairfax Court House, Va.
Martini, John William	New York	Dec 1, '63	Enlisted July 17, '63 & mustered in as Pvt., Co. I, Sep 2, '63. Appointed Cpl. Sep 2, '63; Sgt. Dec 1, '63. Reduced to Cpl. Dec 26, '63. Captured Aug 8, '64 at Fairfax. Reduced Oct 20, '64. Paroled Feb 22, '65 at James River. Reappointed Cpl. Mar 2, '65; Sgt. June 9, '65.
Merkle, Fabian	New York	Aug 16, '64	Enlisted Aug 1, '63 & mustered in as Pvt., Co. I, Sep 2, '63. Appointed Cpl. Feb 26, '64; Sgt. Aug 16, '64. Reduced July 8, '65. Also borne as Fabian Myrkle.
Richter, Otto	New York	Sep 2, '63	Enlisted June 2, '63 & mustered in as Pvt., Co. I, June 8, '63. Appointed 1st Sgt. Sep 2, '63. Reduced to Sgt. May 15, '64; reduced to Pvt. May 28, '64. Appointed Cpl. Aug 17, '64 & Sgt. Oct 20, '64. Mustered out with detachment Aug 17, '65 at Washington. Also served in 5th Missouri Volunteer Cavalry.
Vandevelde, Alexander	New York	Sep 2, '63	Enlisted June 12, '63 & mustered in as Pvt., Co. I, Sep 2, '63.

Appendix A

Name & Rank	Enrolled at	Date of Rank	Remarks
Wicks, Thomas	New York	Sep 2, '63	Appointed Sgt. Sep 2, '63. Discharged June 13, '65 for disability. Enlisted & mustered in as Pvt. Co. I, May 9, '63. Appointed Q-M Sgt. Sep 2, '63. Mustered out with detachment Aug 17, '65 at Washington.

Company K Roster

Name & Rank	Enrolled at	Date of Rank	Remarks
CAPTAINS			
McNichol, Ronald	Albany	June 15, '63	Enrolled & mustered in June 15, '63 as Capt., Co. K. Dismissed Oct 23, '63
Gaylord, Henry M.			See Field & Staff–Adjutants
1ST LIEUTENANTS			
Bailey, Wells S.	New York	Nov 23, '63	Mustered in as 1st Lt., Co. K, Sep 22, '63. Resigned Feb 4, '64. Re-enrolled & mustered in as 1st Lt., Co. M, Apr 1, '64. Recommissioned 1st Lt. Mar 25, '64. Mustered out Nov 28, '64 to accept appointment in Veteran Reserve Corps.
Tuck, Matthew			See Co. G.
Dow, Henry G.			See Co. B.
Farnsworth, Charles H.			See Co. G.
2ND LIEUTENANTS			
Hildebrand, Henry A.			See Co. E.
Barnes, Thomas G.			See Co. I
French, George F.			See Co. E.
SERGEANTS			
Bennett, Theo. L.	Greenburgh	Jan 11, '65	Enlisted Aug 14, '63 & mustered in as Pvt., Co. K, Sep 22, '63. Appointed Cpl. Feb 18, '64.

Roster of Officers and Sergeants

Name & Rank	Enrolled at	Date of Rank	Remarks
Brown, Duncan L.	Rochester	—	Reduced Nov 28, '64. Appointed Sgt. Jan 11, '65. Deserted Mar 28, '65 at Vienna, Va. Enlisted Aug 14, '63 & mustered in as Pvt., Co. K, Sep 22, '63. Appointed Sgt. & reduced, no dates stated. Discharged for disability June 23, '65 at Washington.
Carey, Edward	Buffalo	—	Enlisted Aug 20, '63 & mustered in as Pvt., Co. K, Sep 22, '63. Appointed Sgt. & Commissary Sgt., no dates given. Reduced to ranks Nov 26, '64. Prior service in Co. G., 28th New York Volunteers.
Collins, William	Albion	—	Enlisted June 22, '63 & mustered in as Pvt., Co. K, Aug 8, '63. Wounded in action at Leesburg, Va. Apr 20, '64. Captured June 24, '64 near Chantilly, Va. Released Dec 6, '64 at Charleston, S.C. Appointed Sgt., date not stated. Reduced June 28, '65. Prior service in Co. G, 28th New York Volunteers.
Collyer, William H.	Greenburgh	—	Enlisted Sep 2, '63 & mustered in as Pvt., Co. K, Sep 22, '63. Appointed Sgt., date not stated. Reduced to ranks Feb 18, 64. Appointed Cpl. Nov 26, '64. Prior service in Co. K, 1st New York Volunteers.
Dahlgreen, Gustavus	Mt. Pleasant	Mar 14, '64	Enlisted Sep 14, '63 & mustered in as Pvt., Co. K, Sep 22, '63. Appointed Cpl. Feb 18, '64; Sgt. Mar 14, '64. Captured at Berks Station, Va. June 29, '64. Released at Jacksonville, Fla. Apr 28, '65. Mustered out July 1, '65 at New York.
Diezelsky, Ernest	Mt. Pleasant	Mar 15, '64	Enlisted Sep 9, '63 & mustered in as Pvt., Co. K, Sep 22, '63. Appointed Sgt. Mar 15, '64. Dis-

Name & Rank	Enrolled at	Date of Rank	Remarks
Haviland, Patrick	Yonkers	—	charged for disability June 10, '65 at McDougall General Hospital, New York Harbor. Enlisted Aug 11, '63 & mustered in as Pvt., Co. K, Sep 22, '63. Appointed Sgt. date not stated. Reduced Nov 11, '63. Appointed QM-Sgt. Jan 27, '64. Reduced Nov 26, '64. Appointed Cpl. Jan 11, '65. Reduced June 28, '65.
Lane, Stephen	Rochester	—	Enlisted June 10, '63 & mustered in as Pvt. Co. K, Aug 8, '63. Appointed Sgt., date not stated. Reduced Mar 9, '64. Captured at Falls Church, Va. Oct 18, '64. Released at James River Feb 22, '65. Prior service in Co. G, 38th New York Volunteers.
MacDonald, Dugald	New York	—	Enlisted June 11, '63 & mustered in as Pvt., Co. K, Sep 22, '63. Appointed Sgt., no date stated. Deserted Feb 6, '64 as Pvt. at Camp Stoneman, Washington. Also appears as Dugal McDonald.
McGuire, Charles	New York	—	Enlisted Apr 30, '63 & mustered in as Pvt., Co. K, Sep 22, '63. Captured at Dranesville, Va. Feb 22, '64. Paroled at Vicksburg, Miss. Apr 21, '65. Appointed Cpl. & Sgt., dates not shown. Mustered out June 23, '65 at New York.
Mudge, Volney	Rochester	Feb 22, '64	Enlisted Aug 25, '63 & mustered in as Pvt., Co. K, Sep 22, '63. Appointed Cpl., date not shown; Sgt. Feb 22, '64. Prior service in Co. K, 27th New York Volunteers.
Newman, Lewis	Rochester	—	Enlisted July 15, '63 & mustered in as Pvt., Co. K, Sep 22, '63. Appointed Cpl. & Sgt., dates not stated. Appointed Commissary Sgt. Nov 26, '64. Reduced to ranks June 5, '65. Discharged for disability June 23, '65 at Washington.

Roster of Officers and Sergeants

Name & Rank	Enrolled at	Date of Rank	Remarks
Raymond, Harry	Mt. Pleasant	—	Enlisted Sep 9,'63 & mustered in as Pvt., Co. K, Sep 22,'63. Appointed Cpl. & Sgt., dates not stated. Appointed Hospital Steward Jan 27,'64. Returned to company as Pvt. June 24,'64. Discharged Aug 1,'64 by reason of enlistment in the Navy.
Starr, John M.	New York	Nov 26,'64	Enlisted & mustered in as Pvt., Co. K, Jan 29,'64. Appointed QM-Sgt. Nov 26,'64. Prior service in Co. D, 10th New York Volunteers.
Williams, Joshua R.	Greenburgh	Jan 1,'64	Enlisted Aug 31,'63 & mustered in as Pvt., Co. K, Sep 22,'63. Appointed Regimental Saddler Sgt., to date from Jan 1,'64. Deserted Jan 25,'65 while on furlough at New York.

Company L Roster

Name & Rank	Enrolled at	Date of Rank	Remarks
CAPTAIN			
Leahy, Lawrence	Albany	Feb 14,'62	Enrolled for 2 years as 1st Lt., 9th New York Infantry (Zouaves), May 3,'61. Promoted to Capt., Co. I, Mar 15,'62. Mustered out with company May 20,'63. Wounded & cited for bravery at Antietam. Enrolled in 16th New York Cavalry July 23,'63 & mustered in as Capt., Co. L, Sep 5, '63. Promoted to Maj. (not commissioned) Mar 30,'65 with rank from Feb 18,'65. Mustered out as supernumerary Aug 17,'65 at Washington.
1ST LIEUTENANTS			
Doherty, Edward P.			See Co. B.
Schultz, Joseph N.			See Co. I.
Cannon, Patrick			See Co. I.

Appendix A

Name & Rank	Enrolled at	Date of Rank	Remarks
2ND LIEUTENANTS			
Cannon, Patrick			See Co. I.
Schwaab, Frederick W.	New York	Feb 1, '65	Enlisted Aug 5, '61 & mustered in as Sgt., Co. G, 2nd New York Cavalry, Aug 30, '61. Appointed 1st Sgt., date not stated. Mustered in as 2nd Lt., Co. A, Mar 31, '63. Resigned May 9, '63. Enlisted June 30, '63 & mustered in as Pvt., Co. K, 16th New York Cavalry, Sep 22, '63. Captured at Centerville, Va., June 21, '64. Paroled at Charleston, S.C. Dec 6, '64. Appointed 1st Sgt., date not stated; Sgt.-Maj. Apr 16, '65. Mustered in as 2nd Lt., Co. L, May 16, '65. Also borne as Schwaab, William.
SERGEANTS			
Adams, Richard	Greenburgh	—	Enlisted Sep 3, '63 & mustered in as Pvt. Co. L, Sep 5, '63. Appointed Cpl. Sep 6, '63. Reduced Jan 18, '64. Appointed Sgt., date not stated. In confinement at Port Delaware, Mar '65. Deserted as Pvt., June 15, '65 from Lincoln Barracks. Also borne as R.A. Adams.
Bell, Richard	Greenburgh	Sep 6, '63	Enlisted Aug 18, '63 & mustered in as Pvt., Co. L, Sep 5, '63. Appointed Sgt. Sep 6, '63. Mustered out Aug 17, '65 at Washington. Prior service in Co. I, 9th New York Volunteers.
Corbett, Boston	New York	Oct 31, '64	Enlisted Aug 1, '63 & mustered in as Private, Co. L, Sep 5, '63. Appointed Cpl. Sep 6, '63. Reduced to ranks Feb 26, '64. Captured June 26, '64. Appointed Sgt. Oct. 31, '64. Mustered out Aug 17, '65 at Washington.
Irvin, Gerard	New York	Apr 1, '64	Enlisted Aug 25, '63 & mustered in as Pvt., Co. L, Sep 5, '63.

Name & Rank	Enrolled at	Date of Rank	Remarks
Lynch, Edward H.	Greenburgh	Aug 1, '64	Appointed Cpl. Sep 6, '63; Sgt. Apr 1, '64. Mustered out Aug 17, '65 at Washington. Also borne as Irvine. Enlisted Aug 26, '63 & mustered in as Pvt. Co. L, Sep 5, '63. Appointed Cpl. Sep 6, '63; Sgt. Aug 1, '64.
Mathews, John	New York	Sep 6, '63	Enlisted July 29, '63 & mustered in as Pvt., Co. L, Sep 5, '63. Appointed Sgt. Sep 6, '63. Prisoner of war since Feb 22, '64. Died Aug 15, '64 while prisoner at Andersonville, Ga.
McGlone, William	New York	Aug 1, '64	Enlisted & mustered in as Pvt., Co. L, Feb 3, '64. Appointed Cpl. Apr 1, '64; Sgt. Aug 1, '64. Reduced Jan 2, '65.
Minchon, Thomas	New York	Sep 6, '63	Enlisted Aug 1, '63 & mustered in as Pvt., Co. L, Sep 5, '63. Appointed Sgt. Sep 6, '63. Reduced, date not stated. Again appointed Sgt. Aug 1, '64; 1st Sgt. Jan 10, '65. Mustered out Aug 17, '65 at Washington. Also borne as Minchin.
Murphy, John	Greenburgh	Oct 20, '63	Enlisted & mustered in as Pvt. Co. L, Aug 18, '63. Transferred from Co. M. Appointed 1st Sgt. Oct 20, '63. Reduced at his own request Dec 15, '63 & appointed Sgt. Dec 16, '63. Deserted Apr 4, '64 at Plattsburgh.
Noonan, Edward	New York	Jan 1, '64	Enlisted July 29, '63 & mustered in as Pvt. Co. L, Sep 5, '63. Appointed Cpl. Sep 6, '63; Sgt. Jan 1, '64. Died of disease Aug 8, '64 at hospital Andersonville, Ga. Date of capture not stated.
Norris, William	Greenburgh	Sep 6, '63	Enlisted Aug 27, '63 and mustered in as Pvt., Co. L, Sep 5, '63. Appointed Sgt. Sep 6, '63; QM-Sgt., date not stated. Reduced to ranks Dec 27, '63. Deserted, no

Name & Rank	Enrolled at	Date of Rank	Remarks
			date stated. Prior service in Co. H, 9th New York Volunteers.
Quinn, Hugh	New York	Sep 6, '63	Enlisted July 18, '63 & mustered in as Pvt., Co. L, Sep 5, '63. Appointed Sgt. Sep 6, '63. Reduced to ranks Aug 1, '64. Appointed Cpl. Dec 26, '64. Prior service in Co. G, 9th New York Volunteers.
Sproules, William	New York	Sep 6, '63	Enlisted Aug 17, '63 & mustered in as Pvt., Co. L, Sep 5, '63. Appointed Sgt. Sep 6, '63. Reduced, date not stated. Prisoner of war Mar 31, '65. Returned to unit by Aug '65. Prior service in Co., I, 10th New York Volunteers.
Surrell, Joseph	Beekmantown	Jan 7, '65	Enlisted Feb 22, '64 & mustered in as Pvt., Co. L, Mar 4, '64. Appointed Cpl., date not stated; Sgt. Jan 7, '65. Reduced June 1, '65.

Company M Roster

Name & Rank	Enrolled at	Date of Rank	Remarks
CAPTAINS			
Fleming, James Henry	Albany	Oct 14, '63	Enrolled as 2nd Lt, Co. I, 9th New York Infantry (Zouaves), May 3, '61. Mustered as 1st Lt. Feb 14, '62. Mustered out with company May 20, '63. Mustered in as 1st Lt. & QM, Washington Light Cavalry, July 28, '63. Not commissioned. Through consolidation, mustered as Capt., Co. M, 16th New York Cavalry, Oct 19, '63. Killed in action at Fairfax Station Aug 8, '64.
Gail, Samuel P.			See Field & Staff–Adjutants
1ST LIEUTENANTS			
Kavanaugh, William J.			See Co. B.
Bailey, Wells S.			See Co. K.

Roster of Officers and Sergeants

Name & Rank	Enrolled at	Date of Rank	Remarks
2ND LIEUTENANT			
Maroney, Michael H.	Albany	Oct 14, '63	Enrolled Sep 9, '62 & mustered in as 1st Lt., Co. C, 155th New York Infantry, Nov 18, '62. Discharged Feb 6, '63 at Suffolk, Va. Enrolled Oct 14, '63 & mustered in as 2nd Lt., Co. M, 16th New York Cavalry, Oct 19, '63. Dishonorably dismissed Apr 23, '64, "for conduct unbecoming an officer and gentleman."
SERGEANTS			
Armstrong, Robert W.	New York	Oct 18, '63	Enlisted Sep 11, '63 & mustered in as Sgt., Co. M, Oct 18, '63. Appointed QM-Sgt. Sep 17, '63. Discharged as Sgt. Apr 18, '64 for promotion to 2nd Lt. U.S. Colored Troops.
Bannatyne, Daniel C.	Greenburgh	Mar 1, '64	Enlisted Sep 9, '63 & mustered in as Pvt., Co. M, Oct 18, '63. Appointed Cpl. Oct 19, '63; QM-Sgt. Mar 1, '64.
Fitzgerald, Richard F.	New York	Oct 18, '63	Enlisted Oct 15, '63 & mustered in as 1st Sgt, Co. M, Oct 18, '63. Reduced Feb 24, '64. Discharged for disability May 15, '64.
Hart, Josiah George	New York	Oct 19, '63	Enlisted Oct 5, '63 & mustered in as Pvt., Co. M, Oct 18, '63. Appointed Sgt. Oct 19, '63. Discharged as Commissary Sgt. May 4, '65 to accept commission in U.S. Colored Troops.
Henschall, Otto W.	New York	Oct 18, '63	Enlisted Oct 6, '63 & mustered in as Sgt., Co. M, Oct 18, '63. Appointed Commissary Sgt. Oct 19, '63. Also borne as Otto W. Hanschkel.
Keefe, Edward	New York	Sep 16, '63	Enlisted Aug 24, '63 & mustered in as Pvt., Co. L, Sep 5, '63. Transferred to Co. M Sep 10, '63. Appointed Sgt. Sep 16, '63. Reduced to ranks, date not stated. Appointed Cpl. July 1, '64; Sgt. Dec 27, '64. Mustered out Aug

Appendix A

Name & Rank	Enrolled at	Date of Rank	Remarks
McEvoy, John	New York	May 4, '65	17, '65 at Washington. Prior service in Co. F, 32nd New York Infantry. Enlisted & mustered in as Pvt., Co. M, Apr 20, '64. Wounded Aug 8, '64. Appointed Sgt. May 4, '65. Mustered out June 19, '65 at Sickel's U.S. Army General Hospital, Washington. Also borne as John I. McEvoy.
Pielman, Henry	New York	Oct 19, '64	Enlisted Sep 25, '63 & mustered in as Pvt. Co. M, Oct 18, '63. Appointed Sgt. Oct 19, '64. Prior service in 25th New York Infantry. Also borne as Henry A. Pielman.
Pryor, James	New York	Dec 27, '64	Enlisted Oct 13, '63 & mustered in as Pvt., Co. M, Oct 18, '63. Appointed Cpl. July 1, '64; Sgt. Dec 27, '64. Prior service in 15th New York Volunteers. Also borne as Prior.
Ryan, Mathew	New York	—	Enlisted Sep 25, '63 & mustered in as Pvt., Co. M, Oct 18, '63. Appointed Sgt., no date stated. Reduced June 24, '64. Captured Aug 8, '64. Released Feb 22, '65 at James River.
Singer, John Adolph	New York	Oct 18, '63	Enlisted Oct 8, '63 & mustered in as Sgt., Co. M, Oct 18, '63. Reduced, date not stated. Appointed Cpl. May 14, '64. Reduced Nov 12, '64. Prior service in 20th New York Infantry.
Singleton, John	New York	Oct 15, '63	Enlisted Sep 7, '63 & mustered in as Sgt., Co. M, Oct 15, '63. Appointed 1st Sgt. May 4, '65. Discharged for disability June 1, '65 at Washington.
Smith, George	New York	—	Enlisted Aug 28, '63 & mustered in as Pvt., Co. L, Sep 5, '63. Transferred to Co. M Nov 1, '63. Appointed 1st Sgt., date not stated. Prior service in Co. D, 11th New York Volunteers. Also borne as Smith, George R.

Roster of Officers and Sergeants

Name & Rank	Enrolled at	Date of Rank	Remarks
Zisgen, Joseph	New York	May 14, '64	Enlisted Oct 14, '63 & mustered in as Pvt. Co. M, Oct 18, '63. Appointed Sgt. May 14, '64. Reduced to ranks Dec 26, '64. Prior service in 1st U.S. Infantry.

Field and Staff Roster

Name & Rank	Enrolled at	Date of Rank	Remarks
COLONELS			
Lazelle, Henry M.	Washington	Oct 14, '63	Formerly Capt., 8th U.S. Infantry, Assistant Commissary General of Prisoners. Resigned commission as Colonel Oct 18, '64.
Sweitzer, Nelson B.	Washington	Oct 25, '64	Formerly Capt., 1st U.S. Cavalry and Aide-de-Camp to Gen. George B. McClellan. Mustered out Sep 21, '65.
LIEUTENANT COLONELS			
Olmstead, Spencer H.	Albany	Aug 19, '63	Date of rank, Aug 19, '63, date of enrollment. Dishonorably dismissed Nov 21, '63, "with loss of all pay and allowances, for receiving both transportation in kind and travelling expenses, for the same journey, and for the unauthorized and improper use of transportation blanks, furnished by the Quartermaster General of the State of New York" (War Dept. S.O. No. 518, dated Nov 21, '63).
Hollister, George S.	Washington	Nov 25, '63	1860 graduate of the U.S. Military Academy & formerly Capt., 7th U.S. Infantry. Dishonorably dismissed Oct 7, '64 for conduct (War Dept. S. O. No. 337, dated Oct 7, '64), later changed to "honorably mustered out of the Volunteer service" (War Dept. S.O. No. 32, dated Jan 25, '66).
Nicholson, John	Buffalo	Oct. 7, '65	Native of Scotland, originally enrolled May 1, '61 as 2nd Lt. Co. K, 21st New York Infantry. Resigned Aug 6, '61 and enrolled

Name & Rank	Enrolled at	Date of Rank	Remarks
			as Capt., Co. C, 100th New York Infantry Dec 3, '61. Discharged Mar 6, '63. Enrolled as 1st Lt., Co. B, 16th New York Cavalry, May 8, '63; Capt. June 1, '63; Major Nov 12, '63; Lieutenant Colonel Feb 4, '65.
MAJORS			
Hazzard, Morris	Albany	June 15, '63	Mustered in at Albany June 15, '63. Dishonorably dismissed "for habitual intemperance and neglect of duty" (War Dept. S.O. No. 526, Nov 27, '63).
Nicholson, John	Buffalo	Nov 11, '63	Native of Scotland, originally enrolled May 1, '61 as 2nd Lt. Co. K, 21st New York Infantry. Resigned Aug 6, '61 and enrolled as Capt., Co. C, 100th New York Infantry Dec 3, '61. Discharged Mar 6, '63. Enrolled as 1st Lt., Co. B, 16th New York Cavalry, May 8, '63; Capt. June 1, '63; Maj. Nov 12, '63; Lt. Col. Feb 4, '65.
Bosworth, George	Washington	Dec 9, '63	Originally enrolled Oct 15, '61 as Maj., 87th New York Infantry. Discharged for disability July 17, '62 at Harrisons Landing, Va. Prior service as enlisted man, Co. B, 8th Militia. Mustered in as Maj., 16th New York Cavalry Jan 9, '64.
Horton, Giles G.	Albany	Aug 19, '63	Originally enlisted in Co. E, 15th Connecticut Infantry on Aug 25, '62. Enrolled and mustered in as Maj., 16th New York Cavalry, Aug 19, '63. Mustered out Apr 2, '63.
ADJUTANTS			
Gaylord, Henry M.	Buffalo	Feb 11, '63	Originally enrolled as Capt., Co. B, 21st New York Infantry, May 10, '61. Resigned Aug 9, '62. Mustered with 16th New York Cavalry as 1st Lt. & Adjutant Feb 12, '63; Capt., Co. K, Mar 24, '64.
Thompson, James	New York	Nov 11, '63	Enlisted June 3, '63 & mustered in as 1st Sgt., Co. H, Aug 13, '63. Appointed Sgt.-Maj. Jan 15, '64.

Roster of Officers and Sergeants

Name & Rank	Enrolled at	Date of Rank	Remarks
Gail, Samuel P.	Washington	Apr 22, '64	Mustered in as 1st Lt. & Adjutant Apr 16, '64. Mustered May 21, '61 as 2nd Lt., Co. F, 21st New York Infantry; 1st Lt., Co. K, May 1, '62; Adjutant, Oct 1, '62. Wounded at Fredericksburg, Dec 13, '62. Mustered out with field & staff May 18, '63. Mustered May 3, '64 as 1st Lt., Co. M, 16th New York Cavalry, May 5, '64 as Adjutant; Dec 3, '64 as Capt. Co. M.
Quartermaster			
LaDue, Albert	Albany	Mar. 4, '63	Former Sheriff of Plattsburgh, NY. Mustered Mar. 10, '63 as 1st Lt. & Quartermaster.
Commissary			
Wilber, Albert. B.	Washington	Nov 10, '63	Mustered Dec 2, '63 as 1st Lt. & Regimental Commissary.
Surgeon			
Horniston, Joseph M.	Albany	Sep 3, '63	Mustered in at Albany as Surgeon, Westchester Light Infantry, Apr 6, '63; not commissioned. Enrolled as Surgeon, 16th New York Cavalry, Oct 9, '63; commissioned Nov 20, '63.
Assistant Surgeons			
Drake, Nelson S.	Albany	Aug 19, '63	Union College Class of '52. Living in Brooklyn and serving as Acting Assistant Surgeon, Fort Columbus, New York Harbor in '63. Commissioned Asst. Surgeon Nov 20, '63. Dismissed May 11, '64 per general court-martial, Washington, D.C.
Vondersmith, Samuel P.	New York	Oct 19, '63	Enrolled as Asst. Surgeon, 6th New York (N.G.) Infantry Regt., May 14, '61; mustered out July 31, '61 at New York. Enrolled Apr 2, '63 as Asst. Surgeon, Westchester Light Infantry; not commissioned. Commissioned again as

Appendix A

Name & Rank	Enrolled at	Date of Rank	Remarks
			Asst. Surgeon, 6th New York Infantry (N.G.) June 22, '63 for 30 days Mustered out July 22, '63. Mustered in as Asst. Surgeon, 16th New York Cavalry Oct 19, '63.
CHAPLAIN			
Loyd, Hinton Summerfield	—	Nov 18, '63	Appointed initially per Headquarters Sprague Light Cavalry S.O. No. 29, dated June 20, '63, signed by Spencer H. Olmstead, Colonel, Commanding. 1858 theology graduate of Madison Univ. (now Colgate), then a Baptist institution. Appointed Pastor of First Baptist Church of Peekskill, Westchester County, in May '59.

Appendix B
Regimental Deaths in Andersonville and Other Prisons

In all, 54 men of the 16th New York were sent to Andersonville Prison. Twenty-eight died there, most of scurvy or severe diarrhea, the latter most likely from contaminated drinking water. Co. L had the greatest number of deaths—ten between January and November 1864.[1]

Among those who survived, were exchanged and returned to duty with the 16th, was Sergeant Boston Corbett of Co. L, the man who killed Lincoln assassin John Wilkes Booth. Held at Andersonville for five months, Corbett wrote that "God was good to me, sparing my life while only another and myself lived to return out of fourteen men of my own Company [captured at Culpepper on June 24, 1864]." While imprisoned, Corbett—the deeply religious and evangelical future Methodist pastor—claimed that "bless the Lord, a score of souls were converted, right on the spot where I lay for three months without any shelter."[2]

Conditions at Andersonville were deplorable, even by 19th century standards. Few, if any, prisoners had adequate shelter, sanitary facilities were rudimentary and contaminated the available water supply, there was barely enough food to keep a man alive, and medical care was virtually non-existent. Pvt. John Lynch of the 13th New York Cavalry, which often fought beside the 16th, was captured on July 6, 1864, at Aldie, Virginia. Sent to Andersonville, he was finally paroled April 27, 1865, at Lake City, Florida. In 1876, he described his ordeal and that of his fellow prisoners in a lengthy and detailed statement. Among his recollections:

> We had no shelter whatever to protect us from sun or storm; for this there was no excuse whatever, a pine forest being close at hand which would have afforded ample materials to erect a shed as protection from the hot sun, if they would only grant us the privilege of going out ... [some] would rip up their shorts and stitch them together, three or four united, which they would put up as a shelter....
>
> When rations were issued, they were in quantity and quality as follows: one day we received nearly a pint of black stock beans, cooked with a good mixture of worms, hulls, husks, etc., etc., nothing else; next day we were given a small piece of coarse

corn bread, poorly baked, with sometimes about two ounces of rotten beef or pork; the next day we received a half pint of coarse corn-meal, with sometimes a little salt....
 I have seen hundreds of men lying on the hot sand, fully exposed to the rays of a scorching sun, suffering beyond description from fever, scurvy, diarrhea, etc., crying feebly, in God's name, for some relief, and begging to be dragged down and thrown in the creek, to relieve them of their heart-rending agonies.... From fifteen to sixty dead bodies were laid daily at the gate, awaiting the dead-wagon, into which they were thrown head and points, then hauled out and tossed into a trench, two feet deep, and roughly covered over, without ceremony or token of respect.[3]

One opportunity to escape offered by their Confederate captors in 1864 was for the Union soldiers confined at Andersonville to volunteer for service in the Confederate Army. Three men from the 16th New York accepted the offer: Privates Richard Allison of Co. D (captured at Boggs Station—now in West Virginia—on June 24), Martin Bishop of Co. E (captured near Centreville on June 25), and William Myers of Co. F (captured at Annandale on June 26). All three enlisted in the 10th Tennessee Infantry at Andersonville. They all were recaptured by Union forces at Egypt Station, Mississippi, on December 28, 1864, and confined at the Alton, Illinois Military Prison. They subsequently re-enlisted in the 5th U.S. Infantry in April 1865.[4]

Deaths at Andersonville

Name	Company	Date of Death	Cause
John Baker	K	October 30, 1864	Scurvy
Peter Bender	M	October 17, 1864	Disease
Thomas Boyle	L	November 12, 1864	Scurvy
Oliver Clemon	F	August 15, 1864	Diarrhea
Charles Clifford	B	April 30, 1864	Diarrhea
Martin Dooley	L	August 30, 1864	Disease
Grafe H. Eldrichsburg	K	Sept. 16, 1864	Disease
Richard Hore	L	August 19, 1864	Diarrhea
George Howe	M	October 1, 1864	Diarrhea
William J. Kearney	K	October 2, 1864	Scurvy
Gottlob Keil	K	Sept. 14, 1864	Disease
Charles Lewis	M	November 7, 1864	Scurvy
John Martin	L	August 20, 1864	Scurvy
Edward Noonan	L	January 1, 1864	Scurvy
Robert Pollock	L	July 31, 1864	Massive Edema
Godfrey Pontius	K	August 2, 1864	Scurvy
Anton Rose	L	October 3, 1864	Scurvy
Edwin Salisbury	D	October 11, 1864	Scurvy
Alex Senter	H	May 29, 1864	Diarrhea
Levi St. Dennis	F	October 4, 1864	Scurvy
Henry R. Thompson	K	November 26, 1864	Unknown
August Torbeck	L	July 20, 1864	Scurvy
Francis Troville	L	June 24, 1864	Scurvy
Thomas Turner	B	June 7, 1864	Diarrhea

Name	Company	Date of Death	Cause
Jacob Weidmann	H	October 15, 1864	Scurvy
Daniel Westbrook	K	October 24, 1864	Disease
Lawrence Williams	L	August 26, 1864	Scurvy
George A. Winters	L	October 26, 1864	Scurvy

The men at Andersonville were not the only members of the 16th New York Cavalry to be taken prisoner. Another 90 were captured or declared missing in action. Many were held in southern Virginia prison camps until paroled at Aikens Landing on the James River. Some were sent further south to New Bern and Salisbury, North Carolina.

Conditions at the Confederate prison at Salisbury, a stockade at a former cotton factory, were much better than those at Andersonville, at least initially. With a surge in prisoners in October 1864 to 10,000 by the end of the month, however, conditions became intolerable: "those without shelter dug burrows in an attempt to stay warm and dry. Rations and potable water were scarce." These conditions were made worse by an "unusually cold and wet winter. Disease and starvation began to claim lives."[5]

Fourteen men from the 16th New York died at prisons in Virginia and North Carolina, six at Salisbury.

Deaths in Virginia and North Carolina

Name	Company	Date of Death	Cause	Prison
George Beaton	C	April 28, 1865	Disease	New Bern, NC
August Fisher	E	January 21, 1865	Diarrhea	Salisbury, NC
Jacob Leonard	K	June 25, 1864	Disease	Richmond, VA
Albert O. Martin	B	February 21, 1864	Disease	Richmond, VA
William N. McLean	B	December 8, 1864	Diarrhea	Salisbury, NC
John Miers	K	December 10, 1864	Disease	Danville, VA
Massi Moole	B	February 29, 1864	Disease	Richmond, VA
Patrice O'Connor	B	February 8, 1864	Disease	Richmond, VA
Waldron Salisbury	E	February 21, 1864	Disease	Richmond, VA
Charles Schaeffel	H	February 10, 1865	Disease	Salisbury, NC
John H. Snedwin	H	February 10, 1865	Disease	Salisbury, NC
William W.S. Stephens	E	November 26, 1864	Disease	Salisbury, NC
William Wagner	K	February 22, 1865	Diarrhea	Danville, VA
William White	E	November 4, 1864	Intermit. Fever	Salisbury, NC[6]

Chapter Notes

Introduction

1. Margaret Leech, *Reveille in Washington 1860–1865* (New York: Harper and Brothers, 1941) (Time, Inc. Reprint, 1962), 321.
2. *Ibid.*, 334.
3. Benjamin F. Cooling and Walton H. Owen, *Mr. Lincoln's Forts: A Guide to the Civil War Defenses of Washington* (Shippensburg, PA: White Mane, 1988), 5–12.
4. Benjamin F. Cooling, *Symbol, Sword and Shield: Defending Washington during the Civil War* (Shippensburg, PA: White Mane, 1991), 142–144.
5. U.S. National Park Service, "Civil War Defenses of Washington—Historic Resource Study," Appendix I: Civil War Defenses of Washington Chronology, October 2004. Online at: http://www.cr.nps.gov/history/online_books/civilwar/hrst.htm.
6. Howard R. Crouch, *Like a Hurricane: The Men, Mounts, Arms, and Tactics of Colonel John S. Mosby's Command* (Catlett, VA: SCS Publications, 2013), 34–35; V.C. Jones, "Action Along the Union Outposts in Fairfax," *Historical Society of Fairfax County, Virginia, Yearbook* (Vol. 3, 1954), 6.
7. *The War of the Rebellion, A Compilation of the Official Records of the War of the Union & Confederate Armies*, Series I, Vol. 21 (Washington, D.C.: Government Printing Office, 1890–1901), 902–904. Hereafter referred to as O.R.
8. Bvt. Maj. Gen. J. G. Barnard, *A Report on the Defenses of Washington to the Chief of Engineers, U.S. Army*, Professional Papers of the Corps of Engineers, U.S. Army, No. 20 (Washington, D.C.: General Printing Office, 1871), 104.
9. Frederick H. Dyer, *A Compendium of the War of the Rebellion* (Des Moines, IA: Dyer Publishing Co., 1908), 374–382.
10. Cooling, *Symbol, Sword and Shield*, 151–152.
11. O.R., Series I, Vol. 25, Part 2, 515–516.
12. *Ibid.*
13. O.R., Series I, Vol. 25, Part 2, 542–543.
14. O.R., Series I, Vol. 27, Part 2, 225–226, 244–245.
15. *Ibid.*, 283.
16. *Ibid.*, 334–335.
17. *Ibid.*, 373.
18. *Ibid.*, 323, 331–332, 378.
19. *Ibid.*, 358.
20. Dyer, 1,379.
21. Jones, "Actions Along the Union Outposts of Fairfax," 6.
22. James J. Williamson, *Mosby's Rangers: A Record of the Operations of the 43d Battalion Virginia Cavalry from its Organization to the Surrender*, Second Edition (New York: Sturgis & Walton Co., 1909), 47.
23. Jones, 7.
24. James A. Ramage, *Gray Ghost: The Life of Col. John Singleton Mosby* (Lexington: University Press of Kentucky, 1999), 367, n.9; Crouch, *Like a Hurricane*, 49–50.
25. Crouch, 9.
26. *Ibid.*, 9–16.
27. Augustus P. Green Autobiography, Augustus P. Green Collection, New-York Historical Society, New York, NY, 237–240.
28. O.R., Series I, Vol. 43, Part 2, 272–273.

Chapter One

1. New York State, *Third Annual Report of the Bureau of Military Record, Transmitted to the Legislature February 2, 1866* (Albany: C. Wendell, Printer, 1866), 17–18 (New York State Archives).
2. "Military Affairs in New York," *The Union Army: A History of Military Affairs in the*

Chapter Notes—One 229

Loyal States, 1861–1865 (Madison, WI: Federal Publishing Co., 1908), 18–49.
3. William F. Fox, *Regimental Losses in the American Civil War* (Albany: Augustus S. Brandow, 1898), 5.
4. Earl J. Coates and Dean S. Thomas, *An Introduction to Civil War Small Arms* (Gettysburg, PA: Thomas Publications, 1990), 45–46, 94.
5. *Ibid.*, 54–56.
6. Steven G. Miller, unpublished papers, Lake Villa, Illinois, 2014.
7. *New York Times*, October 5, 1861.
8. *Plattsburgh* (New York) *Republican*, January 24, 1863.
9. New York State, *Town Clerks' Registers of Men Who Served in the Civil War, 1861–1865* (Albany: New York State Archives), Collection (N-Ar) 137745, Box 31, Roll 18.
10. *Plattsburgh Republican*, January 24, 1863.
11. *Plattsburgh Republican*, March 2, 1872.
12. *The Frontier Palladium* (Malone, NY), March 23, 1863.
13. "See the Elephant" was a term used by both Confederate and Union troops to describe battle. If you were in a battle (or skirmish), you "saw the elephant."
14. New York State Military Museum and Veterans Research Center website @ www.dmna.state.ny.us/historic/reghist/civil/cavalry/16thCav/16thCavCWN.htm.
15. New York State, *Town Clerks' Registers of Men Who Served in the Civil War, 1861–1865*; New York State, *Annual Reports to the New York State Legislature, 1846–1995, by the Adjutant General of the New York National Guard, 1863, Vol. I, and 1867, Vol. 2* (Saratoga: New York State Military Museum).
16. James H. Smith, *History of Livingston County, New York* (Syracuse: D. Mason & Co., 1881), 446–447; Frederick Phisterer, *New York in the War of the Rebellion, 1861 to 1865, Third Edition* (Albany: J.B. Lyon Co., State Printers, 1912), 1,010–1,049.
17. *Plattsburgh Republican*, April 11, 1863.
18. *Plattsburgh Republican*, May 4, 1861 and October 26, 1861.
19. *Plattsburgh Republican*, April 11, 1863.
20. *The Union Army: A History of Military Affairs in the Loyal States 1861–65—Records of the Regiments in the Union Army—Cyclopedia of Battles—Memoirs of Commanders and Soldiers, Volume II* (Madison, WI: Federal Publishing Co., 1908), 65.
21. *Civil War Muster Roll Abstracts of New York State Volunteers, United States Sharpshooters, and United States Colored Troops, 1861–1900*, Albany: New York State Archives. Hereafter *Civil War Muster Roll Abstracts*.
22. 1860 U.S. Federal Census; *U.S. Civil War Soldier Records and Profiles, 1861–1865*, Historical Data Systems, Inc., Duxbury, MA (Ancestry.com); *The Plattsburgh Republican*, September 12, 1863.
23. New York State Military Museum and Veterans Research Center @ http://dmna.ny.gov/historic/reghist/civil/rosters/Infantry/118th_Infantry_CW_Roster.pdf.
24. George H. Anderson Letters, Clinton County Historical Association, Plattsburgh, NY.
25. *Plattsburg Sentinel*, January 16, 1891.
26. New York State Military Museum and Veterans Research Center @ http://dmna.ny.gov/historic/reghist/civil/rosters/Infantry/16th_Infantry_CW_Roster.pdf.
27. Moore Family Papers, State University of New York at Plattsburgh, Special Collections, File 66.7f, Folder 2/3/24.
28. New York State Military Museum and Veterans Research Center website @ www.dmna.state.ny.us/historic/reghist/civil/cavalry/16thCav/16thCavCWN.htm.
29. *Plattsburgh Republican*, April 11, 1863.
30. William P. Bacon, *Fourth Biographic Record of the Class of Fifty-Eight, Yale University, 1858–1897* (New Britain, CT: Adkins Printing Co., 1897), 235–236.
31. Albert B. Wilbur Diaries, The Andersonville Guild, Andersonville, GA.
32. *Ibid.*
33. Special Orders No. 29, June 20, 1863, Plattsburgh, N.Y., Hinton Summerfield Loyd Papers, Special Collections and University Archives, A1024, Colgate University Libraries, Hamilton, NY.
34. Guide to the Hinton Summerfield Loyd Papers, Special Collections and University Archives, Colgate University Libraries, Hamilton, NY; *New York Civil War Muster Roll Abstracts, 1861–1900*, Archive Collection #13775–83, Box 894, Roll 550, New York State Archives, Albany, NY (Ancestry.com).
35. Peter Ross, *A History of Long Island From Its Earliest Settlement to the Present Time, Vol. II* (New York: The Lewis Publishing Company, 1902), 96; "Civil War Biographies: Head-Hoodless," Green-Wood Cemetery (Brooklyn) website @ http://www.green-wood.com/2015/civil-war-biographies-head-hoodless.
36. *Ibid.*; U.S. Civil War Soldier Records and Profiles, 1861–1865, Ancestry.com; New York Civil War Muster Roll Abstracts, 1861–1900, New York State Archives (Ancestry.com).
37. New York State Military Museum and Veterans Research Center @ www.dmna.state.ny.us/historic/reghist/civil/cavalry/16thCav/16thCavCWN.htm.
38. Wayne Diercks, *The Story of the Louis*

Abend Drum (Zumbrota, MN: Zumbrota Area Historical Society, July 2010); *Army Register of Enlistments, 1798–1914*, January 1855–September 1857 (Fold3.com. image 310825789).
39. *Civil War Muster Rolls and Related Records, 1861–1866*, Records of the Department of Military and Veteran's Affairs, Record Group 19, Series 19.11, Pennsylvania Historical and Museum Commission, Harrisburg, PA (Ancestry.com).
40. *Civil War Muster Roll Abstracts, 1861–1900*, New York State Archives (Fold3.com).
41. Diercks, *The Story of the Louis Abend Drum*.
42. New York State Military Museum and Veterans Research Center @ http://dmna.ny.gov/historic/reghist/civil/infantry/125thInf/125thInfMain.htm.
43. Francis T. Hagadorn, "Reminiscences of Civil War Experiences, 1861–1866: Manuscript," New York State Library, Albany, MSC 12212 (hereafter, Hagadorn Manuscript), 54.
44. *Ibid.*, 58.
45. *U.S. Census, 1860*; *Williams-Reed Family Tree* (Ancestry.com).
46. *New York Times*, May 25, 1863.
47. *Albany Evening Journal*, June 22, 1863.
48. *Plattsburgh Republican*, June 13, 1863.
49. *Hagadorn Manuscript*, 62–63.
50. *Plattsburgh Republican*, August 8, 1863.
51. *Plattsburgh Republican*, June 13, 1863.
52. New York State Adjutant General's Office, *Annual Report of the Adjutant General of the State of New York for the Year 1894, Volume IV—Registers of the 13th—18th Regiments of Cavalry*, Albany: New York State Library. Hereafter *16th Cavalry Regimental Roster*.
53. Hagadorn Manuscript, 64.
54. Hagadorn Manuscript, 84.
55. Albert G. Martin Papers, William L. Clements Library, University of Michigan, Ann Arbor.
56. *Ibid.*
57. *Ibid.*
58. Hagadorn Manuscript, 85.
59. *New York Herald*, August 12, 1863.
60. Biographical notes prepared by Kenneth Robison II and posted on William West Hammell's obituary page on Find-a-Grave @ www.findagrave.com.
61. Phisterer, Part 3, 279, 389; *New York Herald*, August 12, 1863.
62. New York State Adjutant General's Office, *A Record of the Commissioned Officers, Non-Commissioned Officers and Privates of the Regiments Which Were Organized in the State of New York and Called into Service of the United States to Assist in Suppressing the Rebellion* (Albany: Weed, Parsons & Co., 1867).
63. New York State Military Museum and Veterans Research Center @ www.dmna.state.ny.us/historic/reghist/civil/cavalry/16thCav/16thCavCWN.htm.
64. Hagadorn Manuscript, 64.
65. Charles F. Moore Letters Collection, The Alice T. Miner Museum, Chazy, NY. (Digital collection available on the museum website at: http://www.minermuseum.org.)
66. *New York Tribune*, August 1, 1863.
67. Hagadorn Manuscript, 86.
68. *Plattsburgh Republican*, August 22, 1863; Hagadorn Manuscript, 94.
69. Hagadorn Manuscript, 95.
70. *New York Times*, August 15, 1863.
71. Hagadorn Manuscript, 100–102; *U.S. Civil War Soldier Records and Profiles, 1861–1865* (Ancestry.com).
72. "Giesboro Point Cavalry Depot, Parking for 30,000 Horses," Civil War Washington, D.C. Blog, August 17, 2011 (http://civilwarwashingtondc1861-1865.blogspot.com/2011/08/geisborough-point-cavalry-depot-parking.html).
73. Kenneth W. Munden and Henry Putney Beers, *The Union: A Guide to Federal Archives Relating to the Civil War* (Washington, D.C.: National Archives and Records Administration, 1986), 338.
74. "Camp Life. The First Step in 'Going to War'—Nicknames—Breaking in Cavalrymen-Memories of a Tin Cup," *New York Evening Post*, July 31, 1897, 11.
75. *Ibid.*
76. *Ibid.*
77. National Archives and Records Administration (hereafter, NARA), "Letter to Commanding Officer, 16th New York Cavalry," dated October 29, 1863, Records of Cavalry Depots and Depot Camps, RG393, pt. II, e6835, Letters Sent, Vol. 299.
78. *Plattsburgh Republican*, September 12, 1863.
79. NARA, Order, dated November 8, 1863, from Col. McIntosh, HQs Cavalry Depot, to Capt. Leahy, 16th New York Cavalry, Records of Cavalry Depots and Depot Camps, RG393, pt. II, e6835, Letters Sent, Vol. 299.
80. NARA, Case Files of Approved Pension Applications, Attachment to Application WC84130, Edwin Noonan, Letter dated November 8, 1863, Camp Stoneman (Fold3.com, image 280570843).
81. James Henry Fleming Letters, courtesy of Ms. Louise Brown, Witney, Oxfordshire, UK.
82. *New York State Soldier Burials at The Falls Church During the Civil War* (Falls Church, VA: The Falls Church Episcopal Church, undated), 23.
83. NARA, Court Martial Case Files,

Records of the Judge Advocate General, Lt. Joseph N. Schultz, Co. I, 16th New York Cavalry, RG 153, File MM-1288, November 1863.
84. NARA, Camp of Instruction, Camp Stoneman, Roster of Officers of the 16th New York Cavalry, Records of Cavalry Depots and Depot Camps, RG393, pt. II, e6838, Circulars, Vol. 232.
85. NARA, Court Martial Case Files, Records of the Judge Advocate General, Lt. Joseph N. Schultz, Co. I, 16th New York Cavalry, File LL-1521, January 1864.
86. Albert G. Martin Letters.
87. O.R., Series I, Vol. 29, Part 1, 68–70.
88. *Ibid.*
89. James McLean, *California Sabers: The 22nd Massachusetts Cavalry in the Civil War* (Bloomington: Indiana University Press, 2000), 54; Albert G. Martin Letters.
90. Charles F. Moore Letters Collection.
91. *Ibid.*
92. Albert G. Martin Papers.
93. "Cavalryman's Picket Duty. One of the Most Trying Requirements of a Soldier—The Terrors of a Night-Watch—A Deserter's Fate," *New York Evening Post*, August 28, 1897, 11.
94. *Ibid.*
95. *Philadelphia Press*, September 17, 1863.
96. Carol Bundy, *The Nature of Sacrifice: A Biography of Charles Russell Lowell, Jr., 1835–64* (New York: Farrar, Straus and Giroux, 2005), 241.
97. McLean, 59.
98. Genealogy website maintained by Rod A. MacDonald, Ed.D., Niagara Falls, Ontario, Canada @ www.r-a-macdonald.ca.
99. Ron Baumgarten, "Contraband Camps Established in Northern Virginia: May–June 1863, Part II," June 13, 2013, All Not So Quiet Along the Potomac Blog @ http://dclawyeronthecivilwar.blogspot.com.
100. Letter from the Secretary of War Transmitting a Copy of the Report of the Judge Advocate General Upon the Case of First Lieutenant W. J. Keays, of the Sixteenth New York Cavalry, January 29, 1870, Ex. Doc. No. 105, U.S. House of Representatives, 41st Congress, 2nd Session (hereafter Judge Advocate General Report).
101. Baumgarten, "The Fallout from the Raid on Camp Beckwith: Lt. Keays Takes the Heat," October 10, 2013, All Not So Quiet Along the Potomac Blog. Also see Rod MacDonald's website.
102. Judge Advocate General Report.
103. *Ibid.*
104. Albert G. Martin Letters.
105. Baumgarten, "The Fallout from the Raid on Camp Beckwith."
106. New York State Military Museum and Veterans Research Center @ http://dmna.ny.gov/historic/reghist/civil/infantry/100thInf/100thInfMain.htm.
107. New York State Military Museum and Veterans Research Center @ http://dmna.ny.gov/historic/reghist/civil/infantry/81stInf/81stInfMain.htm.
108. Lazelle Family Papers, James Carson, Vienna, VA.
109. For more on Henry M. Lazelle, see James Carson, *Against the Grain: Colonel Henry M. Lazelle and the U.S. Army* (Denton: University of North Texas Press, 2015).

Chapter Two

1. NARA. Return of the Cavalry Forces, Defences of Washington South of the Potomac, Dept. of Washington for the Month of October 1863: H.M. Lazelle, Col., 16th Reg't N.Y. Cav, Commanding Camp, Vienna, Va., Records of Named Departments, 1821–1920, RG 393.4.
2. Connie P. and Mayo S. Stuntz, *This Was Vienna, Virginia: Facts and Photos* (Vienna, VA: Privately printed, 1987), 117.
3. Charles A. Humphries, *Field, Camp, Hospital and Prison in the Civil War, 1863–1865* (Boston: Press of Geo. E. Ellis Co., 1918), 3–4.
4. Edward W. Emerson, *Life and Letters of Charles Russell Lowell* (New York: Houghton, Mifflin, 1907), 314–315, 445 (n.1).
5. "Freeman Store," National Register of Historic Places Registration Form, VDHR No. 153–002, dated September 27, 2011, @ http://www.dhr.virginia.gov/registers/Counties/Fairfax/153–0002_Freeman_Store_2012_NRHP_ FINAL.pdf.
6. *Ibid.*
7. Stuntz, 95 and 123.
8. Stuntz, 123–126.
9. Map 170–132, "Position of Block Houses at Vienna," Records of the Office of the Chief of Engineers, Fortification Files, RG77, National Archives at College Park, College Park, MD.
10. Grenville M. Dodge, "Use of Block-Houses During the Civil War," *Annals of Iowa*, Vol. 6, No. 4, 1904, 297–301.
11. O.R., Series I, Vol. 29, Part 2, 523; Vol. 33, 1047–1050; Frank J. Welcher, *The Union Army, 1861–1865—Organization and Operations, Vol. I, The Eastern Theater* (Bloomington: Indiana University Press, 1989), 169–175.
12. Charles Wells, ed, *The Memoirs of Colonel John S. Mosby* (Norwood, MA: Russell Boston Little Brown & Co., 1917), 265. See also, Williamson, *Mosby's Rangers*, 407–408.
13. War Department, Adjutant General's

Office, Special Orders No. 518, para. 30, dated November 21, 1863 (Fold3.com/image/ #316381340); New York Civil War Muster Roll Abstracts, 1861–1900; New York State Archives Collection #13775–83, Box 895, Roll 551 (Ancestry.com).
14. *New York Civil War Muster Roll Abstracts, 1861–1900*, Archive Collections # 13775–83, New York State Archives, Albany, New York (available online @ Ancestry.com).
15. Charles F. Moore Letters Collection.
16. "Scouting in the Blue Ridge. A Disregarded Order—Good Use of Repeating Rifles—Encounter with a 'Poor White,'" *New York Evening Post*, August 7, 1897, 11.
17. O.R., Series I, Vol. 29, Part 1, November 16, 1863, 652.
18. O.R., Series I, Vol. 29, Part 1, November 26, 1863, 658.
19. O.R., Series I, Vol. 29, Part 1, December 13, 1863, 977.
20. O.R., Series I, Vol. 29, Part 1, December 22, 1863, 987.
21. O.R., Series I, Vol. 29, Part 1, December 31, 1863, 994–995.
22. John S. Mosby, *The Memoirs of Colonel John S. Mosby*, Foreword by J. O. Tate (Nashville, TN: J.S. Sanders & Company, 1995), 266 (original edition published in 1917 by Little, Brown & Company).
23. O.R., Series I, Vol. 33, January 27, 1864, 432.
24. O.R., Series I, Vol. 33, January 28, 1863, 438, 442.
25. Mosby, 269–270.
26. O.R., Series I, Vol. 33, February 21–22, 1864, Skirmishes near Circleville and Dranesville, Va., 159–160.
27. *Ibid*. (For a full account, see Williamson, 141–146.)
28. *Ibid*.
29. Williamson, 147.
30. O.R., Series I, Vol. 51, Part 1, February 25–26, 1864, Scout from Vienna to Farmwell Station, Va., Report of Maj. Casper Crowninshield, 2nd Mass. Cavalry, 214–215.
31. Ramage, *Gray Ghost*, 137.
32. Williamson, 149.
33. O.R. Series I, Vol. 33, February 29, 1864, 617.
34. Jack and Carol Lundquist, *Civil War Prisons Database* @ www.civilwarprisoners.com; "Roster of New York Cavalry Regiments During the Civil War," New York State Military Museum and Veterans Center, Saratoga Springs, NY.
35. NARA, Carded Records Showing Military Service of Soldiers Who Fought in Volunteer Organizations During the American Civil War, 1890–1912, Records of the Adjutant General's Office, 1762–1984, RG94. Fold3.com images: 314787036 and 314743273–314743300.
36. *Ibid*.
37. *Ibid*.; O.R., Series 1, Vol. 33, February 7, 1864, 536.
38. *New York Evening Post*, August 28, 1897, 11.
39. NARA, Records of the Office of the Judge Advocate General (Army), Court Martial Case Files, File LL-1296.
40. *New York Evening Post*, August 28, 1897, 11.
41. The Second Mass and Its Fighting Californians web page @ http://2mass.omnica. com/References/ormsby.html.
42. Steven G. Miller, *An Informal History of the 16th New York Volunteer Cavalry* (Mundelin, IL: unpublished manuscript, March 1997). Also see Stuntz, *This Was Vienna*, 119–120.
43. "Roster of the New York Cavalry Regiments During the Civil War," New York State Military Museum and Veterans Research Center, Saratoga Springs, NY.

Chapter Three

1. E.B. Long, *The Civil War Day by Day: An Almanac 1861–1865* (Garden City, NY: Doubleday, 1971), 470–474.
2. Williamson, 148.
3. O.R. Series I, Vol. 33, March 22, 1864, 714; Albert B. Wilber Diaries, March 19–20, 1864, The Andersonville Guild, Andersonville, GA.
4. O.R. Series I, Vol. 33, April 5, 1864, 807.
5. Albert B. Wilber Diaries, April 4, 1864.
6. *The Diary of Valorus Dearborn*, April 6, 1864, http://www.2mass.reunioncivilwar.com/ References /dearborn.htm.
7. *Ibid*., April 14–15, 1864.
8. O.R. Series I, Vol. 33, April 15, 1864, 874.
9. D. Hamilton Hurd, *History of Clinton and Franklin Counties, New York* (Philadelphia: J.W. Lewis, 1880), 241–242.
10. *Richmond Daily Dispatch*, April 20, 1864, 1.
11. *Plattsburgh Republican*, May 7, 1864, 2.
12. William R. Cutter, *Genealogical and Family History of Northern New York* (New York: Lewis Historical Publishing Company, 1910), 706.
13. Hurd, 242.
14. Williamson, 157.
15. O.R. Series I, Vol. 33, 308.
16. Mosby, *Memoirs*, 272.
17. O.R. Series I, Vol. 33, 308; Williamson, 157.

18. *Roll of Honor (No. XIV): Names of Soldiers Who in Defense of the American Union, Suffered Martyrdom in the Prison Pens Throughout the South,* Quartermaster General's Office, General Orders No. 7, February 20, 1868 (Washington, D.C.: Government Printing Office, 1868).
19. NARA, Court Martial Case Files, Records of the Judge Advocate General, Captain John J. Schlaefer, Co. F, 16th New York Cavalry, RG 153, File NN-2082, April 1864.
20. Albert B. Wilbur Diaries, April 30, 1864.
21. *New York Civil War Muster Roll Abstracts, 1861–1900,* Archive Collections # 13775–83, box 894, roll 550, New York State Archives, Albany, New York (Ancestry.com).
22. Williamson, 158.
23. O.R. Series I, Vol. 33, 315–316.
24. Williamson, 158.
25. O.R. Series I, Vol. 33, 315–316.
26. *Ibid.*
27. *New York Evening Post,* September 25, 1897, 13.
28. *Ibid.*
29. O.R. Series 1, Vol. 37, Part 1, 446.
30. O.R., Series I, Vol. 37, Part 1, 453, 485.
31. "Yankee Davis: Colonel Lowell's Scout," The Second Mass and Its Fighting Californians web page http://www.2mass.reunioncivilwar.com/References/Yankee%20Davis.htm
32. Williamson, 110–111.
33. Steve Meserve, "Charles Binns of Loudoun County," *Bulletin of the Loudoun County Historical Society,* 2004, 76–77.
34. *Ibid.,* 79–80.
35. "Headquarters, Dept. Washington, 22d Army Corps, January 18, 1864," Charles Binns Vertical File, 2004.011-B, Thomas Balch Library, Leesburg, VA.
36. Meserve, 82.
37. "Report to Accompany H.R. 11453, Committed to the Committee of the Whole House, Charles E. Binns," January 11, 1901, House of Representatives, 56th Congress, 2nd Session, Report No. 2240. (Charles Binns Vertical File, Thomas Balch Library, Leesburg, VA.)
38. Thomas J. Evans and James M. Moyer, *Mosby Vignettes, Vol. I* (N.p.: Privately printed, 1993), 80.
39. Albert B. Wilbur Diaries, May 14–17, 1864.
40. McLean, 79.
41. Albert B. Wilbur Diaries, June 4, 1864.
42. *U.S. Civil War Records and Profiles, 1861–1865;* Tuck Family Tree and Roberta Tuck Kantner Gromley Family Tree, Ancestry.com.
43. O.R., Series I, Vol. 37, Part 2, 167–169.
44. *Ibid.*
45. Williamson, 177; Mosby, 274.
46. *Roll of Honor (No. XIV): Names of Soldiers Who in Defense of the American Union, Suffered Martyrdom in the Prison Pens Throughout the South*; "Roster of the New York Cavalry Regiments During the Civil War," New York State Military Museum and Veterans Research Center, Saratoga Springs, NY.
47. McLean, 80.

Chapter Four

1. "The Battle of Monocacy, 9 July 1864," The Army Historical Foundation website at www.armyhistory.org.
2. "Battle of Fort Stevens," The Civil War Trust website at: http://www.civilwar.org/battlefields/fort-stevens.html.
3. McLean, 87–88; Mosby, 275–276.
4. O.R. Series I, Vol. 37, Part 2, 170–171, 543; McLean, 91–93, 116.
5. O.R., Series I, Vol. 37, Part 2, 245–246
6. Bradley E. Gernand, *A Virginia Village Goes to War: Falls Church During the Civil War* (Virginia Beach, VA: The Donning Company Publishers, 2002), 113–114, 178–179.
7. Albert B. Wilbur Diaries, July 13, 1864.
8. James Henry Fleming Letters, Fort Buffalo, July 31, 1864.
9. Long, *The Civil War Day by Day,* 537–542.
10. O.R., Series I, Vol. 37, Part 2, 290, 312, 336–337, 354.
11. O.R., Series I, Vol. 37, Part 2, 364.
12. NARA, Court Martial Case Files, Records of the Judge Advocate General, Lt. Col. George S. Hollister, 16th New York Cavalry, RG 153, File NN-2376.
13. NARA, Court Martial Case Files, Records of the Judge Advocate 1st Lt. Col. George S. Hollister, 7th Infantry, RG 153, File LL-317.
14. Special Orders No. 32, War Department, Adjutant General's Office, Washington, January 25, 1866; Thomas P. Lowry, *Sexual Misbehavior in the Civil War: A Compendium* (Xlibris Corp., 2006), 199.
15. McLean, 106–109.
16. O.R., Series I, Vol. 37, Part 2, 387–388.
17. *Ibid.*
18. O.R., Series I, Vol. 37, Part 2, 389–390.
19. O.R., Series I, Vol. 37, Part 2, 481–482.
20. O.R., Series I, Vol. 37, Part 2, 362–363.
21. O.R., Series I, Vol. 37, Part 2, 497–498.
22. O.R., Series I, Vol. 37, Part 2, 511, 530.
23. Long, *The Civil War Day by Day,* 533; see also John L. Heatwole, *The Burning: Sheri-*

dan in the *Shenandoah Valley* (Charlottesville, VA: Howell Press, 1998), 7–16.
24. Mosby, *Memoirs*, 283–286.
25. O.R., Series I, Vol. 37, Part 2, 575.
26. O.R. Series I, Vol. 43, Part 1, 684.
27. O.R. Series I, Vol. 43, Part 1, 721–722.
28. O.R. Series I, Vol. 43, Part 1, 729; Williamson, 204.
29. Williamson, 205.
30. *Skirmish at St. Mary's*, The Historical Marker Database http://www.hmdb.org/marker.asp?marker=186; Williamson, 205–206.
31. J. Marshall Crawford, *Mosby and His Men* (New York: G.W. Carleton, 1867), 236–237.
32. O.R. Series I, Vol. 43, Part I, 742–43, 762; Williamson, 206; Albert B. Wilbur Diaries, August 10, 1864.
33. O.R. Series I, Vol. 43, Part I, 742–743, 777.
34. *New York Tribune*, undated clipping, courtesy of Ms. Louise Brown, Witney, Oxfordshire, UK.
35. "Danville National Cemetery, Danville, Virginia," U.S. National Park Service website http://www.nps.gov/nr/travel/national_cemeteries/virginia/Danville_VA_National_Cemetery.html; "Roster of the New York Cavalry Regiments During the Civil War," New York State Military Museum and Veterans Research Center, Saratoga Springs, NY.
36. O.R. Series I, Vol. 43, Part 1, 784–785, 793–794.
37. O.R. Series I, Vol. 43, Part 1, 801,813–814, 832–833, 862; Albert B. Wilber Diaries, August 20, 1864.
38. O.R. Series I, Vol. 43, Part 1, 862, 871–873.
39. Cooling, *Symbol, Sword and Shield*, 221.
40. O.R. Series I, Vol. 43, Part 1, 873.
41. O.R. Series I, Vol. 43, Part 1, 890, 910–911.
42. O.R. Series I, Vol. 43, Part 1, 899.
43. Williamson, 218.
44. O.R. Series I, Vol. 43, Part 1, 638.
45. *Ibid.*; Williamson, 218–219.
46. Williamson, 219–220.
47. Charles F. Moore Letters Collection, August 25, 1864; Augustus P. Green Collection, 217–219.
48. Southern Claims Commission, Claim of James Purdy; Records of the Ordinance of Succession, Fairfax County Circuit Court Archives, cited in the Dutkowski/Schneider/Kennell Family Tree, Ancestry.com http://person.ancestry.com/tree/54514926/person/1367676 1380/facts.
49. O.R. Series I, Vol. 43, Part 1, 638.
50. "Curriculum Vitae de Joseph Schneider," undated, Schneider Family Papers, courtesy of Robert Snapper, Kew Gardens, NY.
51. *Ibid.*
52. KDUTMAN Family Tree, Ancestry.com; additional background information courtesy of Kathy Manese; "Roster of the New York Cavalry Regiments During the Civil War," New York State Military Museum and Veterans Research Center, Saratoga Springs, NY.
53. Charles F. Moore Letters Collection, August 25, 1864.
54. O.R. Series I, Vol. 43, Part 1, 920, 933.
55. O.R. Series I, Vol. 43, Part 1, 942–943.
56. O.R. Series I, Vol. 43, Part 1, 943–944.
57. O.R. Series I, Vol. 43, Part 1, 955.
58. *Ibid.*
59. O.R. Series I, Vol. 43, Part 1, 963.
60. O.R. Series I, Vol. 43, Part 1, 971; Albert B. Wilbur Diaries, August 31, 1864.

Chapter Five

1. Long, *The Civil War Day by Day*, 564.
2. Mosby, *Memoirs*, 283.
3. O.R., Series I, Vol. 43, Part 2, 5.
4. *Ibid.*
5. Williamson, 223–226.
6. Williamson, 232–233; O.R. Series I, Vol. 43, Part 2, 90.
7. Mosby, *Memoirs*, 298.
8. Williamson, 233, 250.
9. O.R., Series I, Vol. 43, Part 2, 146.
10. O.R., Series I, Vol. 43, Part 2, 85, 94, 97.
11. *New York Herald*, September 24, 1864.
12. *New York Evening Post*, July 17, 1897.
13. *Elmira* (NY) *Morning Telegram*, August 6, 1888.
14. O.R., Series 1, Vol. 43, Part 2, 133–134.
15. *New York Herald*, September 24, 1864.
16. *Ibid.*
17. Letter, dated April 15, 1886, to Captain Eugene Carter, Recorder Board of Adjudication, Washington, D.C., from Captain H.M. Lazelle, 8th Infantry, Lazelle Family Papers; O.R., Series 1, Vol. 43, Part 2, 275.
18. *New York Evening Post*, July 17, 1897.
19. *New York Herald*, September 24, 1864.
20. O.R., Series 1, Vol. 43, Part 2, 133.
21. *New York Evening Post*, July 17, 1897.
22. O.R., Series 1, Vol. 43, Part 2, 133–134.
23. *New York Herald*, September 24, 1864.
24. *Lockport* (New York) *Daily Journal*, July 28, 1887.
25. *New York Evening Post*, July 17, 1897.
26. *Ibid.*
27. *Ibid.*
28. O.R., Series 1, Vol. 43, Part 2, 134.
29. Albert B. Wilbur Diaries, September 2021, 1864.
30. O.R., Series 1, Vol. 43, Part 2, 134.

31. "Roster of the New York Cavalry Regiments During the Civil War," New York State Military Museum and Veterans Research Center, Saratoga Springs, NY.
32. O.R., Series 1, Vol. 43, Part 2, 145.
33. O.R., Series 1, Vol. 43, Part 2, 166.
34. O.R., Series 1, Vol. 43, Part 2, 211.
35. Colonel W.H. Powell, *List of Officers of the Army of the United States from 1779 to 1900* (New York: L.R. Hamersly, 1900), 202.
36. Special Orders. No. 327, War Department, Adjutant General's Office, Washington, October 1, 1864 (www.fold3.com/image/#31639 5064).
37. Journal of the Proceedings of the Senate of the United States in Executive Session, Part II: February 13, 1866 to July 28, 1866, Executive Journal, July 26, 1866, 1099, U.S. Senate, 39th Congress, 1st Session.
38. Williamson, 247.
39. O.R., Series 1, Vol. 43, Part 2, 155.
40. O.R., Series 1, Part 2, 165.
41. O.R., Series 1, Vol. 43, Part 2, 178.
42. O.R., Series 1, Vol. 43, Part 2, 211, 219.
43. O.R., Series I, Vol. 43, Part 2, 291–292.
44. Charles F. Moore Letters Collection, October 6, 1864.
45. *Ibid.*
46. O.R., Series 1, Vol. 43, Part 2, 268.
47. O.R., Series 1, Vol. 43, Part 2, 272–273.
48. Mosby, *Memoirs*, 307–309.
49. O.R., Series 1, Vol. 43, Part 2, 301.
50. Albert B. Wilber Diaries, October 7, 1864.
51. O.R., Series 1, Vol. 43, Part 2, 312.
52. O.R., Series 1, Vol. 43, Part 2, 319.
53. O.R., Series 1, Vol. 43, Part 2, 312.
54. Williamson, 266–267.
55. O.R., Series, I, Vol. 43, Part 1, 618–619; Williamson, 266–267; Augustus P. Green Autobiography, 222–224.
56. O.R., Series, I, Vol. 43, Part 1, 618–619.
57. Augustus P. Green Autobiography, 224.
58. Williamson, 269–270.
59. Williamson, 270–271; see also O.R. Series I, Vol. 43, Part 2, 394–398.
60. O.R., Series I, Vol. 43, Part 2, 403–406.
61. Ramage, *Gray Ghost*, 147.
62. Virgil Carrington Jones, *Ranger Mosby* (Chapel Hill: University of North Carolina Press, 1944) (reprinted by EPM Publications, McLean, VA, 1972), 179.
63. O.R. Series I, Vol. 43, Part 2, 414–415. See also Evans and Moyer, *Mosby Vignettes, Vol. I*, 46–54.
64. Crawford, *Mosby and His Men*, 277–278.
65. Williamson, 271.
66. Crawford, 277; Evans and Moyer, 48.
67. O.R. Series I, Vol. 43, Part 2, 414–415.
68. Albert B. Wilbur Diaries, October 19, 1864.
69. Evans and Moyer, 51.
70. O.R., Series I, Vol. 43, Part 2, 403.
71. NARA, H. M. Lazelle File, RG94, 26214 ACP 1874.
72. *Ibid.*
73. *Philip Henry Sheridan Correspondence, 1831–1888*, Letter dated October 16, 1864, to Horatio Seymour (OCoLC: 314107062), New York State Library, Albany.
74. NARA, Letters Received by the Office of the Adjutant General, Main Series, 1861–1870, RG94, M619B, L804.
75. Stuntz, 26–27.

Chapter Six

1. Bvt. Maj.-Gen. George W. Cullum, *Biographical Register of the Officers and Graduates of the U.S. Military Academy from Its Establishment in 1802 to 1890, Volume II* (Boston: Houghton, Mifflin, 1891), 543–544.
2. *New York Evening Post*, October 2, 1897.
3. O.R., Series I, Vol. 43, Part 2, Special Orders No. 289, Headquarters, Department of Washington, November 19, 1864, 645–646; General Orders No. 120, Headquarters, Department of Washington, November 29, 1864, 699.
4. *Ibid.*
5. *Ibid.*
6. O.R., Series I, Vol. 43, Part 2, 671–672.
7. P.H. Sheridan, *Personal Memoirs of P. H. Sheridan, General, United States Army, Vol. II* (New York: Charles L. Webster & Co., 1888), 99–100.
8. O.R., Series I, Vol. 43, Part 2, 699–701.
9. O.R., Series I, Vol. 43, Part 2, 701, 731.
10. Sheridan, 100.
11. Virgil Carrington Jones, *Ranger Mosby* (Chapel Hill: University of North Carolina Press, 1944), 241.
12. NARA, Letters Received by the Office of the Adjutant General, Main Series, RG94, M619, L820.
13. *New York Evening Post*, October 2, 1897.
14. *Ibid.*
15. *Ibid.*
16. O.R., Series I, Vol. 43, Part 2, 768.
17. O.R., Series I, Vol. 43, Part 2, 806–807.
18. Charles F. Moore Letters Collection, December 20, 1864.
19. O.R., Series I, Vol. 43, Part 2, 810–811, 825.
20. Nancy C. Baird, ed., *Journals of Amanda Virginia Edmonds, Lass of the Mosby Confederacy, 1857–1867* (Stephens City, VA: Commercial Press, 1984), 209–210.

21. O.R., Series I, Vol. 43, Part 2, 810–811, 831–832.
22. Mosby, *Memoirs*, 337–338.
23. *Ibid.*, 341–342.
24. O.R., Series I, Vol. 43, Part 2, 832.
25. O.R., Series I, Vol. 43, Part 2, 843–844.
26. *Ibid.*
27. Crawford, *Mosby and His Men*, 324; Williamson, 338.
28. O.R., Series I, Vol. 46, Part 2, 17, 92.
29. Albert B. Wilbur Diaries, January 5, 18–19, 1865.
30. O.R., Series I, Vol. 46, Part 2, 73, 110, 142.
31. Albert B. Wilbur Diaries, January 20–23, 1865.
32. Augustus P. Green Autobiography, 229–236.
33. *Ibid.*
34. *Ibid.*
35. Albert B. Wilbur Diaries, February 8, 1865.
36. NARA, Court Martial Case Files, Records of the Judge Advocate General, Captain Charles Robin, Co. H, 16th New York Cavalry, January 1865, RG 153, File NN-3658.
37. *Ibid.*; *New York Civil War Muster Roll Abstracts, 1861–1900*, Archive Collections # 13775–83, box 895, roll 551, New York State Archives, Albany, New York (available online @ Ancestry.com).
38. Albert B. Wilbur Diaries, February 8, 1865.
39. O.R., Series I, Vol. 46, Part 2, 734; Albert B. Wilbur Diaries, February 28, 1865.
40. Welcher, *The Union Army 1861–1865, Vol. I*, 1046–1047.
41. O.R., Series I, Vol. 46, Part 2, 798.
42. O.R., Series I, Vol. 46, Part1, 541–542.
43. *Ibid.*
44. 2nd Lt. John Frank Hoover had originally mustered in as Commissary Sergeant, Company D, in June 1863 and had been reduced to private in August 1864. He was mustered in as 2Lt., Company B, February 12, 1865, with a date of rank of November 15, 1864, replacing Lt. Henry P. Field, who had been discharged in October 1864.
45. O.R., Series I, Vol. 46, Part1, 541–542.
46. O.R., Series I, Vol. 46, Part 2, 853.
47. O.R., Series I, Vol. 46, Part 2, 911.
48. *New York Civil War Muster Roll Abstracts, 1861–1900*, Archive Collections # 13775–83, box 892, roll 548 and box 361, roll 3–4, New York State Archives, Albany, New York (available online @ Ancestry.com); O.R., Series I, Vol. 46, Part 1, 545–546.
49. O.R., Series I, Vol. 46, Part 2, 883.
50. Albert B. Wilbur Diaries, March 7–8, 1865.
51. O.R., Series I, Vol. 46, Part 1, 546–547.
52. O.R., Series I, Vol. 46, Part 1, 548.
53. O.R., Series I, Vol. 46, Part 1, 546.
54. *Ibid.*
55. *New York Civil War Muster Roll Abstracts, 1861–1900*, Archive Collections # 13775–83, box 361, roll 3–4, New York State Archives, Albany, New York (available online @ Ancestry.com).
56. O.R., Series I, Vol. 46, Part 2, 850–851, 911, 921.
57. *The Virginia State Journal*, Volume 3, Number 913, March 11, 1865, 3.
58. O.R., Series I, Vol. 46, Part 1, 551; Vol. 46, Part 2, 943–944.
59. O.R., Series I, Vol. 46, Part 1, 551; Vol. 46, Part 2, 944, 955; *The Virginia State Journal*, Volume 3, Number 915, March 14, 1865, 3; Albert B. Wilbur Diaries, March 13–14, 1865.
60. O.R., Series I, Vol. 46, Part 1, 551; Vol. 46, Part 2, 955.
61. O.R., Series I, Vol. 46, Part 2, 922.
62. O.R., Series I, Vol. 46, Part 1, 552.
63. *Ibid.*
64. O.R., Series, I, Vol. 46, Part 3, 25, 47–48, 84.
65. Albert B. Wilbur Diaries, March 20, 1865.
66. Albert B. Wilbur Diaries, March 20, 1865; Charles F. Moore Letters Collection, March 26, 1865.

Chapter Seven

1. Albert B. Wilbur Diaries, April 2–3, 1865.
2. Charles F. Moore Letters Collection, April 5, 1865.
3. O.R., Series, I, Vol. 46, Part 3, 638, 661–662.
4. O.R., Series, I, Vol. 46, Part 1, 1307–1308.
5. Williamson, 367.
6. O.R., Series, I, Vol. 46, Part 1, 1307–1308.
7. Albert B. Wilbur Diaries, April 10, 1865.
8. Mosby, *Memoirs*, 357–358.
9. O.R., Series, I, Vol. 46, Part 3, 700–701.
10. O.R., Series, I, Vol. 46, Part 3, 715.
11. O.R., Series, I, Vol. 46, Part 3, 750–751.
12. O.R., Series, I, Vol. 46, Part 3, 752–773.
13. John Wells Buckley, "The War Hospitals," in Marcus Benjamin, ed., *Washington During War Time: A Series of Papers Showing the Military, Political, and Social Phases During 1861 to 1865* (Washington, D.C.: National Tribune Press, 1902), 138–153.
14. *New York Evening Post*, June 5, 1897.
15. O.R., Series, I, Vol. 46, Part 3, 819.

16. Charles F. Moore Letters Collection, April 16/22, 1865.
17. O.R., Series, I, Vol. 46, Part 3, 801–802.
18. Charles F. Moore Letters Collection, April 16/22, 1865.
19. Albert B. Wilbur Diaries, April 20, 1865.
20. O.R., Series, I, Vol. 46, Part 3, 902–903.
21. O.R., Series, I, Vol. 46, Part 3, 949.
22. O.R., Series, I, Vol. 46, Part 3, 949, 988.
23. Albert B. Wilbur Diaries, April 25, 1865.
24. O.R., Series, I, Vol. 46, Part 3, 962.
25. O.R., Series, I, Vol. 46, Part 1, 1317.
26. O.R., Series, I, Vol. 46, Part 1, 1318; "Pursuit and Death of John Wilkes Booth," *The Century Illustrated Monthly Magazine*, November 1889 to April 1890, 446–447.
27. O.R., Series, I, Vol. 46, Part 1, 1318; William C. Edwards, ed., *The Lincoln Assassination: The Reward Files* (Google e-book, 2012), 211.
28. This account, unless otherwise noted, is taken from Doherty's official report: O.R., Series I, Vol. 46, Part 1, 1317–1322.
29. "Pursuit and Death of John Wilkes Booth," *The Century Illustrated Monthly Magazine*, November 1889 to April 1890, 446–447.
30. "A Cavalryman's Account of the Chase and Capture of John Wilkes Booth," Abraham Lincoln's Assassination website @ http://rogerjnorton.com/Lincoln73.html.
31. Albert B. Wilbur Diaries, April 28, 1865.
32. *The New York Evening Post*, June 5, 1897.
33. O.R., Series, I, Vol. 46, Part 3, 817.
34. Mosby, *Memoirs*, 360–361.
35. O.R., Series, I, Vol. 46, Part 3, 910.
36. Mosby, *Memoirs*, 397–399.

Chapter Eight

1. Albert B. Wilbur Diaries, May 16, 1865.
2. O.R., Series 1, Vol. 46, Part 1, 1114.
3. O.R., Series 1, Vol. 46, Part 3, 1173.
4. O.R., Series 1, Vol. 46, Part 3, 1171.
5. Albert B. Wilbur Diaries, June 27–30, 1865.
6. *Ibid.*, July 3, 1865.
7. *Ibid.*, July 10–11, 1865; *Daily National Intelligencer*, Washington, D.C., July 20, 1865.
8. Copy of original courtesy of Rod A. MacDonald, Niagara Falls, Ontario, Canada.
9. *Daily National Intelligencer*, Washington, D.C., July 20, 1865.
10. Steven G. Miller, *Officers of the Sixteenth NY Cavalry and the Lincoln Avengers Medals/Certificates* (Lake Villa, IL: unpublished memo, August 3, 2016).

11. "Headquarters, First Separate Brigade, Department of Washington, Special Orders No. 117, dated June 29, 1865," New-York Historical Society, Civil War Collection, Miscellaneous: Military Orders & Documents, June 20, 1861–April 6, 1868.
12. Augustus P. Green Autobiography, 300–304.
13. Albert B. Wilbur Diaries, July 9, 1865.
14. Phisterer, *New York in the War of the Rebellion*, 329.
15. *Courier and Republic*, Buffalo, N.Y., August 19, 1865, citing report from the Washington *Evening Star*.
16. *Ibid.*
17. *National Daily Republican*, Washington, D.C., August 18, 1865.
18. *Ibid.*
19. Albert B. Wilbur Diaries, August 27, September 9, 1865.
20. Phisterer, *New York in the War of the Rebellion, Vol. 2*, 1010–1011.
21. Fox, *Regimental Losses*, 474.
22. William T. Sherman, *Memoirs, Vol. II* (New York: D. Appleton & Co., 1875), 385.
23. Ramage, *Gray Ghost*, 346.
24. Jeffrey D. Wert, *Mosby's Rangers* (New York: Simon and Schuster, 1990), 292.
25. Ramage, 344.

Chapter Nine

1. Leech, *Reveille in Washington*, 516.
2. George F. Price, *Across the Continent with the Fifth Cavalry* (New York: D. Van Nostrand, 1883), 298–299.
3. Charles Morris, ed., *Men of the Century: An Historical Work Giving Portraits and Sketches of Eminent Citizens of the United States* (Philadelphia: L.R. Hamersly, 1896), 229.
4. Cullum, *Biographical Register of the Officers and Graduates*, 543–544.
5. "A Special Lincoln Medal," July 17, 2013, and "Letters to the Editor: More on the Lincoln Avengers," February 2, 2015, *The Rail Splitter: A Journal for the Lincoln Collector*, online @ railsplitter.com; Frederick von Allendorfer, *The Cross of Lincoln's Avengers: Was It Produced and Issued?*, memorandum prepared for the 25th Convention of the Orders and Medals Society of America, August 9–12, 1984.
6. *New York Times*, March 8, 1898; *1890 Veterans Schedules*, Ancestry.com; Arlington National Cemetery Website, http://www.arlingtoncemetery.mil/Explore-the-Cemetery/Find-a-Grave.
7. James Carson, *Against the Grain: Colonel Henry M. Lazelle and the U.S. Army* (Denton: University of North Texas Press, 2015).

8. Lowry, *Sexual Misbehavior in the Civil War*, 199.
9. NARA, Letters Received by the Commission Branch of the Adjutant General's Office, 1863–1870, RG 94 (M1064, roll 98, file H1194 CB 1864 and roll 264, file H50 CB 1866).
10. NARA, Letters Received by the Commission Branch of the Adjutant General's Office, 1863–1870, RG 94 (M1064, roll 264, file H50 CB 1866).
11. *Ibid.*
12. *Ibid.*
13. NARA, Court Martial Case Files, Records of the Judge Advocate General, Capt. George S. Hollister, 7th U.S. Infantry, January 1868, RG 153, File OO-2903, January 1868.
14. John Y. Simon, ed., *The Papers of Ulysses S. Grant, Vol. 18, October 1, 1867–June 30, 1868* (Carbondale: Southern Illinois University Press, 1991), 343–344.
15. *Ibid.*
16. *Ibid.*
17. Lowry, 199; *U.S. Census, 1860*.
18. NARA, Court Martial Case Files, Records of the Judge Advocate General, Capt. George S. Hollister, 7th U.S. Infantry, January 1868, RG 153, File OO-2903, January 1868.
19. *Ibid.*
20. *Ibid.*
21. NARA, Headquarters of the Army General Court Martial Orders No. 18, Washington, May 25, 1868; Headquarters, Third Military District General Orders No. 84, Atlanta, June 1, 1868. Letters Received by the Commission Branch of the Adjutant General's Office, 1863–1870, RG 94 (M1064, roll 401, file H94 CB 1868).
22. NARA, Returns from U.S. Military Posts, 1800–1916, Omaha Barracks, May 1869, RG 94 (M617, roll 879); Camp Douglas, June 1869, RG 94 (M617, roll 324).
23. NARA, Returns from U.S. Military Posts, 1800–1916, Camp Douglas, July 1869–April 1870, RG 94 (M617, roll 324); George W. Cullum, *Biographical Register of the Officers and Graduates*, 766.
24. Letters Received by the Commission Branch of the Adjutant General's Office, 1863–1870, RG 94 (M1064, roll 98, file H1194 CB 1864).
25. Lowry, 200; Francis B. Heitman, *Historical Register and Dictionary of the United States Army from Its Organization, September 29, 1789, to March 2, 1903, Vol. 1* (Washington, D.C.: Government Printing Office, 1903), 538; NARA, General Index to Pension Files, 1861–1934, T288, roll 222, Hollister, George S., Application No. 513582.

26. *Janesville Daily Gazette*, Janesville, Wisconsin, September 14, 1901.
27. *U.S. Census, 1860*.
28. *Janesville Daily Gazette*, September 14, 1901.
29. *U.S. Census, 1870 & 1880*.
30. *Christian Intelligencer of the Reformed Dutch Church*, May 20, 1858 (Ancestry.com); New York State Census, 1875 (Ancestry.com).
31. Peter Ross, *A History of Long Island*, 96; *The Brooklyn Daily Eagle*, April 9, 1879, 3; *Annual Reports Submitted to the New York State Legislature, 1846–1995*, Adjutant General of the New York National Guard, 1870, 1873, 1874, and 1875 (fold3.com).
32. *The Boston Post*, April 9, 1879, 3.
33. "Civil War Biographies: Head-Hoodless," Green-Wood Cemetery (Brooklyn) website http://www.green-wood.com/2015/civil-war-biographies-head-hoodless.
34. *The Brooklyn Daily Eagle*, March 17, 1879; "New York Wills and Probate Records, 1659–1999," New York County, District and Probate Courts (Ancestry.com); NARA, U.S. Civil War Pension Index: General Index to Pension Files, 1861–1934 (Ancestry.com); Green-Wood Cemetery database @ http://www.green-wood.com/burial_search/.
35. *History of Clinton and Franklin Counties, New York* (Philadelphia: J.W. Lewis, 1880), 241–242; William Richard Cutter, ed., *Genealogical and Family History of Northern New York, Volume II* (New York: Lewis Historical Publishing Co., 1910), 705–706.
36. *Plattsburgh Sentinel*, November 19, 1868.
37. *Plattsburgh Sentinel*, November 4, 1881.
38. *Ibid.*
39. *Plattsburgh Sentinel*, August 31, 1883.
40. *Plattsburgh Sentinel*, August 3, 1883.
41. *Ibid.*
42. *U.S. Census, 1900 & 1910*; *New York State Census, 1905*.
43. KDUTMAN Family Tree, Ancestry.com.
44. *Ibid.*
45. O.R., Series 1, Vol. 46, Part 3, 847.
46. Robert G. Wick, "Battle for the War Department Rewards for the Capture of John Wilkes Booth," *Journal of the Abraham Lincoln Association*, Vol. 32, No. 2, 2011.
47. *Ibid.*
48. Taken variously from "New York Civil War Muster Rolls Abstracts, 1861–1900," New York State Archives, Collections No. 13775–83, Box 897, Roll 553 (Ancestry.com) and NARA, "Organizational Index to Pension Files of Veterans Who Served Between 1861 and 1900," T289 (Fold3.com).
49. NARA, *Letters Received by the Commis-*

sion Branch of the Adjutant General's Office, 1863–1870, RG94, M12064, Roll 253.
50. NARA, Returns from U.S. Military Posts, 1800–1916, Posts at Columbia and Aiken, S.C., RG94, M617, roll 228.
51. NARA, Letters Received by the Commission Branch of the Adjutant General's Office, 1863–1870, RG94, M12064, Roll 253.
52. NARA, Returns from U.S. Military Posts, 1800–1916, Post at Atlanta, RG94, M617, roll 50.
53. NARA, Letters Received by the Commission Branch of the Adjutant General's Office, 1863–1870, RG94, M1065, Roll 407.
54. George F. Price, Across the Continent, 142, 513–514.
55. NARA, Returns from U.S. Military Posts, 1800–1916, Fort D.A. Russell, RG94, M617, roll 1050.
56. NARA, Letters Received by the Commission Branch of the Adjutant General's Office, 1863–1870, RG94, M617, roll 253.
57. NARA, Letters Received by the Commission Branch of the Adjutant General's Office, 1863–1870, Unsigned Letter, dated July 30th, postmarked Washington, D.C., to General W. Sherman, RG94, M617, roll 1050.
58. NARA, Letters Received by the Commission Branch of the Adjutant General's Office, 1863–1870, Memorandum, dated September 7, 1870, from Headquarters, Detachment, 5th U.S. Cavalry. Fort D.A. Russell, to 1st Lieut. N. C. Forbush, Adjutant, 5th U.S. Cavalry, Fort McPherson, RG94, M1064, Roll, 253, files D184–413.
59. NARA, Letters Received by the Commission Branch of the Adjutant General's Office, 1863–1870, "Charges and Specification Preferred Against 1st Lieut. Edward P. Doherty, 5th U.S. Cavalry," RG94, M1064, files D184–413.
60. NARA, Letters Received by the Commission Branch of the Adjutant General's Office, 1863–1870, Special Orders No. 294, Adjutant General's Office, Washington, D.C., November 3, 1870, and "Case 29, No. 44 on List, 1st Lieut. E.P. Doherty, 5th Cavalry," RG94, M1064, files D184–413; NARA, Returns from U.S. Military Posts, 1800–1916, Fort D.A. Russell, RG94, M617, roll 1050.
61. District of Columbia, Select Marriages, 1830–1921 (Ancestry.com); U.S. Census, 1880.
62. NARA, Letters Received by the Commission Branch of the Adjutant General's Office, 1863–1870, RG94, M12064, Roll 253.
63. Index to Reports of Committees of the House of Representatives for the First Session of the Forty-Fourth Congress, 1875–76, "Testimony Taken Before the Committee on the Post-Office and Post-Roads in Relation to Mail Contracts" (Washington, D.C.: Government Printing Office), 636.
64. The Times-Picayune, New Orleans, August 18, 1879.
65. House of Representative, 48th Congress, 1st Session, Ex. Doc 1, pt. 2, vol. II, "Annual Report of the Chief Of Engineers, United States Army, to the Secretary of War for the Year 1883," Part II, 1136; House of Representatives, 48th Congress, 2nd Session, Ex. Doc. 1, Part 2, "Report of the Secretary of War," Vol. II, Part 2, 1884, 1322 (Washington D.C.: Government Printing Office).
66. NARA, Letters Received by the Commission Branch of the Adjutant General's Office, 1863–1870, RG94, M12064, Roll 253; New York Times, April 4, 1897.
67. For a comprehensive treatment of Cobett's life, see Scott Martelle, The Madman and the Assassin: The Strange Life of Boston Corbett, the Man Who Killed John Wilkes Booth (Chicago: Chicago Review Press, 2015).
68. George R. Prowell, The History of Camden County, New Jersey (Philadelphia: L.J. Richards, 1886), 476.
69. "To Whom it may concern," signed by F. Taylor Heiss, Boston Corbett Correspondence, Kansas Memory Project, Kansas Historical Society, Folder 3, 1869; U.S. Census, 1870; Camden, New Jersey City Directory, 1874 (Ancestry.com).
70. Cleveland Plain Dealer, April 19, 1875; Cleveland City Directory, 1875 (Ancestry.com); Martelle, The Madman and the Assassin, 136–137.
71. Cleveland Plain Dealer, May 17, 1875 (cited in Martelle, The Madman and the Assassin).
72. Cleveland, City Directory, 1875; New Hampshire Gazette (reproduced @ http://roger jnorton.com/Lincoln32.html).
73. Letter, dated January 12, 1878, Boston Corbett Correspondence, Folder 5, 1878; Camden City Directory, 1878.
74. U.S. Census, 1880. "Boston Corbett" page on Camden, New Jersey History website @ http://www.dvrbs.com/people/Camden People-BostonCorbett.html
75. E.F. Hollibaugh, Biographical History of Cloud County, Kansas, Biographies of Representative Citizens (Cloud County, KS: Wilson, Humphrey & Co., 1903), 444–445.
76. Ibid.
77. Christian Harvester (monthly), Cleveland, Ohio, February 1887.
78. Hollibaugh, 247–249.
79. Kansas Memory Project, Kansas Historical Society, item no. 206535.
80. Letter to Professor David Dary, University of Kansas, dated March 24, 1972, from

Helen DeFord Bush, Kansas Memory Project, Kansas Historical Society, item no. 307437.
 81. Ibid.
 82. *Bonner County* (Idaho) *Daily Bee*, January 10, 24 & 31, 2009.
 83. *U.S. Census, 1910*; "Vrooman Family Tree 4," Ancestry.com.
 84. "Dowler-Wilkinson-Tufts-Felter" Family Tree, Ancestry.com; "Pvt. John William Millinton," Findagrave.com; *1870, 1880, 1900 & 1910 U.S. Census; Iowa State Census, 1995* (Ancestry.com); Randol B. Fletcher, *Hidden History of Civil War Oregon* (Charleston, SC: The History Press, 2011), 27–28.
 85. Fletcher, 28.
 86. *U.S. Census, 1870, 1880, 1900, 1910, 1920*.
 87. Fletcher, 28.
 88. www.findagrave.com.
 89. Abraham W. Snay Family Tree, Ancestry.com; *U.S. Census, 1870–1920; New York State Census, 1875, 1925*; findagrave.com.
 90. James I. Robertson, Jr., "Houses of Horror: Danville's Civil War Prisons," *Virginia Magazine of History and Biography*, Vol. 69, No. 3 (July 1961), 330.
 91. Robertson, 340–341.
 92. *The Herald and Torch Light* (Hagerstown, MD), September 27 and November 1, 1865 and May 26, 1869.
 93. *The Herald and Torch Light*, May 14, 1873; Washington County Free Library, *Marriage Records* (Ancestry.com).
 94. *U.S. Census, 1880; Baltimore Maryland City Directory*, 1874–1885 (Fold3.com).
 95. *The Baltimore Sun*, March 8, 1901; Find-a-Grave web site @ findagrave.com.
 96. Rod A. MacDonald, Ed.D., *William Jeremiah Keays*, Biography web site @ http://www.r-a-macdonald.ca; *1871 Ontario Canada Census* (Ancestry.com).
 97. MacDonald; Isaiah Wright, "A Family History Notebook," unpublished manuscript, 1903, 9–10 (courtesy of Rod A. MacDonald, Niagara Falls, Ontario, Canada).
 98. MacDonald.
 99. Richard M. Bruno, ed., *The American Insolvency Reports*, Vol. I, January 1878 to January 1883 (New York: H. Campbell and Company, 1883).
 100. Letter to the Honorable Alexander MacKenzie, Premier of Canada, dated July 10, 1878, Canadian Department of Justice File No. 984, 1878; Appointment Acceptance Letter, dated August 15, 1878. Both cited and reproduced in MacDonald.
 101. *1889 Buffalo City Directory* (Ancestry.com); Welcome to Conesus Lake New York website http://www.conesuslakeny.org/cl_people_keays_william.htm; McDonald.

102. Mcdonald; *1889 and 1890 Buffalo City Directories* (Ancestry.com).
 103. *1895, 1897 & 1899 Buffalo City Directories* (Ancestry.com); *U.S. Census, 1900 & 1910; New York State Census, 1905; New York, Find-a-Grave Index, 1660–2012* (Findagrave.com).
 104. NARA, *Historical Register of National Homes for Disabled Volunteer Soldiers, 1866–1938*, RG 15, M1749 (Ancestry.com).
 105. *The Plattsburgh Sentinel*, Plattsburgh, New York, November 30, 1877.
 106. *U.S. Census, 1870; Troy, New York City Directory, 1870* (Ancestry.com).
 107. Moore Family Papers, Letter dated November 17, 1874, Folder 66.7f, File 2/3/28.
 108. *Troy* (New York) *City Directory, 1874* (Ancestry.com).
 109. *New York Tribune*, November 29, 1877.
 110. *Plattsburgh Sentinel*, November 30, 1877.
 111. *Plattsburgh Sentinel*, July 20, 1894.
 112. *Troy Weekly Times*, Troy, NY, November 29, 1877.
 113. Bacon, *Fourth Biographical Record of the Class of Fifty-Eight, Yale University*, 236.
 114. *Ibid.*, 237; U.S. Passport Applications, 1795–1925 (Ancestry.com).
 115. Bacon, 237; *U.S. Census, 1900*.
 116. *U.S. Census*, various; U.S. Cities Directories, 19882–1995; Ward Family Tree (Ancestry.com).
 117. New York State Military Museum and Veterans Research Center @ http://dmna.ny.gov/historic/reghist/civil/rosters/Infantry/16th_Infantry_CW_Roster.pdf.
 118. *New York Times*, December 14, 1893.
 119. *Ibid.*; *U.S. City Directories, Utica and Hartford*, Ancestry.com.
 120. *New York Times*, December 14, 1893.
 121. *The Times of London*, November 18, 1902; *New York Times*, November 23, 1902.
 122. *U.S. Census, 1870*; "Town and Village of Plattsburgh Civil War Soldiers," Town of Plattsburgh, Clinton County, NY (http://townofplattsburgh.com/dept_historian/CIVIL/CivilWar.pdf); Francis M. Kearns, *Assumption of Mary Parish, Redford, New York: Baptisms 1863–1910, Marriages 1853–1923, Burials 1853–1923 and Cemetery Records* (Northern New York American-Canadian Genealogical Society, 1992).
 123. *U.S. Census, 1870; New York State Census, 1875* (Ancestry.com); *Brooklyn New York City Directories, 1885, 1888, and 1889* (Ancestry.com); NARA, *Internment Control Forms, A1 2110-B*, Records of the Office of the Quartermaster General, 1774–1985, RG 92 (Ancestry.com).
 124. Williams-Reed Family Tree (Ancestry.

com); Letter from the Rev. Phillip T. Allen, Pastor, Church of the Assumption, Redford, NY (Ancestry.com); *History of Clinton and Franklin Counties New York*, 358.

125. *U.S. Census, 1880; Plattsburgh Republican*, April 3, 1880 and January 16, 1886.

126. *U.S. Census, 1900; Plattsburgh Republican*, December 8, 1906.

127. *Plattsburgh Republican*, September 25, 1907; *U.S. Census, 1910; Annual Report of the State Board of Charities for the Year 1916, Vol. 2* (Albany: J.B. Lyon, 1917), 139–140.

128. *Plattsburgh Republican*, February 16, 1917; *Town and Village of Plattsburgh Civil War Soldiers*, Town of Plattsburgh, Clinton County, NY (http://townofplattsburgh.com/dept_historian/CIVIL/CivilWar.pdf); Richard Lynch, *St. Joseph's Church Dannamora, New York 1860–1922, Marriages-Births-Deaths* (Northern New York American-Canadian Genealogical Society, No. 7, 2001).

129. *Plattsburgh Sentinel*, September 11, 1908.

130. *U.S. Civil War Solider Records and Profiles, 1861–1865* (Ancestry.com) and *U.S. Civil War Soldiers, 1861–1865*, National Park Service (Ancestry.com).

131. *The Westinghouse Letter: One young Civil War veteran at the crossroads*, Smithsonian National Museum of American History, Kenneth E. Behring Center, March 1, 2011 (http://americanhistory.si.edu/blog/2011/03/the-westinghouse-letter-one-young-civil-war-veteran-at-the-crossroads.html).

132. Kyle Balthaser, *George Westinghouse,* Fall 2006 (http://pabook.libraries.psu.edu/palitmap /bios/ Westinghouse_George.html).

133. *Ibid.*

Appendix B

1. Jack and Carol Lundquist, *Civil War Prisons Database* at www.civilwarprisoners.com; "Roster of New York Cavalry Regiments During the Civil War," New York State Military Museum and Veterans Research Center.

2. Byron Berkeley Johnson, *Abraham Lincoln and Boston Corbett* (Waltham, MA: self-published, 1914), 49–50.

3. *True History—Jefferson Davis Answered—The Horrors of the Andersonville Prison Pen—The Personal Experience of Henry Hernbaker, Jr. and John Lynch* (Philadelphia: Merrihew & Sons, 1876), 8–12.

4. "Roster of New York Cavalry Regiments During the Civil War," New York State Military Museum and Veterans Research Center.

5. U.S. National Park Service, Salisbury National Cemetery web site at www.nps.gov/nr/travel/national_cemeteries/North_Carolina/Salisbury_National_Cemetery.html.

6. *Roll of Honor (No. XIV), Names of Soldiers Who in Defense of the American Union, Suffered Martyrdom in the Prison Pens Throughout the South*, Quartermaster General's Office, General Orders No. 7, February 20, 1868 (Washington, DC: Government Printing Officer, 1868).

Bibliography

Archives and Collections

Anderson, George H. Letters, Clinton County Historical Association, Plattsburgh, NY.
Binns, Charles. Charles Binns Vertical File, 2004.011-B, Thomas Balch Library, Leesburg, VA.
Corbett, Boston. Correspondence. Kansas Memory Project, Kansas Historical Society, Topeka, KS.
Fleming, James Henry. Letters. Courtesy of Ms. Louise Brown, Witney, Oxfordshire, UK.
Green, Augustus P. "Augustus P. Green Autobiography," Green Collection. New-York Historical Society, New York, NY.
Hagadorn, Francis T. *Reminiscences of Civil War Experiences, 1861–1866: Manuscript.* New York State Library, Albany, NY.
Lazelle Family Papers, available from author upon request.
Lloyd, Hinton Summerfield. Papers. Special Collections and University Archives, Colgate University Libraries, Hamilton, NY.
Martin, Albert G. Papers. William L. Clements Library, University of Michigan, Ann Arbor, MI.
Moore, Charles F. Letters. The Alice T. Miner Museum, Chazy, NY.
Moore Family Papers. Special Collections, State University of New York at Plattsburgh, NY.
New York County, District and Probate Courts. "New York Wills and Probate Records, 1659–1999" (Ancestry.com).
New-York Historical Society. "Civil War Collection, Miscellaneous: Military Orders & Documents, June 20, 1981–April 6, 1868," New York, NY.
New York State. *Annual Reports Submitted to the New York State Legislature, 1846–1995*, Adjutant General of the New York National Guard (www.fold3.com).
New York State Archives. *Census of Inmates in Almshouses and Poorhouses, 1875–1921*, Series A1978, Albany, NY.
———. *New York Civil War Muster Roll Abstracts of New York State Volunteers, United States Sharpshooters, and United States Colored Troops, 1861–1900*, Collection # 13775–83, Albany, NY (Ancestry.com).
———. *Third Annual Report of the Bureau of Military Record, Transmitted to the Legislature February 2, 1866.* Albany, NY: C. Wendell, Printer, 1866.
———. *Town Clerks' Registers of Men Who Served in the Civil War, 1861–1865*, Collection (N-Ar) 137745, Albany, NY.
New York State Library. *Annual Report of the Adjutant General of the State of New York for the Year 1894, Volume IV: Registers of the 13th–18th Regiments of Cavalry*, Albany, NY.

Bibliography

———. *Philip Henry Sheridan Correspondence, 1831–1888.* Albany, NY.
New York State Military Museum and Veterans Research Center. *Annual Reports to the New York State Legislature, 1846–1995, by the Adjutant General of the New York National Guard, 1863, Vol. I, and 1867, Vol. 2,* Saratoga, NY.
———. *Roster of the New York Cavalry Regiments During the Civil War,* Saratoga, NY.
Pennsylvania Historical and Museum Commission. *Civil War Muster Rolls and Related Records, 1861–1866,* Records of the Department of Military and Veteran's Affairs, Record Group 19, Series 19.11, Harrisburg, PA (Ancestry.com).
Schneider, Joseph. Family Papers, courtesy of Robert Snapper, Kew Gardens, NY.
U.S. National Archives and Records Administration. *Carded Records Showing Military Service of Soldiers Who Fought in Volunteer Organizations During the American Civil War, 1890–1912.* Records of the Adjutant General's Office, 1762–1984, Record Group 94 (www.Fold3.com).
———. *Court Martial Case Files, Records of the Judge Advocate General,* Record Group 153. Washington, D.C.
———. *General Index to Pension Files, 1861–1934,* Record Group 15 (T288), Washington, D.C.
———. *Historical Register of National Homes for Disabled Volunteer Soldiers, 1866–1938,* RG 15, M1749 (Ancestry.com).
———. *Internment Control Forms, A1–2110-B,* Records of the Office of the Quartermaster General, 1774–1985, RG 92 (Ancestry.com).
———. *Letters Received by the Commission Branch of the Adjutant General's Office, 1863–1870,* Record Group 94, Washington, D.C.
———. *Letters Received by the Office of the Adjutant General, Main Series,* Record Group 94, Washington, D.C.
———. *Organizational Index to Pension Files of Veterans Who Served Between 1861 and 1900,* Record Group 15, T289 (Fold3.com).
———. *Records of Cavalry Depots and Depot Camps,* Record Group 393. Washington, D.C.
———. *Records of the Office of the Chief of Engineers, Fortification Files,* Record Group 77, College Park, MD.
———. *Records of the Office of the Judge Advocate General (Army), Court Martial Case Files,* Record Group 153, Washington, D.C.
———. *Return of the Cavalry Forces, Defenses of Washington South of the Potomac, Dept. of Washington,* Records of Named Departments, 1821–1920, Record Group 393.4. Washington, D.C.
———. *Returns from U.S. Military Posts, 1800–1916,* Record Group 94, Washington, D.C.
Wilber, Albert B. Diaries. The Andersonville Guild, Andersonville, GA.

U.S. Government Documents

Barnard, Bvt. Maj. Gen. J.G. "A Report of the Defenses of Washington to the Chief of Engineers, U.S. Army," Professional Papers of the Corps of Engineers, U.S. Army, No. 20. Washington, D.C.: General Printing Office, 1871.
United States Army Quartermaster General's Office. "Roll of Honor (No. XIV): Names of Soldiers Who Died in Defense of the American Union, Suffered Martyrdom in the Prison Pens Throughout the South." General Orders No. 7, February 20, 1868. Washington, D.C.: Government Printing Office, 1868.
United States Congress. "Testimony Taken Before the Committee on the Post-Office and Post-Roads in Relation to Mail Contracts." *Index to Reports of Committees of the House of Representatives for the First Session of the Forty-Fourth Congress, 1875–76.*
———. House of Representatives. "Annual Report of the Chief of Engineers, United States Army, to the Secretary of War for the Year 1883," Ex. Doc. 1, pt. 2, vol. II, 48th Congress, 1st Session.

Bibliography

_____. House of Representatives. "Letter from the Secretary of War Transmitting a Copy of the Report of the Judge Advocate General Upon the Case of First Lieutenant W. J. Keays, of the Sixteenth New York Cavalry," Ex. Doc. No. 105, 41st Congress, 2nd Session, January 29, 1870.

_____. House of Representatives. "Report of the Secretary of War," Vol. II, Part 2, Ex. Doc. 1, Part 2, 48th Congress, 2nd Session, 1884.

_____. Senate. "Journal of the Proceedings of the Senate of the United States in Executive Session, Part II: February 13, 1866 to July 28, 1866, Executive Journal, July 26, 1866, 1099, 39th Congress, 1st Session.

United States National Park Service. "Civil War Defenses of Washington—Historic Resource Study," October 2004. On-line at: http://www.cr.nps.gov/history/ online_books/civil-war/hrst.htm.

United States War Department. "War of the Rebellion: A Compilation of the Official Records of the Union and Confederate Armies," 128 volumes. Washington, D.C.: Government Printing Office, 1880–1900.

Books

Annual Report of the State Board of Charities for the Year 1916, Vol. 2. Albany, NY: J.B. Lyon, 1917.

A Record of the Commissioned Officers, Non-Commissioned Officers and Privates of the Regiments Which Were Organized in the State of New York and Called into Service of the United States to Assist in Suppressing the Rebellion. New York State Adjutant General's Office. Albany, NY: Weed, Parsons & Co., 1867.

Baird, Nancy C., ed. *Journals of Amanda Virginia Edmonds, Lass of the Mosby Confederacy, 1857–1867.* Stephens City, VA: Commercial Press, 1984.

Benjamin, Marcus, ed., *Washington During War Time: A Series of Papers Showing the Military, Political, and Social Phases During 1861 to 1865.* Washington, D.C.: National Tribune Press, 1902.

Bruno, Richard M., ed. *The American Insolvency Reports, Vol. I, January 1878 to January 1883.* New York: H. Campbell and Company, 1883.

Bundy, Carol. *The Nature of Sacrifice: A Biography of Charles Russell Lowell, Jr., 1835–64.* New York: Farrar, Straus and Giroux, 2005.

Carson, James. *Against the Grain: Col. Henry M. Lazelle and the U.S. Army.* Denton: University of North Texas Press, 2015.

Coates, Earl J., and Dean S. Thomas. *An Introduction to Civil War Small Arms.* Gettysburg, PA: Thomas Publications, 1990.

Cooling, Benjamin F. *Symbol, Sword and Shield: Defending Washington During the Civil War.* Shippensburg, PA: White Mane Publishing Co., 1991.

_____, and Walton H. Owen. *Mr. Lincoln's Forts: A Guide to the Civil War Defenses of Washington.* Shippensburg, PA: White Mane Publishing Co., 1988.

Crawford, J. Marshall. *Mosby and His Men.* New York: G.W. Carleton & Co., 1867.

Crouch, Howard R. *Like a Hurricane: The Men, Mounts, Arms and Tactics of Colonel John S. Mosby's Command.* Catlett, VA: SCS Publications, 2013.

Cullum, Bvt. Maj.-Gen. George W. *Biographical Register of the Officers and Graduates of the U.S. Military Academy from Its Establishment in 1802 to 1890, Volume II.* Boston: Houghton, Mifflin, 1891.

Cutter, William R., ed. *Genealogical and Family History of Northern New York.* New York: Lewis Historical Publishing Company, 1910.

Dyer, Frederick H. *A Compendium of the War of the Rebellion.* Des Moines, IA: The Dyer Publishing Co., 1908.

Edwards, William C., ed. *The Lincoln Assassination: The Reward Files.* Google e-book, 2012.

Bibliography 245

Emerson, Edward W. *Life and Letters of Charles Russell Lowell.* New York: Houghton, Mifflin, 1907.
Evans, Thomas J., and James M. Moyer. *Mosby Vignettes, Vol. I.* Fairfax, VA: Privately printed, 1993.
Fletcher, Randol B. *Hidden History of Civil War Oregon.* Charleston, SC: The History Press, 2011.
Fox, William F. *Regimental Losses in the American Civil War.* Albany, NY: Augustus S. Brandow, 1898.
Gernand, Bradley E. *A Virginia Village Goes to War: Falls Church During the Civil War.* Virginia Beach, VA: The Donning Company Publishers, 2002.
Heatwole, John L. *The Burning: Sheridan in the Shenandoah Valley.* Charlottesville, VA: Howell Press, 1998.
Heitman, Francis B. *Historical Register and Dictionary of the United States Army from Its Organization, September 29, 1789, to March 2, 1903, Vol. 1.* Washington, D.C.: Government Printing Office, 1903.
History of Clinton and Franklin Counties, New York. Philadelphia: J.W. Lewis & Co., 1880.
Hollibaugh, E.F. *Biographical History of Cloud County, Kansas, Biographies of Representative Citizens.* Cloud County, KS: Wilson, Humphrey & Co., 1903.
Humphries, Charles A. *Field, Camp, Hospital and Prison in the Civil War, 1863–1865.* Boston: Press of Geo. E. Ellis Co., 1918.
Hurd, D. Hamilton. *History of Clinton and Franklin Counties, New York.* Philadelphia: J.W. Lewis, 1880.
Jones, Virgil Carrington. *Ranger Mosby.* Chapel Hill: University of North Carolina Press, 1944 (reprinted by EPM Publications, McLean, VA, 1972).
Kearns, Francis M. *Assumption of Mary Parish, Redford, New York: Baptisms 1863–1910, Marriages 1853–1923, Burials 1853–1923 and Cemetery Records.* Dannemora, NY: Northern New York American-Canadian Genealogical Society, 1992.
Leech, Margaret. *Reveille in Washington 1860–1865.* New York: Harper and Brothers, 1941 (Time, Inc. Reprint, 1962).
Long, E.B. *The Civil War Day by Day: An Almanac 1861–1865.* Garden City, NY: Doubleday, 1971.
Lowry, Thomas P. *Sexual Misbehavior in the Civil War.* N.p.: Xlibris, 2006.
Lynch, Richard. *St. Joseph's Church Dannemora, New York 1860–1922, Marriages-Births-Deaths.* Dannemora, NY: Northern New York American-Canadian Genealogical Society, No. 7, 2001.
Martelle, Scott. *The Madman and the Assassin: The Strange Life of Boston Corbett, the Man Who Killed John Wilkes Booth.* Chicago: Chicago Review Press, 2015.
McLean, James. *California Sabers: The 2nd Massachusetts Cavalry in the Civil War.* Bloomington: Indiana University Press, 2000.
Morris, Charles, ed. *Men of the Century: An Historical Work Giving Portraits and Sketches of Eminent Citizens of the United States.* Philadelphia: L.R. Hamersly, 1896.
Mosby, John S. *The Memoirs of Colonel John S. Mosby,* Foreword by J.O. Tate. Nashville, TN: J.S. Sanders & Company, 1995. (Original edition published in 1917 by Little, Brown, New York.)
Munden, Kenneth W., and Henry Putney Beers. *The Union: A Guide to Federal Archives Relating to the Civil War.* Washington, D.C.: National Archives and Records Administration, 1986.
New York State Soldier Burials at The Falls Church During the Civil War. Falls Church, VA: The Falls Church Episcopal Church, undated.
Phisterer, Frederick. *New York in the War of the Rebellion, Third Edition.* Albany, NY: J.B. Lyon Co., State Printers, 1912.
Powell, Colonel W.H. *List of Officers of the Army of the United States from 1779 to 1900.* New York: L.R. Hamersly & Co., 1900.

Price, George F. *Across the Continent with the Fifth Cavalry.* New York: D. Van Nostrand, 1883.
Prowell, George R. *The History of Camden County, New Jersey.* Philadelphia: L.J. Richards, 1886.
Ramage, James A. *Gray Ghost: The Life of Col. John Singleton Mosby.* Lexington: The University Press of Kentucky, 1999.
A Record of the Commissioned Officers, Non-Commissioned Officers and Privates of the Regiments Which Were Organized in the State of New York and Called into Service of the United States to Assist in Suppressing the Rebellion. New York State Adjutant General's Office. Albany: Weed, Parsons & Co., 1867.
Ross, Peter. *A History of Long Island From Its Earliest Settlement to the Present Time, Vol. II.* New York: The Lewis Publishing Company, 1902.
Scott, John. *Partisan Life with Mosby.* London: Sampson Low, Son, and Marston, 1867.
Sheridan, P.H. *Personal Memoirs of P. H. Sheridan, General, United States Army, Vol. II.* New York: Charles L. Webster & Co., 1888.
Sherman, William T. *Memoirs.* New York: D. Appleton, 1875.
Simon, John Y., ed. *The Papers of Ulysses S. Grant, Vol. 18, October 1, 1867—June 30, 1868.* Carbondale: Southern Illinois University Press, 1991.
Smith, James H. *History of Livingston County, New York.* Syracuse, NY: D. Mason, 1881.
Stuntz, Connie P., and Mayo S. Stuntz. *This Was Vienna, Virginia: Facts and Photos.* Vienna, VA: Privately printed, 1987.
The Union Army: A History of Military Affairs in the Loyal States 1861–65—Records of the Regiments in the Union Army—Cyclopedia of Battles—Memoirs of Commanders and Soldiers, Vol. II. Madison, WI: Federal Publishing Co., 1908.
Welcher, Frank J. *The Union Army, 1861–1865—Organization and Operations, Vol. I, The Eastern Theater.* Bloomington: Indiana University Press, 1989.
Wells, Charles, ed. *The Memoirs of Colonel John S. Mosby.* Norwood, MA: Russell Boston Little Brown & Co., 1917.
Wert, Jeffrey D. *Mosby's Rangers.* New York: Simon & Schuster, 1990.
Williamson, James J. *Mosby's Rangers: A Record of the Operations of the 43d Battalion Virginia Cavalry.* New York: Ralph B. Kenyon, Publisher, 1896 (reprinted by Time-Life Books, Inc., 1982).

Articles

Allendorfer, Frederick von. "The Cross of Lincoln's Avengers: Was It Produced and Issued?" Memorandum prepared for the 25th Convention of the Orders and Medals Society of America, August 9–12, 1984.
Cooling, B.F., and Wally Owen. "Washington's Civil War Defenses and the Battle of Fort Stevens." *Hallowed Ground.* The Civil War Preservation Trust, Vol. 9, No. 3, Fall, 2008, pp. 24–32.
Diercks, Wayne. "The Story of the Louis Abend Drum." Zumbrota, MN: Zumbrota Area Historical Society, July 2010.
Dodge, Grenville M. "Use of Block-Houses During the Civil War." *Annals of Iowa,* Vol. 6, No. 4, 1904, 297–301.
Jones, V.C. "Actions Along the Union Outposts in Fairfax." *Historical Society of Fairfax County, Virginia, Yearbook,* Vol. 3, 1954.
"Military Affairs in New York." *The Union Army: A History of Military Affairs in the Loyal States, 1861–1865.* Madison, WI: Federal Publishing Co., 1908.
"Pursuit and Death of John Wilkes Booth." *The Century Illustrated Monthly Magazine,* November 1889 to April 1890, 446–447.
Robertson, James I., Jr. "Houses of Horror: Danville's Civil War Prisons." *Virginia Magazine of History and Biography,* Vol. 69, No. 3 (July 1961).

Wick, Robert G. "Battle for the War Department Rewards for the Capture of John Wilkes Booth." *Journal of the Abraham Lincoln Association*, Vol. 32, No. 2, 2011.

Newspapers and Journals

Albany Evening Journal, Albany, NY.
The Baltimore Sun, Baltimore, MD.
Bonner County Daily Bee, Sandpoint, ID.
Boston Post, Boston, MA.
Brooklyn Daily Eagle, Brooklyn, NY.
The Century Illustrated Monthly Magazine, New York, NY.
Christian Harvester, Cleveland, OH.
Christian Intelligencer of the Reformed Dutch Church (Ancestry.com)
Cleveland Plain Dealer, Cleveland, OH.
Courier and Republic, Buffalo, NY.
Daily National Intelligencer, Washington, D.C.
Elmira Morning Telegram, Elmira, NY.
The Frontier Palladium, Malone, NY.
The Herald and Torch Light, Hagerstown, MD.
Janesville Daily Gazette, Janesville, WI.
Lockport Daily Journal, Lockport, NY.
National Daily Republican, Washington, D.C.
New Hampshire Gazette (reproduced @ http://rogerjnorton.com/Lincoln32.html).
New York Evening Post, New York, NY.
New York Herald, New York, NY.
New York Times, New York, NY.
New York Tribune, New York, NY.
Philadelphia Press, Philadelphia, PA.
Plattsburgh Republican, Plattsburgh, NY.
Plattsburgh Sentinel, Plattsburgh, NY.
Richmond Daily Dispatch, Richmond, VA.
The Times of London, London, UK.
The Times-Picayune, New Orleans, LA.
Troy Weekly Times, Troy, NY.
The Virginia State Journal, Alexandria, VA.

Websites

"Abraham Lincoln's Assassination" website http://rogerjnorton.com/Lincoln.html.
Abraham W. Snay Family Tree @ Ancestry.com.
Arlington National Cemetery website http://www.arlingtoncemetery.mil/Explore-the-Cemetery/Find-a-Grave.
Balthaser, Kyle. "George Westinghouse." http://pabook.libraries.psu.edu/palitmap/bios/Westinghouse_George.html.
Baltimore Maryland City Directory, 1874–1885 @ www.Fold3.com.
"Battle of Fort Stevens." The Civil War Trust website www.civilwar.org.
"The Battle of Monocacy, 9 July 1864," The Army Historical Foundation website www.armyhistory.org.
Baumgarten, Ron. "All Not So Quiet Along the Potomac" Blog website http://dclawyeronthecivilwar.blogspot.com.
Buffalo City Directory @ Ancestry.com.
"A Cavalryman's Account of the Chase and Capture of John Wilkes Booth." Abraham Lincoln's Assassination website @ http://rogerjnorton.com/Lincoln73.html.

Bibliography

"Civil War Biographies." Greenwood Cemetery, Brooklyn, NY, website @ www.green-wood.com.
"Civil War Washington, D.C." Blog @ http://www.civilwarwashingtondc1861–1865.blogspot.com.
Cleveland City Directory @ Ancestry.com.
"Danville National Cemetery, Danville, Virginia." U.S. National Park Service website https://www.nps.gov/nr/travel/national_cemeteries/virginia/Danville_VA_National_Cemetery.html.
The Diary of Valorus Dearborn, April 6, 1864, @ http://www.2mass.reunioncivilwar.com/References/dearborn.htm.
District of Columbia, Select Marriages, 1830–2921 @ Ancestry.com.
Dowler-Wilkinson-Tufts-Felter Family Tree @ Ancestry.com.
Dutkowski/Schneider/Kennell Family Tree @ Ancestry.com.
"Giesboro Point Cavalry Depot, Parking for 30,000 Horses." Civil War Washington, D.C. Blog, August 17, 2011 http://civilwarwashingtondc1861–1865.blogspot.com/2011/08/geisborough-point-cavalry-depot-parking.html.
Historical Marker Database http://www.hmdb.org.
"Kansas Memory." Kansas Historical Society website http://www.kansasmemory.org.
KDUTMAN Family Tree @ Ancestry.com.
Lundquist, Jack, and Carol Lundquist. "Civil War Prisons Database." www.civilwarprisoners.com.
MacDonald Genealogy Website, Rod A. MacDonald, Niagara Falls, Ontario, Canada www.r-a-macdonald.ca.
"Military Affairs in New York." *The Union Army: A History of Military Affairs in the Loyal States, 1861–1865*. Madison, WI: Federal Publishing Co., 1908. New York State Military Museum, http://dmna.ny.gov/historic/reghist/civil/MilAffairsNY.htm.
"New York Wills and Probate Records, 1659–1999," New York County, District and Probate Courts @ Ancestry.com.
Ontario Canada Census @ Ancestry.com.
The Rail Splitter: A Journal for the Lincoln Collector www.railsplitter.com.
"The Second Mass and Its Fighting Californians." http://www.2mass.reunioncivilwar.com/index.htm
"16th Cavalry Regiment." New York State Military Museum and Veterans Research Center website www.dmna.state.ny.us/historic/reghist/civil/cavalry/16thCav/16thCavCWN.htm.
Swenson, Timothy. "Charles S. Eigenbrodt, Alvarado Civil War Hero." Creative Commons, Attribution-Non-Commercial-ShareAlike, 2005 www.museumoflocalhistory.org/pages/eigenbrodt.pdf.
Town and Village of Plattsburgh Civil War Soldiers, Town of Plattsburgh, Clinton County, New York http://townofplattsburgh.com/dept_historian/CIVIL/CivilWar.pdf.
Troy New York City Directory @ Ancestry.com.
"21st Infantry Regiment, Civil War, First Buffalo Regiment," New York State Military Museum and Veterans Research Center http://dmna.ny.gov/historic/reghist/civil/infantry/21stInf/21stInfMain.htm.
Tuck Family Tree and Roberta Tuck Kantner Gromley Family Tree @ Ancestry.com.
U.S. Civil War Soldier Records and Profiles, 1861–1865 @ Ancestry.com.
U.S. Federal Census @ Ancestry.com.
Vroomman Family Tree 4 @ Ancestry.com.
Welcome to Conesus Lake New York www.conesuslakeny.org.
"The Westinghouse Letter: One young Civil War veteran at the crossroads." Smithsonian National Museum of American History, Kenneth E. Behring Center http://americanhistory.si.edu/blog/2011/03/the-westinghouse-letter-one-young-civil-war-veteran-at-the-crossroads.html).
Williams-Reed Family Tree @ Ancestry.com.

Unpublished Papers and Interviews

Miller, Steven G., Lake Villa, Illinois. Unpublished background information on Spencer Olmstead; the origins of the 16th New York Cavalry; officers and men of the 16th New York Cavalry; and the patrol that captured John Wilkes Booth.

_____. "An Informal History of the 16th New York Volunteer Cavalry," unpublished manuscript, Mundelein, IL: March 1997.

_____. "Officers of the Sixteenth NY Cavalry and the Lincoln Avengers Medals/Certificates," unpublished manuscript, Lake Villa, IL: August 2016.

Wright, Isaiah. "A Family History Notebook," unpublished manuscript, 1903 (courtesy of Rod A. MacDonald, Niagara Falls, Ontario, Canada).

Index

Numbers in ***bold italics*** indicate pages with photographs.

Abend, Pvt. Louis 23, *24*, 25
Abendorff, Capt. John 26
Aldie, Virginia 10, 55–56, 58, 60, 64, 66, 70, 73, 83–84, 92–93, 116, 119, 130, 132
Alexandria, Loudoun and Hampshire Railroad 50, 54
Alexandria, Virginia 4, 6, 10, 32–33, 39–40, 50, 69, 77, 80, 83, 85, 102, 105–106
Allison, Pvt. Richard 62
Anderson, Lt. George H. 20
Andersonville Prison, Georgia 44, 59–60, 62, 66, 73–74, 86, 148, 170–172, 225–227
Anker, Samuel 57–60, 71, 150
Annandale, Virginia 19, 37, 41–42, 57, 59, 72, 76–83, 85, 89–92, 94–95, 103, 107, 113, 150
Army of Northern Virginia 6
Army of the Potomac 5–9, 19, 23, 37, 63, 83–84
Ashby's Gap, Virginia 95, 114, 130
Augur, Maj. Gen. Christopher C. 12, *67*, 68–69, 76–77, 83, 86–88, 92, 95–96, 101–103, 105, 107, 109, 111, 114, 118–119, 122–123, 125–129, 132–135, 142–143
Ayr Hill, Vienna, Virginia 50–51, 60

Babcock, Sgt. A.G. 106
Bailey's Cross-Roads, Virginia 126, 133
Baker, Pvt. David 165
Baker, Capt. Francis M. 100, 123, 143, 145
Baker, Col. Lafayette 136–137, 139, 141
Baker, Luther B. 137–139
Balls Mills, Virginia 127
Battle of Cedar Creek 80
Battle of Monocacy 75–76
Battle of the Wilderness 69
Bealeton Station, Virginia 122
Belle Isle Prison, Virginia 29
Belle Plain, Virginia 70, 137, 139
Berryville, Virginia 95, 130
Billy Gooding's Tavern 40–41

Binns, Chares "Charlie" ***70***, 71
Birdsall, Maj. James 109
Bishop, Pvt. Martin 62
Bloomfield, Virginia 107
Booth, John Wilkes 1, 12, 30, 135, 137–139, 141, 144, 148, 164, 166, 171, 173, 225
Bosworth, Maj. George 46, 100–101, 120, 144
Botts, John Minor ***104***
bounty jumping 29
Bowling Green, Virginia 138
Bowman, Josiah 50, 52–53
Bristoe Station, Virginia 77
Brooks, Frank 108
Brown, Pvt. Dennis 28
Brown, Pvt. George 28
Bull Run (Mountains) 4, 6, 10, 33, 42, 56–57, 59, 83, 123, 130,
Bunn, Pvt. George 179–180
Burke Station, Virginia 4, 85, 107, 131
Byrne, Pvt. William 165

Camp Barry, Washington D.C. 133, 146–148
Camp Beckwith, Virginia 43–44
Camp Norton, New York ***18***, 28, 31, 34
Camp Sprague (Staten Island), New York 34–36, 66
Camp Stoneman (Giesboro Point), Washington DC 35–37, 39, 46
Cannon, Lt. Patrick 47
Cavalry Bureau 35
Centreville, Virginia 3, 39–42, 55, 57–59, 64, 72–74, 77, 85, 95, 107, 122–123
Chamberlain, Lot 15, 20
Chantilly, Virginia 40, 64, 95
Chester Gap 87–88, 116
Coan River, Virginia 135–136
Cobbler Mountain, Virginia 106,
Columbia Baptist Church 108
Commins, Moses A. 52–53
Conger, Everton J. 137–139

251

Conger, Pvt. William 27
Conway's Ferry, Virginia 137
Corbett, Sgt. Boston 12, 30, 73–74, 137, *138*, 139–141, 164, 170–172, 225
Corbett, Samuel J. 61
Corcoran, Brig. Gen. Michael 53
Coulton, Sgt. Thomas 28
Craozia, Sgt. Benjamin 27
Culpeper (Station)(Court House), Virginia 78, 82–84, 87–88, 96–97, 100, 102–104, 151, 175

Danville Prison 86–87, 101, 175
Darnestown, Maryland 125
Davies, Col. Thomas 20
Davis, Alexander G. "Yankee" 70
Dearborn, Cpl. Valorus 2, 61, 65
Deleplane, Virginia 106,
DeRussy, Brig. Gen. Gustavus 53, 108,
deserters 27–28, 60–62
Dietz, Pvt. Frederick 165
Dix, Maj. Gen. John 156
Dix-Hill Cartel 48
Doherty, Edward P. 1, 12, 101, 121, 136, *137*, 138–140, 144–145, 164, 166–170
Dow, Lt. Henry G. 47, 120
Dranesville, Virginia 40, 58–59, 120, 126, 150

Early, Gen. Jubal 75, 77, 79, 83, 87, 94, 96–97, 103–104
8th Illinois Cavalry 84, 91–93, 113, 122–123, 127, 131–133
Eldrichburg, Pvt. Grafe H. 59
Elkton, Virginia 88

Fairfax Court House, Virginia 4, 6, 10, 36–37, 42, 53, 55–56, 65, 70–72, 78, 89–90, 92, 94–95, 113, 116, 124, 133, 146
Fairfax Station, Virginia 6, 38, 57, 82, 85, 113, 116, 133, 146
Fairman, Col. James 18
Falls Church, Virginia 53, 66–67, 72, 76–77, 79–80, 82, 86–87, 89–91, 93–95, 99, 105, 107–109, 113, 115, 126, 150
Farmwell, Virginia 119, 126
Farnsworth, Lt. Charles H. 136, 145, 147–148
Farrell, Lt. William 78, 145
Field, Lt. Henry P. 101
Field, Sgt. Henry 67
15th Virginia (Cavalry) Regiment 87, 122
5th Pennsylvania Artillery 106, 113, 143
1st Separate Brigade 113
1st Virginia Cavalry 10
Fleming, Capt. James H. 2, 37–38, 46, 77, 85–86, 148
Flint Hill, Virginia 40, 53, 57, 124, 128
Foote, Dr. J. Platt 19
Forbes, Maj. William 64, 73
Fort Buffalo 19, 77, 80, 82–83, 94, 96, 100, 107

Fort Corcoran 108
Fort DeRussy 76
Fort Ethan Allen 41, 78, 83, 102
Fort Head 109
Fort Ramsay 77
Fort Reno 102
Fort Stevens 32, 76
43rd Battalion, Virginia Cavalry 11, 149
Frazar, Maj. Douglas 64, 117–118
Fredrich, Pvt. Jacob 25
Freedom Hill, Virginia 119, 126
Freeman, Anderson 52
French, Lt. George 99, 101, 175–176
Front Royal, Virginia 102, 105, 116
Frying Pan, Virginia 107, 119

Gail, Lt. Samuel P. 47
Gamble, Col. Willliam 113–114, 116, 118–119, 121–123, 125–133
Gansevoort, Col. Henry S. 78–79, 88, 95, 10, 105–107, 109,
Garrett, Richard Henry 1, 138–139
Garrett's Farm Patrol 164–165
Gault, Lt. Olney K. 124–125
Gaylord, Lt. Henry M. 19, 47, 54, 100, 116, 148
Germantown, Virginia 42, 55–56
Gettysburg, Pennsylvania 8, 9, 32
Goode, Mary Ann 147–148
Goose Creek, Virginia 4, 55, 58, 77, 91, 120, 127
Gordonsville, Virginia 103–104
Grace, Pvt. James 28
Grant, Gen. Ulysses S. 12, 63, 83, 102, 105, 114, 121–122, 129–130, 135, 143, 146, 157–158, 169
Green, Maj. Augustus 2, 11, 106–107, 119–120, 146
Gum Springs, Virginia 40, 58–59, 92–93

Hagadorn, Pvt. Francis T. 2, 25–29, 32, 34–35
Halleck, Henry W. 1, 5, 6, 8, 10, 12, 44, 102, 105, 111, 114, 132, 149
Hamilton, Virginia 127
Hammell, Col. William W. 30
Hancock, Maj. Gen. Winfield Scott 128, 131–132, 141–142
Harmony, Virginia 130
Hatch, Capt. Charles H. 120
Hazzard, Maj. Morris 14, 31–32, *33*, 39, 42–43, 45, 54
Heintzelman, Maj. Gen. Samuel P. 3, 4, 6, 8, 10, 43–44
Herold, David 136, 138–139, 144, 164
Hildebrand, Lt. Henry A. 47
Hollister, Lt. Col. George 46, 54, 78–79, 110, 121, 156–160
Homiston, Dr. Joseph M. 22, *23*, 144, 146–148, 156, 160–161
Hooker, Maj. Gen. Joseph 5–6, 8

Index

Hoover, Lt. John F. 146
Hornsby (Hormsby), Cpl. Michael 164, 173
Horton, Maj. Giles G. 88, 91–93, 99, 121, 125, 144
Howe, Pvt. George 59
Hoyt, Pvt. Godfrey Phillip 165
Humphreys, Charles 50
Hunter, Dr. James 111
Hunter's Mill, Virginia 40, 52, 56, 64, 66, 109, 119

Independent Cavalry Brigade 5, 9, 50, 75, 94

Jett, Capt. Willie 138–139
Jones, Pvt. Alpheus 28

Keays, Lt. William Jeremiah *43*, 44–46, 54, 144, 146, 176–177
Kelley, Pvt. Martin 165
Kelly's Ford, Virginia 97–101
Kenelty, Edward 26, 180–181
Kenelty, James 26, 180–181
Kenelty, John 26, 180–181
Kershaw, Maj. Gen. Joseph P. 97, 100, 102, 104, 151
Kincheloe's partisans 72, 103
King George Court House, Virginia 137
Kleinschmidt, Capt. Otto 36, 38–39, 47, 74

Ladue, Lt. Albert *19*, 36, 144
LaFeaver, Pvt. John 28
Lake, Ludwell 117–118
Langley, Virginia 56
Larned, Lt. Henry S. 101
Lawrence, Pvt. Ralph J. 28
Lazelle, Col. Henry M. 46–47, *48*, 49–50, 52–55, 58, 66, 71–74, 76–78, 80–88, 90–92, 94–97, 99–105, 107, 109–111, 113, 149–150, 153–155, 175
Leahy, Capt. Lawrence 36, *37*, 46–47, 84, 99, 101, 133
Leesburg, Virginia 63, 68, 83–84, 87, 119, 125–127, 130, 132
Lewinsville, Virginia 29, 42–44, 53, 56, 60, 76–77, 80, 82–83, 95, 119
Libby Prison 23, 65
Lincoln, Pres. Abraham 6, 24, 30, 63, 132–134, 141, 144, 146, 164, 177, 225
Lonkey (Lonpay), Oliver 164
Lowell, Col. Charles R. 8, 39–43, 50, 52–53, 56–57, 60–61, 66, 68–71, 73, 76, 79–80
Loyd, Rev. Hinton Summerfield *22*, 109, 115, 1129
Lunzeford, John H. 106
Lydecker, Abram 51–52

Manassas (Gap) (Junction), Virginia 10, 76–77, 82–83, 87, 102, 105–106, 122
Manassas Gap Railroad 56, 102–103, 105–107, 115

Maroney, Lt. Michael H. 47, 68
Martin, Cpl. Albert G. 2, 28–29, 39–41, 45
McClellan, Maj. Gen. George B. 3, 19, 46–47, 112
McDaniel (McDaniels), Pvt. Frank (Franklin) 165
McDowell, Brig. Gen. Irvin 3
McIntosh, Col. J.B. 36
McLean, Pvt. William M. 101
McMenamin, Capt. John 85
McNealy, Thomas 126
McNichol, Capt. Ronald 54
McPherson, Capt. James A. *17*, 18, 145–146
McQuade, Pvt. William 165
Meade, Maj. Gen. George 63, 159, 166
Merritt, Maj. Gen. Wesley 114
Meyers (Myers, Mayers), Pvt. John 165
Mickles, Capt. Philo D. 47, 70, 90, 101
Middleburg, Virginia 56, 58, 64, 68, 71, 92, 116–118
Miers, Pvt. John 86
Millar, Pvt. Abraham 28
Millington, Pvt. John 139, 165, 173–174
Mitchell's Station, Virginia 97
Montjoy, Capt. Richard P. 108–109
Moody, Lt. Horace D. 47
Mooney, Capt. Nathan H. 19, *33*, 47, 65–66, 161–163
Moore, Lt. Charles F. 2, 20–21, 32–33, 40–41, 47, 54, 91, 104, 116, 128–129, 133, 177–179
Morse, Capt. Charles E. 47
Mosby, John Singleton 1, 3, *9*, 10–12, 39–41, 53, 55–59, 68, 76, 82–84, 89, 91–92, 95–96, 107, 111, 117–119, 125–126, 141–142, 149–151
Mosby's Rangers 1, 39–41, 56–58, 60, 63–64, 66, 70–71, 73, 85–87, 89–90, 94, 103, 105–106, 108–109, 114, 124, 127, 129–131, 139, 142–143, 149
Mount Gilead, Virgina 119
Mount Zion Church 56–57, 64, 70
Mountjoy, Capt. (Mosby's Rangers) 89
Mountville, Virginia 119
Mudd, Dr. Samuel 141
Muddy Branch, Maryland 42, 58, 72, 84, 92, 121, 125
Mudge, Sgt. Volney 99
Munson's Hill, Virginia 126

New Baltimore, Virginia 122–123
New Dorp, New York 19
Newgarten (Neugarten), Cpl. Herman (Herron) 164
Nichols, Pvt. William 27
Nicholson, Lt. Col. John 46, 55, 59, 63, 73, 99, 121, 133, 135–136, 144, 160, 166
Noonan, Pvt. Edwin 37
Northern Neck, Virginia 130, 135–136

O'Beirne, Maj. James 141
Occoquan River 4, 116

Olmstead, Spencer H. 15, 18, 22, 44–45, 54
Orange and Alexandria Railroad 4, 6, 78, 82–83, 88, 102–105, 113, 133, 145
Orange Court-House, Virginia 103, 138
Ormsby, Pvt. William E. 60–61

Paraday, Pvt. Emery 165, 173–174
parole system 48
Peach Grove, Virginia 126
Pettit, Lt. John 17
Pickett, Pvt. Edmund J. 26, 181–182
Piedmont, Virginia 102, 107,
Plattsburgh, New York 1, 14–17, 20–21, 26–27, 29, 31, 34
Pontius, Pvt. Godfrey 59
Pope, Maj. Gen. John 157–158
Port Conway, Virginia 137
Port Royal, Virginia 139
Potomac River 4, 6, 8, 33, 42–43, 53, 58, 75–77, 81–84, 105–106, 115, 125, 133, 135–138, 144–145
Prospect Hill 113, 116, 119–120, 146
Purcellville, Virginia 107
Purdy, James S. 90
Putnam, Pvt. Henry 165

Raccoon Ford, Virginia 97
Randall, Pvt. James 56
Rapidan River (Station) 78, 82, 84, 96–97, 123, 144, 150
Rappahannock River (Station) 6, 70, 77–78, 83–84, 87, 97, 99, 104, 122–123, 135–137, 139, 145
Raymond, Pvt. Henry 147–148
Read, Rev. John D. *108*, 109, 150
Rectortown, Virginia 11, 68, 89, 105, 107
Richter, Sgt. Otto 124–125
Robin, Capt. Charles L.J. 121, 156
Rose, Pvt. Anton 59
Roundhill, Virginia 107
Rugen, Pvt. Jacob 101
Russell, Capt. Edward 122–124, 126
Ryan (Rina), Pvt. John 165

St. Dennis, Pvt. Levi 66
St. Mary's Church 85–87
Salem, Virginia 105, 123, 141–142
Salisbury Prison, North Carolina 227
Sangster's Station, Virginia 57, 82
Savage, Pvt. Lewis 165
Schlaefer, Capt. John J. 25, 47, *64*, 66–67
Schneider, Capt. Joseph *89*, 90–91, 95, 103, 107, 122–125, 136–137, 146, 150, 163–164
Schnepf, Col. Engleberth 30
Schultz, Lt. Joseph N. 38–39
2nd Massachusetts Volunteer Cavalry 8, 9, 39–40, 43, 50, 53, 57–58, 60, 63–64, 66, 68, 71–73, 75–76, 79–80, 149–150
Seward, William 79, 132
Seymour, Gov. Horatio 110

Shepard, QM-Sgt. Cyrus G. 2, 35–36, 41–42, 60, 69, 97–99, 112, 115–116, 132, 141
Sheridan, Maj. Gen. Philip 12, 75–76, 83–84, 87–88, 94, 101–103, 105, 110, 112, 114, 116, 118, 121–122, 129, 143
Shields, Pvt. John 28
Singer, Pvt. John Adolph 165
Smith, Pvt. Henry 96
Smith, Pvt. Thomas 86
Snay (Genay), Pvt. Abraham (Abram) 165, 174
Snicker's Gap 10, 55, 58, 95
Snickersville, Virginia 114, 129
Sperryville, Virginia 126, 129
Sprague, John T. 1, 47–48, 157
Sprague Light Cavalry 15–17, 19, 22, 26–27, 29–31, 54, 157
Springfield Station, Virginia 113
Stafford Court House 70
Stahel, Maj. Gen. Julius H. 5, 6, 8
Stanton, Edwin 3–6, 44, 136, 156
Staten Island, New York 1, 19, 31, 37
Steinbrigge (Steinbrugge), Pvt. Carl 165
Stephens, Pvt. William W.S. 101
Stevensburg, Virginia 97
Stoughton, Brig. Gen. Edwin 9–10
Strasburg, Virginia 102
Stuart, Gen. J.E.B. 3–4, 9–10, 53, 57, 64
Sulfur Springs, Virginia 122
Sweitzer, Col. Nelson B. 46, 110, 112, *113*, 114, 116, 121, 125–127, 130, 135–136, 143–145, 152–153

Taylor, Lt. Col. J.H. 80, 92, 109, 132
13th New York Cavalry 9, 11, 40–41, 43, 50, 58, 64, 72, 76, 80, 83, 85, 90, 95–96, 103, 105, 108–109, 113–115, 119–121, 146
35th Virginia Cavalry 40, 44
Thornton's Gap 88
Thoroughfare Gap 10, 77, 84, 116
Torbeck, Pvt. August 59
Tuck, Lt. Matthew 72–74, 78, 84, 146
20th Veterans Infantry 29–30
22nd Army Corps 4–6, 9
202nd Pennsylvania (Infantry) Volunteers 113
Tyler, Brig. Gen. Robert O. 53, 58, 65
Tyson's Corner, Virginia 109, 119

Uniac (Uniace), Cpl. Michael 165
Upperville, Virginia 55, 68, 91–92, 130
Upton's Hill, Virginia 77, 126

Vandersmith, Asst. Surgeon Samuel P. 146, 156
Vienna, Virginia 9, 11, 36, 39–40, 43, 46, 50–53, 55, 57–58, 61, 65–66, 70–72, 78–80, 92, 111, 113, 115–116, 119–120, 124, 126–127, 130, 133, 143, 149

Wagner, Pvt. William 86
Waite, Maj. John 92–93

Index

Walz (Wallz), Cpl. John 165
Wambolt, Pvt. Philip 121
Ward, Eliza 147
Warrenton, Virgina 6, 55, 87–88, 96, 122–124
Washburn, Capt. A. Livingston 78, 100, 156
Washington Light Cavalry 29–30, 38
Waterford, Virginia 84, 126–127
Wells, Lt. Col. Henry H. 88
Wendell, Sgt. Andrew 164
Westinghouse, Cpl. George 23, 182
White, Col. Elijah 40, 44, 64, 85, 127
White, Pvt. William 101
White Plains, Virginia 116
Wicomico River, Maryland 135

Wilbur, Lt. Albert B. 2, 21–22, 68, 71, 77, 80, 8, 93, 100, 105, 119–121, 124, 126, 128–130, 135–136, 140, 143–144, 179
Williams, Pvt. Lawrence 60
Williamson, James J. 2, 59, 68, 71, 85, 106–107, 119
Winchester, Virginia 80, 103, 131
Windsbecker, Capt. Julius 148
Winter, Pvt. John 165
Wolf Run Shoals, Virginia 59, 116

Zimmer, Cpl. Charles 165
Zisgen, Pvt. Joseph 165

www.ingramcontent.com/pod-product-compliance
Ingram Content Group UK Ltd.
Pitfield, Milton Keynes, MK11 3LW, UK
UKHW041934140426
5217IPUK00014B/479